Essays in Political Economics

Other books by the editor

The Making of Marx's Critical Theory

Marx's Critique of Political Economy:
Intellectual Sources and Evolution (two volumes)

Essays in Political Economics

Public Control in a Democratic Society

Adolph Lowe
Emeritus Professor of Economics
New School for Social Research, New York
and Goethe Universität, Frankfurt-am-Main

Edited and Introduced by

Allen Oakley
Senior Lecturer in Economics
University of Newcastle, Australia

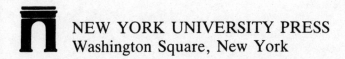

NEW YORK UNIVERSITY PRESS
Washington Square, New York

First published in the USA in 1987 by
NEW YORK UNIVERSITY PRESS
Washington Square,
New York, NY10003

Library of Congress Cataloging-in-Publication Data

Lowe, Adolph, 1893–
   Essays in political economics.

   Bibliography: p.
   1. Economic development.   2. Economic policy.
I. Oakley, Allen.   II. Title.
HD82.L693 1987   338.9   87–11219
ISBN 0–8147–6168–2

I wish to express my profound gratitude and sincere admiration to Dr Allen Oakley for the outstanding work he has performed in preparing this book for publication. Not only has he succeeded in creating a unity of many disparate parts, but he offers in his Introduction a most lucid exposition of my basic ideas.

Adolph Lowe

Contents

Preface

Adolph Lowe (1893–), emeritus professor of economics from The New School for Social Research, New York and the Goethe Universität, Frankfurt-am-Main, wrote his two already extant main works, *On Economic Knowledge* (1965) and *The Path of Economic Growth* (1976), after the age of 70 years. And soon, a trilogy will be completed when *The Prospect for Freedom* is published.

This remarkable pattern of writing, in which I found a highly congenial approach to economic analysis and issues, led me to enquire into the long intellectual gestation of these erudite books. With my curiosity whetted by reading a substantial part of Professor Lowe's earlier writings, I took up an interesting correspondence with him and, early in 1985, I went to meet him in his very active 'retirement' in West Germany. The present volume resulted from these events.

Professor Lowe's output over the past 70 years of writing has been considerable in both its intellectual scope and quantity, as the bibliography at the end of this volume attests. Judicious selection was, therefore, required in order to prepare a collection of essays constrained by length. Fortunately, Professor Lowe's themes of *structural analysis* and *instrumental analysis*, and their confluence in his *political economics* as the science of the controlled economy, are able to be clearly defined as his main contributions to the evolution of economics. The essays selected here, and my 'Introduction' to them, emphasize these themes. Through these essays, the reader will be introduced to a profound and radically distinct set of ideas about economy and society designed to help 'transform the historical process from blind motion into responsible action.'

In preparing this collection for publication, I have benefited greatly from the guidance and support of Professor Lowe. My 'Introduction' was also read by Robert Heilbroner, Geoffrey Harcourt and Phil O'Hara and I thank them all, without implication, for their interest in the project. The whole book was typed by the very able and accurate Lorraine King. I am grateful for her enthusiastic assistance.

Allen Oakley
November 1986
Newcastle, Australia

Introduction: Adolph Lowe's Contribution to the Development of a Political Economics

Allen Oakley

Adolph Lowe (1893–) is an economic theorist who has always had an abiding concern with the problems of the 'real world'. The range of issues to which he has applied his analytical acumen and the transdisciplinary scope of his scholarship make him truly worthy of the appellation 'Worldly Philosopher'.[1]

This assessment will be confirmed by a reading of the erudite essays collected in the present volume. They have been selected to reflect Lowe's two main contributions to economics, namely his integrated development of what he calls *structural analysis* and *instrumental analysis*. If his life's work is thought of as an ellipse, these two theoretical achievements constitute the foci. They are separately identifiable, but both are essential for the existence of the body of his thought and are linked by their common situation. The *raison d'être* of these interdependent aspects of theory has been for Lowe the formulation of *political economics* as a science of controlled economic systems.

While it has become something of a cliché, Lowe's interest in economic theory has been inspired by a perceived need for increased relevance. In contradistinction to many economists and other critics who bemoan the parlous 'state' of economics, Lowe has devoted his long life to doing something to correct the situation, albeit in different ways over time. The yawning void between the nature of 'real-world' capitalism and that version of it which is the object of most orthodox analysis used to guide policy and to teach in the classroom, has been his main concern.

This concern was evident in Lowe's earliest work on economic theory at Kiel University in Germany in the mid 1920s. He established a high reputation at that time for his critical assessment of the state of business-cycle theory and for his propositions concerning its reformulation.[2] His approach involved re-emphasizing the need for a theory of motion of

1

economic systems through time to replace the static neoclassical theory that largely dominated the explanatory analysis of real-world conditions. A second aspect of this endeavour was to provide an economic–analytical core which would have general application in explaining particular phases and phenomena of motion. But, in contrast to most received business cycle theory, Lowe envisaged a reformulation that would explain motion in an *endogenous* way rather than by the accepted means of introducing exogenous disturbances into otherwise stationary conditions.

Lowe and his co-worker at Kiel, Fritz Burchardt, found the basis of their future work in the reproduction schema formulated by Marx in volume II of *Capital*. In this respect Burchardt made a profound contribution to the progress of the Kiel school's research by comparing, contrasting and uniting the 'circular' and 'linear' perceptions of production. The particular subjects of Burchardt's study were Marx who emphasized the former perception, and Eugen von Böhm-Bawerk whose concern was with the latter in his period-of-production analyses.[3] The potential insight provided by this eclectic reformulation of the framework for motion analysis was increased further by Lowe's suggestion that the key sector I of Marx's reproduction model, in which means of production are produced, should be divided into two subsectors: one producing means of production for intrasector appli- cation and the other producing them for application in the consumption commodity sector.[4] At first sight, this appears to have been a rather elementary extension towards a more 'realistic' representation of industrial *structure*. Its full implications for the process of adjustment to the conditions of motion in response to change, such as technological change, were not to be made explicit until Lowe's work on structural analysis some years later.

After moving to Manchester in the early 1930s, Lowe's attention turned to a reconsideration of the essential theoretical premises and tenets upon which 'positive' economic analysis depends. His argument was that, although these essentials appeared to be general, they actually followed from very strict structural and behavioural assumptions. This especially applied to that fundamental device of most economic analysis, the so-called 'law' of supply and demand.[5]

In particular, the 'law' assumes that human economic behaviours are confined to particular mechanistic responses to price–quantity signals. No consideration is given to the *spontaneity* that characterizes much of human behaviour, taking shape in various and varying expectations concerning future states of the market. Moreover, the 'law' requires that the economy is so structured that all productive resources are perfectly flexible and mobile. Under these assumptions, expectations can indeed be disregarded, because decisions in response to price–quantity signals involving physicotechnical structural adjustments can be carried out instantaneously.

These critical realizations by Lowe marked the beginning of his scepticism about the very viability of orthodox economic theory. The problems that he saw then did not concern theory *per se* or the use of the 'scientific' (deductive) method. Rather there was a need to ensure that the structural and behavioural premises from which theoretical reasoning begins are abstracted from 'real-world' conditions. It was to be this point that led Lowe to baulk at any further pursuit of 'positive' explanatory theory of motion in a capitalist economy. His recognition of the rigidities of modern industrial structures, in conjunction with the diversity of individual motivations, expectations and behaviours that pervade modern capitalism, added up to a highly problematical object for theory. It is not possible, he concluded, to abstract from such a profile of characteristics any general premises from which deductive reasoning can draw empirically reliable inferences. For Lowe, the challenge became to preserve the rigour of the 'scientific' method while ensuring that the resulting theory remains relevant to its object, modern industrial capitalism.

Lowe's proposed solution to the puzzle of maintaining theoretical rigour in the face of such an intractable object is simple but radical. Rather than seeking to reform orthodox theory *per se*, Lowe chose to *reform the empirical object of theory*—the actual economic process—in order to effect his reconstruction.

As the papers selected for the present collection will detail, this reconstruction of theory, with its now clearly defined and regularized object, is comprised of the two interdependent components of structural and instrumental analysis. The former argues that the fundamental base from which economic analysis should work is the *physicotechnical* dimension of the production process. Having defined clearly the structural conditions of any particular historical period, the challenge for theory and policy management is to ensure that these structures operate optimally *vis-à-vis* the politically devised goals to be served. The task of instrumental analysis is then to define rigorously the set of motivations and behaviours of individual economic decision makers that would ensure the realization of this optimal performance. And, having defined these conditions, the analysis must proceed to design a controlled institutional environment that would, as far as possible, induce voluntary conformity to the required behavioural outcomes. This combination of structural and instrumental analysis constitutes

Lowe's political economics that is developed most extensively in his two *magna opera*: *On Economic Knowledge* (1965) and *The Path of Economic Growth* (1976).

A first step in coming to grips with Lowe's work is to be clear about what *he* means by 'economics'. Economic behaviour is *modal* in the sense that it is a means to providing for the realization and fulfilment of other human potentials and enjoyments. For most people, solving 'the economic problem' is not an end in itself. This modal status of economics is reinforced by interpreting the key problem to be addressed as the process of material provisioning in the face of quantitative and qualitative constraints imposed by nature. This problem is confronted each day, in one way or another, by all people in their endeavours to survive or achieve any state of material welfare beyond such a minimal outcome. Thus, the economy is perceived by Lowe as essentially an 'engine of provision' and the details of choice and allocation, so much the exclusive concern of orthodoxy, are but elements within this context.

Moreover, economics is about processes, activities and change rather than about 'states of mind'. Its events and phenomena are set in historical time with its excruciating interface between an immutable past and a perfidious future. Economic analysis that fails to take cognisance of this situation is bound to be largely irrelevant to an understanding of the human condition.

Lowe's analyses have a plutological emphasis. The neoclassical focus on the catallactical niceties of harmonious exchange is overruled in favour of portraying the competitive struggles of accumulation and technological change. Such analyses are appropriately founded upon an understanding of production rather than of exchange. Indeed, economics from this perspective might best be called a 'science of production'. However, as Lowe clearly recognizes in the development of his structural analysis, the continuity of production is conditional upon its unity with the appropriate sociopolitically determined exchange–circulation, distribution and final consumption processes.

In his emphasis on understanding production, Lowe stresses the need to distinguish the physicotechnical structures involved and the behavioural–operational processes which give 'life' to those structures. Economic analysis is, therefore, required to portray a structural core to which the motivations and behaviours induced by the final and modal goals of the economic actors must be firmly secured. Dealing with given resources such as to realize material goals is primarily a technical problem. It requires first and foremost an understanding of the laws of nature and the rules of engineering. But, having established the technological–structural foundations of economics, Lowe always keeps its human and social dimensions to the fore as well. The purposive and cognitive behaviours of individual decision makers need to be shown to conform to the dictates of structure if on-going optimum provisioning is to be successfully achieved. This raises a fundamental problem for economics to which Lowe gives intensive critical consideration in the process of reformulating economics as political economics, namely: what is to be done about the spontaneity of human decision making and action that pervades the 'real world'?

Recognition that economics deals with *modal* behaviour immediately suggests that it has an important practical aspect. In Lowe's treatment this is quite clear. Economists are not appropriately treated as 'observers', 'taxonomists' or 'chroniclers' of economic events and phenomena. Their role in a modern industrial economy is rather increasingly an interventionist one. In Lowe's political economics, the unity of theory and practice becomes complete.

As a practical science, economics is brought directly and unavoidably into contact with political structures, processes and constraints. It is in this context that Lowe's apparently paradoxical advocacy of a controlled economy alongside his staunch defence of democratic freedom has been a source of some incredulity amongst his readers. In order to overcome such a reaction, which may well impede a proper understanding of his work, it is necessary to appreciate the concept of freedom that he defends. First, consider the following, often neglected point about economic freedom. Whether they realize it or not, even the most radical libertarians cannot be advocating 'licence' or 'anarchy'. For as Lowe showed more than fifty years ago, their perfectly competitive free market can only function as described if the 'atoms' conform to strict structural and behavioural constraints.[6] A market system in which participants do not overwhelmingly adhere to these constraints cannot generate stable, optimal provisioning through the so-called 'law' of supply and demand.

Lowe's argument is that the very sort of *constrained* freedom implicitly espoused by free marketeers can only be ensured and perpetuated in the context of industrial capitalism if the required constraints are imposed by an appropriate control matrix. This has become necessary because the 'real-world' structures, institutions, motivations and behaviours have departed so radically from those which *laissez-faire* philosophies presupposed. In a capitalist world of monopoly power, large-scale and technically sophisticated production, significant inflexibilities and immobilities of resources, and potential for collusive practices, the 'deregulation' concept of 'freedom' can only be seen as a recipe for a welfare disaster for the majority of people. This form of 'freedom', lifted as it is out of its original *laissez-faire* setting, is unlikely to provide any humanly reasonable provisioning outcome. And, for technologically imposed reasons, actual reversion to the theoretical atomism of such a setting is not feasible. Small may be beautiful, but large is powerful, profitable and well defended (with apologies to E. F. Schumacher).

Lowe's *freedom through control and spontaneous conformity* is, by contrast, designed to elicit by predominantly manipulative means those motivations and behaviours which, given the present technical and other structures, would ensure that the market system delivers provisioning at the socially chosen optimum level and pattern.[7] He advocates no particular provisioning goals and only specifies examples for didactic purposes in his analyses. Such goals are to be decided politically, with Lowe's preference being for the democratic process. His work has been explicitly directed towards the preservation of this sort of political condition and his forthcoming book, *The Prospect for Freedom*, will continue the endeavour. In it, Lowe situates political economics in the social and institutional context that is consistent with democratic control and decentralized operation of the economy.

ANALYSING THE STRUCTURE AND MOTION OF ECONOMIC SYSTEMS

Lowe's work centres on the distinction between a structure and its activation by human behaviour. His seminal endeavours to formalize a structural model upon which the analysis of motion can be based are to be found in the two essays written in the early 1950s, which open the selection below.

In the 1930s, Lowe applied the concept of structure to the framework within which market processes must operate in order to deliver optimal provisioning. The structure concept at that time included the '*natural, psychological and institutional constants* which constitute the meta-economic framework of the individual economic transactions'. These must be such as to secure the 'permanent working of the system' through the appropriate constraints on human behaviour. In addition to this, Lowe briefly introduced the physicotechnical dimension of the production process as comprising the foundations upon which human society is erected. This historical–materialist perspective on structure argues that the optimal provisioning process depends upon the efficient technical operation of the production structure. Consequently, the social relations of production and the related institutional forms and processes should be consistent with and effectively facilitate these technical operations if provisioning is to proceed with stability.

In his 1950s papers, Lowe analysed these ideas more elaborately and formally. His thought returned to the research achievements of the Kiel period and it was production which again became the central theme of the analysis. The analysis of motion, in the form of economic growth, was prominent in the era after Keynes' *General Theory* and Lowe took the opportunity to revive and develop some of the key contributions of the Kiel group. These contributions were neglected by contemporary writers and Lowe set out to reveal the limitations imposed on any understanding of motion as a consequence. In the process, he made his own contributions to the analysis, at first in a 'positive'-explanatory way, but subsequently the beginnings of an instrumental methodology were to become apparent.

What struck Lowe was that the analyses of motion that prevailed in the growth literature had two limiting characteristics. First, the variables were expressed only in value–price terms to the exclusion of any explication of the physicotechnical structures to which they are related. For Lowe, the latter dimension represents a fundamental determinant of and constraint on behaviour and change in an economic system. Analysis which begins from this level is, therefore, likely to provide a more complete insight into the process of motion. Only if resources are perfectly flexible, mobile and adaptable in the face of change can the role of structure legitimately be neglected, especially if full employment is assumed or actually realised as a policy goal.

Secondly, Lowe found the degree of aggregation used in growth analysis to be a factor which obscured the nature of the adjustment processes which constitute motion. By focusing on aggregates, much of the fixed-factor characteristics of production could be overlooked, thus compounding the effect of the first limitation on the analysis. The challenge for Lowe was to formulate a model in which the degree of aggregation is 'high enough to permit analytical manipulation of complex dynamic processes, [and] low enough to reflect those physical properties of an industrial market which affect its general stability'. To this end, Lowe returned to Marx's reproduction schema as providing the most appropriate basis for such a meso-level of analysis.[8]

As we saw previously, while working in Kiel, Lowe made a crucial suggestion for modifying Marx's original format. This consisted of dividing the 'means of production producing sector' into two parts: one producing for intrasector needs and one producing for intersector transfer to the consumption commodity sector. He now combined this revised reproduction format with the attention to intrasector 'linear' production details outlined earlier by his Kiel colleague, Fritz Burchardt. These 'linear' sequences had been analysed by Marx, Böhm-Bawerk and J. B. Clark, but it was Burchardt who formulated the seminal synthesis with the reproduction schema which Lowe applied to the analysis of motion.[9]

This 'synthetic' analytical framework has two additional character-istics. First, the inclusion of 'linear' production sequences within each sector brought out the neglected role of 'working capital' embodied in 'work in progress' while final commodities (equipment or consumer commodities) are technically built up from original resources. Secondly, the distinction between stocks and flows is made explicit. Marx's own analysis related essentially to flows, but Lowe explicitly included the associated stock variables which become especially significant when accumulation and other changes are to be analysed.

As Lowe demonstrated in his 1950s papers, this 'Kiel' model of expanding reproduction provides previously unobtainable insights into the conditions for the establishment, preservation and restoration of stable motion in an economy with short-run fixed-coefficient production. He made this clear most graphically in his analyses of particular types of disturbances to stable motion and the consequent adjustment demands upon the system in the face of profound short-term (at least) rigidities and immobilities at the *physicotechnical* level. That is, Lowe made evident the very real task which the autonomous market system (or any other system of functional forces) faces in order to ensure continuous stable provisioning at the optimum level. Lowe's emphasis on the short-run problematics of adjustment served to emphasize the artificial nature of so-called 'long-run' analyses in which such processes are abstracted from. His approach is to treat the 'long-run' as a sequence of short-run positions and processes involving significant discontinuities of adjustment.[10] The existence of an inherited stock of real means of production of various vintages and various qualitative compositions, with varying degrees of physical 'depreciation' and economic obsolescence, along with the existing complementary 'stocks' of other factors, constitute the structural barriers to short-term responses when quantitative and/or qualitative changes occur. The processes by which these physicotechnical barriers are transcended is the precise focus of Lowe's analyses.

In the earlier of the two papers in focus here, 'A structural model of production' dating from 1952 (Essay 1 below), Lowe introduced his analytical format and purpose along the lines of the above discussion. His first substantive objective was to establish the detailed physicotechn-ical and value conditions for stationary-state equilibrium in the model. A twofold challenge faced him in applying these conditions to meaningful analyses: one was to show that the introduction of changes into the stationary state generates processes of adjustment that are now accessible to exact calculation; the other was to show that the model facilitates the solution of puzzles that have proved refractory in conventional economic theory.

Lowe met the first challenge by referring to three sorts of change which the model can handle: first, a shift in the *quality* of demand for means of production or consumer commodities; secondly, a depletion of, or decreasing returns from, natural resources; and thirdly, technical changes that involve alterations in the ratios of means of production and labour inputs. The model makes explicit the relevant stock-flow interactions involved in these changes and the adjustment processes which they generate in restoring the stationary conditions. Moreover, changes which are generated endogenously as a consequence of introducing lags in the relations of the model can also be treated in a quantitatively exact way.

In meeting the second challenge, Lowe addressed three particular issues. First of all he considered the Harrod–Domar position on equilibrium growth conditions; secondly, he tackled the problem of the upper turning point of the business cycle, using John Hicks' argument as a key example of the genre; and thirdly, he addressed the notion of statistical double counting in the concept of gross national product posited by Gerhard Colm and Simon Kuznets. In each case, Lowe's model facilitated access to aspects of the issue which remain obscured in the treatments in question. Harrod–Domar are shown to provide for necessary rather than sufficient conditions, Hicks is shown to have made special assumptions about the composition of aggregate demand as the turning point is approached and the double-counting problem is revealed to be a *non sequitur*.

The second of the papers to be considered here, that entitled 'Structural analysis of real-capital formation', was prepared by Lowe for a conference in 1953 (Essay 2 below).[11] In spite of its chronological proximity to the earlier paper, it marks a significant step forward in the evolution of his work on this theme. This step has both methodological and substantive dimensions. The papers are, however, complementary in that while the earlier one provides a more detailed exposition of the model itself, the present one extends the formal analysis beyond establishing stationary conditions and analysing 'once-over' adjustments to particular data changes. Lowe now identifies as well the necessary and sufficient conditions for the stable absorption of continuous expansion across the system. This enables him to pursue adjustments in response to the introduction of dynamic disequilibria.

The conditions for stationary and dynamic equilibrium are now argued by Lowe in terms of the maintenance of specific fixed means of production stock ratios and output ratios between the sectors such that the replacement and expansion needs of the sectors are always met. This technique proves to be highly effective, first of all, in a more detailed exposition of 'once-over' adjustments to such changes as an increase in the labour supply and a 'Harrod-neutral' technical change. A more graphic demonstration of the efficacy of the technique comes in the analysis of continuous expansion. Here Lowe considers two basic categories of dynamic processes: those which parallel the stationary analyses in that they focus on constant rates of change and those which parallel the 'once-over' analyses in that they deal with variations in rates of change.

In the first category, the argument again constitutes a critique of the Harrod–Domar conditions for dynamic equilibrium growth. This time, though, a more fully developed set of sufficient conditions is set out as against the necessary conditions devised by the two originators of the theory. In the case of variations in rates of change, Lowe treats in detail the adjustment responses to shifts in investment supply and demand functions, and from amongst the various possible cases of factor-displacing, non-neutral technical change, he analyses fully the effects of a pure labour-displacing change.[12]

From a methodological perspective, the later, 'Real capital formation' paper contains a significant shift of approach towards what was to be formalized as instrumental analysis in due course. The earlier treatment of structural analysis, albeit only one year or so before, had been written entirely in a 'positive' style with the model perceived as providing for explanations of existing 'real-world' phenomena. Lowe's objective was, at that point, to enter the literature of the time in an endeavour to improve the explanatory capacity of the analysis of motion. However, in 1953, his burgeoning pessimism about 'positive' theory turned into an epistemological leap sideways. This was to affect profoundly all of his future work.

Lowe's conclusion concerning his structural analysis was now that its epistemological status is best thought of in what he called at the time 'normative' terms. His intention was to convey that his model sets out the specific conditions which would bring about, maintain and restore certain states of provisioning in a free-market-dominated capitalist economy (although he noted that the model could be applied in any 'functional' form of system). Thus, 'we have not been concerned with the *descriptive* analysis of structural relations and movements as they occur in empirical systems in historical time, but with *normative* analysis, that is, with the structural requirements for the optimal achievement of a postulated goal. . .'. The sense in which the contribution is normative is that the requirements are perceived by Lowe as 'the "efficiency norms" by which the performance of empirical growth processes must be judged. . . [and which] point up and locate the structural and functional deficiencies of any empirical system under observation'. His analysis does not intend, in the usual sense of 'normative', to posit prescriptive imperatives of the '*should*' kind, but rather to set out what *could* be done in order to achieve a given goal in the most efficient way. The instrumental message of this approach to analysis is already evident in the illustrative examples given by Lowe towards the end of the paper. The precise expression of the possibility of an instrumental analysis was to come in a 1959 paper written in German.[13]

In the interim, Lowe maintained his concern to further the general understanding of the optimal requirements for a 'positive' analysis of motion by re-examining the classicals' treatment of the theory of growth and the post classical developments that so changed the ideals of such theory. By referring to the history of economic thought in his 1954 essay 'The classical theory of economic growth' (Essay 3 below), he sought to substantiate his view that meaningful economic analysis should begin from an explication of the relevant metaeconomic 'environment': that is 'the whole natural, social and technical environment of the economic system'. In this respect, the 'classical' growth analyses, as devised by Smith, Ricardo and Marx, were more in touch with the 'dynamics' of capitalist 'reality' than the writings which followed. Economic theory for the former group was socially integrated and comprehensive. The latter sought completely to divorce 'pure' economics from this sociopolitical environment and ended up carrying forward hidden theoretical premises as 'data' which were no longer pertinent to a transformed capitalism. By contrast, the classicals treated as endogenous a much wider range of variables, both economic and metaeconomic. Indeed, for Lowe, the *differentia specifica* of classical theory is this extensive endogeneity.

Now while the historical aspects of Lowe's work are highly significant, our concern here is with the methodological point of the paper. What the classicals demonstrated in this respect was that, as a matter of principle, extensive, endogenously determinate theoretical systems could be formulated such that the explanation of motion did not require exogenous forces or independent variables. This characteristic was lost in the post-Millian rush to 'purify' economics by treating as independent 'data' the natural, psychological, institutional and technological dimensions of the economic problem. As a consequence, modern theory's capacity to explain motion was weakened, although, in general, concern about motion was not dominant in economics anyway.

By means of a proper specification, the classicals' approach to the theory of motion facilitated the accurate logical prediction of paths of evolution. The endogeneity of the whole process, along with the absence of any expected exogenous disturbances made for an equilibrium theory of motion which recalled Lowe's hope in the Kiel period that he could develop a 'realistic' and socially inclusive dynamic theory. He now recognized that the 'closed' mechanism of the classicals was not a viable option. 'Rather, the problem consists in establishing the criteria by which those areas where the economic process does indeed interact with its environment can be distinguished from fields where the "underlying forces" operate as independent variables.' That such criteria do not yet exist in economics was to be regretted, in Lowe's view, but the burgeoning renewed concern with growth theory at least pointed in the direction of a desirable reintegration of the social dimension with the economic. This plea for unity had been made by Lowe some twenty years before[14] and the theme was to re-appear in *The Path of Economic Growth* in 1976.

The final essay included in the first part of the collection, 'Is economic value still a problem?' (Essay 4 below), dates from 1981, nearly thirty years after Lowe first worked out his ideas on structural analysis. Its significance here is that it provides us with some retrospective insights into a vital link between structures and their activation under the guidance of instrumental analysis. Part of this activation process is to identify the vector of relative prices that will most efficiently facilitate the intersector transfer of commodities required to ensure stable and balanced reproduction at the physicotechnical level. The task of any economic system is to ensure that these prices are actually set.

In this 1981 paper, Lowe turned to existing theories of value in a search for some *objective rule* by which the set of appropriate operational prices can be computed. While he does not explicitly link this issue with his work on the structural–instrumental nexus, it is evident that the discovery of such a rule would greatly facilitate the practical application of his methodology.

Lowe's 'test' of the two contending theoretical bases for the existence of value, viz. embodied labour and utility, is a severe one. He posed the question: '*suppose that a universal amnesia were to wipe out the knowledge of all present prices, would there be a rule for reestablishing them?*' (emphasis original). This 'test' effectively rules out any appeal to the 'history' of either prices or the conditions upon which they were based. And, as Lowe goes on to establish, both perceptions of value depend for their theoretical viability on some historically given conditions.

Thus Lowe concludes that the value category can have no *practical* relevance as the basis for specifying empirical prices. Implicitly this also precludes value *per se* from being part of the process of instrumental analysis.[15]

THE METHODOLOGY OF POLITICAL ECONOMICS

Instrumental analysis grew out of Lowe's increasing scepticism concerning the orthodox use of the 'scientific' (deductive) method to explain events and phenomena in a modern industrialized economic system. In effect, he has challenged orthodoxy on two counts that are succinctly expressed by Robert Heilbroner, his most devoted and perceptive disciple. First, 'contemporary economic theory is not—and worse, cannot be—an adequate tool for the control of our social destiny because the very premises on which that theory is based are no longer relevant to social reality'. Secondly, 'a restructured economic theory might become such a tool if economists understood the *changed relationship of theory and reality* in the milieu of industrial capitalism, and altered the nature of their procedure accordingly'.[16]

In accordance with the first of these challenges, Lowe's political economics emphasizes the role of *control*. His generalized objective is to contribute to endeavours 'to transform the historical process from blind motion into responsible action'. Then, in restructuring economic theory to serve this end, he recognized that the modern industrialized economy is highly problematical as an object of scientific method.

In each of the essays included in the second section of the collection below, Lowe details the nature of these elements of his challenge. The most detailed statement is that in his position paper, 'Toward a science of political economics' (Essay 5 below), presented to a conference on his work held at the New School for Social Research in New York early in 1968. A briefer outline is provided in 'What is evolutionary economics? Remarks upon receipt of the Veblen–Commons Award' (Essay 7 below), delivered when Lowe was presented with his award by the Association for Evolutionary Economics in 1979. The other two essays in this section centre on critical reactions to his ideas on political economics. His responses to the papers and remarks at the New York conference are outlined in 'Economic means and social ends: a rejoinder' (Essay 6 below). Then, in the final essay of the collection dating from 1982, 'Is the glass half full or half empty? A self-critique' (Essay 8 below), Lowe undertakes to clarify the intellectual foundations upon which instrumental analysis and political economics are erected.

The Essentials of Instrumental Analysis

As Lowe told his 'Veblen–Commons Award' audience, the 'crucial issue' in his work is the treatment of *theory*. His position is that the application of the hypotheticodeductive method and the formulation of 'positive' theory, usually associated with the natural sciences, requires an object that exhibits two essential qualities.[17] First, the object should have an *autonomous existence* and move independently of man's volition. That is, it has an observable 'life of its own' which follows a particular pattern when it is not disturbed by human actions. Any intrusion by man into this existential state should have no universal or lasting effect. Withdrawal of any exogenously induced distortion should allow the natural state to return automatically. Secondly, Lowe specifies '*inherent orderliness*' as a necessary characteristic of an object of science. The scientific method is designed to reveal laws or probabilistic generalizations about the nature of states and motion. These regularities should not relate only to particular episodes in the 'life' of the object, but are intended to be independent of the place and time of observation.

In the absence of these two qualities, the scientist is unable to produce and test an objective theory of how the object is structured and operates. Most importantly, he cannot make reliable predictions involving cause and effect.

In Lowe's perception, the modern capitalist economic system is an object which lacks both of these important qualities. It is, therefore, not an appropriate object for the application of the traditional scientific method. The extent and reliability of any regularities of structure and behaviour that may be discerned in the system are not sufficient to provide the necessary orderliness. Moreover, the system is a collective human creation and cannot be autonomous in the sense required of a natural scientific object. Its form and evolution depend upon the exigencies of human volition and caprice. Most interventions in the system will permanently affect its structures and/or behaviours and their removal will not restore the original state unless a conscious reversal procedure is implemented.

Autonomy and regularity can, therefore, only be *attributed* to a capitalist economic system by devising idealized assumptions about its structure and the behaviour of its participants that have little or no observed validity. Analytical premises formulated in this way do not have the same epistemological status as those upon which conventional scientific reasoning is based. Theories and predictions which are derived from such premises are strictly only manifestations of the rules of deductive logic. It will only be chance that results in predictions of any accuracy *vis-à-vis* actual events because of the often capricious and diverse behaviours of economic decision makers. Modelling such behaviours in terms of logical analogies cannot hope to capture the realities of capitalist processes. Consequently, in order that the important role to be played by prediction in the policy management of unstable capitalist motion be made effective, Lowe advocates his radically revised approach to theory formulation. His instrumental analysis centres on establishing an object for economic theory that is scientifically viable. Analysis then allows accurate and reliable (at least in a probabilistic sense) policy predictions to be made. On this basis, Lowe develops his political economics as the science of a controlled economic system.

Lowe calls *instrumental–deductive* the method of analysis that is appropriate to establishing such an object. Like all scientific theory, the method involves reasoning from a set of known premises to a set of unknown consequences. In a given case, this amounts to deriving from stipulated ends the means suitable for the realization of those ends. The first step in formulating this type of theory is to establish 'the *initial state* of the system under investigation' and to identify '*certain laws, rules and empirical generalisations*' that are operational within the system. These latter represent the natural, psychological, social and technological structures and functions within and through which economic decisions are made. A further known premise from which the theory works is the politically given terminal state of the system which forms the goal of any policy to be formulated.

On the basis of these initially known premises, a process of regressive inference can be applied in order to establish the unknown means through which the pertinent operational conditions will transform the initial state into the desired goal state. This involves an 'heuristic' search procedure which is effectively a variation of the 'retroductive' method (C. S. Peirce) in that the sequence of means is correctly specified when their actual implementation would necessarily generate the given end state.[18] The result of identifying the means in this way is the formulation of an instrumental–deductive logic in which a chain of causation is known with certainty.

The sequence of unknown means to be specified comprises the following categories of elements: '(1) the *path* or the succession of macro-states of the system suitable to transform a given initial state into a stipulated terminal state; (2) patterns of *micro-behaviour* appropriate to keeping the system to the suitable path; (3) *micro-motivations* capable of generating suitable behaviour; and (4) *a state of the environment* . . . designed to stimulate suitable motivations'. This sequence is such as to ensure that once the unknowns are determined, a process of deductive reasoning will reveal the causal logic of moving from the now known 'state of the environment' to the goal-adequate path of adjustment. In this way, Lowe preserves the analytical rigour that is characteristic of the scientific method.

However, in applying inferential reasoning to economic theory, the analyst must be conscious that his object and its situation are subject to change. The detailed specifications of the knowns, including the chosen macro-goals, and unknowns analytically discovered will be peculiar to a particular economic system at a particular phase of its history. Consequently, '*instrumental inference* of . . . causes or highest-level hypotheses *is an ongoing task of the social theorist . . .*'. Lowe can, therefore, only formulate general principles to be applied *ad hoc*.

Also concerning the object macro-goal state, it should be emphasized that it has a strictly normative status. Its selection, a political decision to be referred to again below, is not to be confused with the process of instrumental analysis by which the means of its realization are established. The instrumental–deductive method itself is quite indepen-dent of any goals selected by sociopolitical consensus or imposition. An additional normative element creeps in, though, where more than one goal-adequate path for the economy is revealed by instrumental analysis. The selection of the path, too, must then come under some sociopolitical criteria.

Consider next the nature of the 'laws, rules and empirical generalis-ations' that will be needed in order to devise the suitable means to realize the object macro-goal state. These knowns appear at first sight very similar to the very empirical statements of reliable cause and effect that Lowe has ruled out for economic analysis through his epistemological critique. However, he insists that, for the most part, the sufficient means can be devised in terms of operational conditions that have a sound epistemological status. To begin with, the most essential relationships between means and ends are technological. Any programme of decision making that would realize the goal set must, at least, be consistent with and bounded by the currently known rules of engineering. The sufficient goal-adequate behaviours that will, in principle, optimize the use of available technology follow as a matter of logic.

A main requirement of instrumental analysis is to establish the unknown motivational conditions and forces that will be perceived by decision makers in such a way as to induce the behaviours that are consistent with a path to the goal state. Here Lowe sees a need to comprehend as completely as possible the potential action directives conducive to realizing a range of individual goals and the associated expectation patterns that decision makers could hold as the bases for their actions. Lowe is optimistic that this requirement can be satisfied and he writes that 'once the behaviour patterns themselves have been regressively derived from the engineering rules governing the path, it is, *in principle*, always possible to infer suitable motivational substructures'.

It is the process of establishing the environmental state that will set in motion 'the instrumentally valid intra-system forces', that have been derived more or less as matters of logic, that causes Lowe the most misgivings about meeting the scientific requirements of his approach. The first thing required here is a full knowledge of the action directives and expectations patterns that are currently actually being applied in the decision-making process. In spite of the obvious practical difficulties that this requirement poses, it is necessary in computing the extent to which these bases of decisions need to be modified by the control environment in order that goal-adequate behaviours are ensured. Here Lowe grants that the analytical problem faced is akin to that which besets 'positive' economics. His concern is that human knowledge of the links between environmental conditions and action directive–expectation responses is quite inadequate for the benefits of political economics to be realized fully. This limitation causes Lowe to make some compromises in handling the design of control measures that will induce a goal-adequate motivational–behavioural nexus. In particular, because the conscious control of expectations formation seems to be more viable than is the case for action directives, the two aspects of motivation need to be treated differently in the design process.

Controls and Goals in Political Economics

We saw previously that instrumental analysis opens the way for the *formal* design of controls that will realize given goals. These controls will specifically ensure that the micro-participants behave in such a way that their economic decisions are consistent with the desired macro-outcome. The process of control forms the ultimate link between the existing and the stipulated goal status of the economic system. As Lowe puts it, control is the '*practical step of intervention*, geared to adapt economic reality to the design fashioned by instrumental analysis' and 'the discovery of *which controls are goal-adequate in a given context* is part of instrumental analysis proper'.

For Lowe, control means providing an 'environment' that will motivate microeconomic decision makers to conform to behaviours that are goal adequate. The choice of controls is immediately constrained by the specification that the maximum degree of freedom consistent with the achievement of the goals pursued must be sustained. In effect, this freedom and the retention of decentralized decision making become goals in themselves. When compared with generally accepted economic management policies currently in use, the controls that Lowe advocates are designed to be more direct in their effects. Orthodox policies attempt to influence micro-behaviours and operations by altering some aspect of the state of the macroeconomy. This most often involves aggregate demand as governments can affect this variable either directly or via some related conditions such as tax rates or interest rates. To these types of controls Lowe applies the term *primary controls*.

Lowe's view is that these controls need to be augmented by the addition of a more directly acting programme of *secondary controls*. The latter would set out to elicit precisely those responses from micro-units that are goal adequate. This can be done in two ways: first, by manipulating volitional responses; secondly, by command. The former relies on rewards for conformity while the latter relies on the wish to avoid the penalties associated with non-conformity. The two are, therefore, quite different in their implications for the kind of society which will surround the economic system. In Lowe's case, the aim is to keep command controls to an absolute minimum. However, he realizes that the degree of control needed to direct a mature capitalist economic system, with all its inflexibilities, uncertainties and instabilities, towards any desired evolutionary path will require some combination of the two control forms. His hope is, though, that command controls will only be required to 'fine tune' the strategy.

As a consequence of this preference for volitional adherence to goal-adequate behaviours, Lowe is led to focus on the market as the object of control. However, he does not argue for structural changes or deregulation that are intent on re-instating a 'competition' of sorts. Rather he advocates dynamic controls that operate more directly on motivations and consequent market behaviours. With these sorts of controls, the necessity for large-scale micro-units in order to maximize the economic benefits from modern technology and management skills is accepted. The two areas of motivation that are potentially controllable are the action directives which micro-units perceive as maximizing their own objectives and the associated pattern of expectations which they form. These two motivational elements combine as the bases for micro decision making.

As already indicated above, Lowe sees these two areas as requiring different treatment in a control programme as a result of certain limitations of current human knowledge. Especially is the control of action directives highly problematical because the sociopsychological transmission mechanism between the action 'environment' and the motivations that lead to particular actions is poorly understood. Lowe concludes that two approaches to this problem are possible. First, the use of command controls could force goal-adequate behavioural conformity. But this move is not consistent with the maximum maintenance of freedom and decentralized decision making, and would probably lead to all sorts of 'underground' responses. Secondly, then, the only viable short-term alternative is *to constrain the choice of macro-goals* such that they are consistent with generally accepted micro-goals and action directives. In the longer term, Lowe is hopeful that education will facilitate a shift of the latter in the direction of more socially desirable macro-objectives.

It is Lowe's view, though, that much more can be achieved in the control of expectations. In this way, the effects of existing action directives can be made to serve more certainly the relevant macro-goals. The primary input to expectations formation that can be brought under control is the flow of information received by micro-units. It is to be expected that private decision makers will welcome any publicly provided expansion and amplification of their information base. For most of them, information is costly and, therefore, limited. A properly designed and continuously revised and updated flow of shared information would reduce individuals' uncertainty about their future and about the behaviours of other economic units and institutions with which they are interdependent.

Little has been said so far about *the choice of the macro-goals* that comprise the terminal state to be realized. As is well known, the setting of objectives for any dimension of society is largely a matter of political discretion. But the choice is constrained by the history of the society and its goal setting and any social inertia that has been generated as a consequence. Thus, once the 'general criteria of social action' are set down, and the relevant technological and social contextual factors are recognized, macroeconomic goal specification becomes 'anything but arbitrary'.

Under a regime of mature capitalism, and given the desire to preserve the maximum possible social, political and economic freedom, some caution is required in suggesting goal patterns to be pursued. Lowe's discussions of the problem reflect this caution. Although major ideological and social–philosophical issues are raised in such discussions, they need not be treated here. What is at stake can be recognized by pondering on the following piece from Lowe: 'Stated in general terms, not all macro-goals are intrinsically compatible with any prevailing order of social relations. Whenever a conflict arises, we are compelled to choose between abandoning the goal or the existing order, the latter at the peril of applying means which may defeat the end?'

Critical Reflections

Here we consider first the mix of criticisms levelled at the tenets of instrumental analysis and political economics by the participants in the New York conference. They were concerned to expose the points of limitation and weakness in Lowe's theses, but his 'Rejoinder' (Essay 6 below) negates each point concisely and effectively.

At the hub of the rationale for instrumental analysis is the factual judgement that the industrialized capitalist system does not exhibit sufficient order and coherence to provide deductive reasoning with reliable premises. This lack of order continues to exist in spite of the range of interventions by governments since the Second World War designed to bring stability to the system. Lowe notes that to argue against this judgement by indicating the increasing degree of rational decision making and operational sophistication at the micro-level is to miss the point. It is a lack of conscious co-ordination of individual processes and goals that leads to suboptimal *macro*-provisioning outcomes in market economies characterized by the exercise of monopoly power. Only the deeper penetration of *secondary* controls can be expected to elicit behavioural patterns that are consistent with macro-goals.

Moreover, the refutation of this objection to the factual judgement of disorder is important to Lowe for methodological reasons. An argument against the development of instrumental analysis is that the use of the deductive method in the natural sciences must contend with a similar diversity of object characteristics from field to field and over time. In order to negate this objection, Lowe observed that in any one field at any one time, the object faced by natural scientists is autonomous and orderly. In economics the situation is quite different. While its object is well defined, it just does not have these 'scientifically' necessary qualities anywhere at the present time.

The subject of macro-goals themselves also confounded Lowe's critics to a considerable extent. This gave him cause to re-emphasise that, however complex the potential goal structures may become with their multitude of options and incompatibilities, it is *not* the task of a political economics to provide the criteria for selecting a goal matrix. To the extent that the feasibility and compatibility of goals are technical issues, instrumental analysis can formerly expose the relevant considerations. But, as Lowe points out, more often than not these difficulties are of a political origin and do not arise as absolute technical limitations; with the case of the full-employment–low-inflation conflict being a well known example.

A further criticism that concerned Lowe is that instrumental analysis must end up applying the very behavioural 'laws' which have been rejected in his critique of orthodox theory. That this is a misunderstanding becomes clear when the nature of the heuristic search procedure that provides the logical 'material' for the instrumental reasoning is fully recognized. The process of regressive inference derives the necessary links 'back' to the motivational patterns that would generate a goal-adequate path of behaviours and structural operations. All these links are of an 'engineering' kind rather than being immediately behavioural. That is, they remain contingent until the final link is activated by the implementation of a set of *secondary* controls that will induce individuals to adopt the motivations and expectations specified.

Lowe readily grants that the sociopsychological process of controlling motivations and expectations is an area for further research. Control design, therefore, acts as a limiting element in the application of instrumental analysis. The effect is to constrain the goals to be pursued to those that are clearly understood and affirmed at the micro-level and that are relatively short range in their realization. Hence Lowe's emphasis on stabilization and balanced growth as gambits in progressively developing a more complex and detailed goal set.

In his 'Self-critique' (Essay 8 below), Lowe was not concerned with criticisms in the sense of the 'mistakes, oversights and other imperfections' referred to above. Rather he used the term critique here to refer to the process of clarification of the intellectual foundations of an author's extant ideas. These foundations are of concern because they are often of a different epistemological status from the ideas themselves. They are 'presuppositions' or 'beliefs' that are refractory to any analytical or experimental refutation and yet they have a fundamental place in the philosophy of science. Lowe's objective was to explore the relevance of such 'beliefs' to the foundations of social science, with particular reference to his own development of political economics.

Lowe identified three categories of such 'beliefs' that act to bring coherence to natural science. First, there are 'metaphysical requirements' that regularize the construction of any theoretical argument, most especially the belief in object 'permanence' and 'stability'. Secondly, science depends on more substantive 'thematic hypotheses' which serve as axiomatic premises for the development of formal analyses, without being in their particularity either empirically or logically necessary. Thirdly, there will exist a paradigm 'in which metaphysical requirements combine with certain thematic hypotheses in a specific "matrix"' that represents a specific way of viewing the object. These 'matrices' provide the accepted boundaries for theoretical and empirical research in a field of science as long as they remain historically dominant.

The issue for Lowe to address is whether or not this taxonomy of 'beliefs' can be applied to economic analyses. His view is that they can. Orthodox economic reasoning begins from a belief in the order, permanence and stability of the capitalist market system. This foundation is made more behaviourally specific by a belief in the universality of the motivational postulate that all economic decision makers choose to minimize 'costs' and maximize 'returns'. The combination of this latter 'thematic hypothesis' with the specified market characteristics constitutes a paradigmatic belief in the maintenance of order and stability by virtue of a self-correcting negative-feedback process that involves responses to particular price–quantity signals.

A key characteristic of economic analysis is that its object changes over time. Consequently there should be an accompanying pattern of change in the paradigmatic basis for analysis. Any simultaneous existence of two alternative paradigms upon which extant analyses of a particular historical economic object are based may mean that one of them is anachronistic—in particular, that one may be sustaining a pattern of beliefs that is no longer relevant to the contemporary object form.

In Lowe's view, this situation has emerged in economics as the capitalist system has become inherently more unstable. This he ascribes to the decreasing influence of any automatic negative-feedback mechanisms that may have operated in the earlier stages of the system's evolution. The trend is towards more destabilizing positive feedbacks and the structural forms of the modern system prohibit any reversal of that trend. Here Lowe uses his 'glass' analogy: while he sees the 'glass' of provisioning in modern capitalism as half empty and likely to become completely so if left to itself, orthodox economists see it as half full and quite capable of being refilled automatically by 'free' market processes.

Thus the issue must be resolved as a practical matter: is action or inaction the more appropriate response to the feedbacks of modern capitalism? Lowe's political economics calls for a very definite set of actions that will try to restore the behavioural requirements for stabilizing negative feedback. And this is to be achieved without having to advocate the impossible task of negating or reversing the structural characteristics of accumulated industrial development and the associated non-competitive markets. By contrast, calls for inaction ignore the influence of structures and market forms that generate positive-feedback behaviours and instability in the first place.

Whatever its current limitations, Lowe's political economics warrants further research and development. The problems that it addresses are very real and, as his arguments indicate, there is little reason to be confident that 'the free market' can cure them. On the contrary. There are well-reasoned arguments for believing that unstable provisioning is a result of uncontrolled markets *in their currently existing structural forms*. Lowe's contributions provide us with guidance as to how we might use existing markets to better human advantage.

NOTES

1. cf. Robert L. Heilbroner, *The Worldly Philosophers*, (New York: Simon and Schuster, 1953) in which this term is coined. Kenneth Boulding, in reviewing *On Economic Knowledge* in *Scientific American*, May 1965, was the first to call Lowe an 'economic philosopher'. Another appreciation of Lowe as a philosopher of the economics of the 'real world' is contained in Heilbroner's 'Portrait: Adolph Lowe', *Challenge*, September–October 1978, pp. 66–7. The scope of Lowe's intellectual reach can be gleaned from the bibliography of his works presented at the end of this volume. There have been three *Festschriften* devoted to Lowe and his work: Harald Hagemann und Heinze D. Kurz (Hrsg.), *Beschäftigung,Verteilung und Konjunktur: Zur Politischen Ökonomik der modernen Gesellschaft*, (Bremen: Universität Bremen, 1984); a special issue of *Social Research*, **50**; (Summer 1983); and a special issue of the *Eastern Economic Journal*, **X** (April–June 1984).
2. See especially 'Wie ist Konjunkturtheorie überhaupt möglich?' (1926). The publication details for this and all subsequent references to Lowe's works can be found in the bibliography at the end of this volume.
3. Fritz Burchardt, 'Die Schemata des stationären Kreislaufs bei Böhm-Bawerk und Marx', *Weltwirtschaftliches Archiv*, **34** (1931) and **35** (1932). The thesis of Burchardt is present also in R. Nurkse, 'The schematic representation of the structure of production', *Review of Economic Studies*, **2** (1935). David Clark's paper 'Confronting the linear imperialism of the Austrians: Lowe's contribution to capital and growth theory', *Eastern Economic Journal*, **X** (April–June 1984), provides an interesting exposition of the Burchardt–Lowe thesis in relation to modern analyses of capital and motion.
4. 'Wie ist Konjunkturtheorie überhaupt möglich?', p. 190n.
5. *See Economics and Sociology: A Plea for Co-operation in the Social Sciences* (1935); 'Economic analysis and social structure' (1936); and the later paper written after Lowe had moved to the United States, 'A reconsideration of the law of supply and demand' (1942). Ultimately, the critique formed a main theme of the *magnum opus*, *On Economic Knowledge: Toward a Science of Political Economics* (1965).
6. This thesis was initially developed in *Economics and Sociology*.
7. In his 1937 pamphlet, *The Price of Liberty*, Lowe used the case of England to illustrate that at a more general social level, order can prevail in what is essentially a free society by means of 'self-restraint and social and mental conformity'. In this case, the conformity is spontaneous and 'it is not felt as a compulsion but as the genuine form of self-realisation'. Thus England provided 'proof that even a great industrial society can function spontaneously' such that freedom is possible without anarchy and order without autocracy. 'Social control of the general dynamics of society, political and technical', is the price of liberty.
8. For a thorough comparative analysis of the alternative Walrasian and classical–Marxian backgrounds to the development of disaggregated circular flow models *see* Edward Nell, 'Theories of growth and theories of value', *Economic Development and Cultural Change*, **16** (1967); and Vivian Walsh and Harvey Gram, *Classical and Neoclassical Theories of General*

Equilibrium: Historical Origins and Mathematical Structure, (New York: Oxford University Press, 1980).

9. E. von Böhm-Bawerk, *The Positive Theory of Capital*, [1891], (New York: G. E. Strechert, 1946), Book II, Section IV. Similar 'linear' perceptions are to be found in Karl Marx, *Theories of Surplus Value*, translated by E. Burns, Part I, (Moscow: Progress Publishers, 1963), pp. 107–47 and J. B. Clark, *The Distribution of Wealth*, (New York: Macmillan, 1899), Chapters XVIII to XX; *Essentials of Economic Theory*, (New York: Macmillan, 1924), Chapters IV, V, XV.

10. cf. Michal Kalecki's thesis that 'the long-run trend is but a slowly changing component of a chain of short-period situations . . .': in *Selected Essays on the Dynamics of the Capitalist Economy*, (Cambridge: Cambridge University Press, 1971), p. 165. This notion was also applied by Joan Robinson throughout her many works on the motion of capitalism.

11. Conference of the Universities-National Bureau Committee for Economic Research held in New York, 6–8 November 1953.

12. Lowe's concern with technological change has always transcended this structural–analytical context. The human dimensions of the issue were explored in two papers that deal with the employment effects of such change. In these papers, 'The social productivity of technical improvements' (1937) and 'Technological unemployment reexamined' (1955), Lowe's concern was to show that extant analyses fail to take due cognisance of the physicotechnical structural rigidities in production and the inflexibilities in the quality of the labour power stock when arguing the 'costs' of the adjustments required by technological change. Human displacement is, consequently, underestimated. His message is that a properly managed, but still voluntaristic and decentralized, market system can achieve much in realizing the 'benefits' of change while minimizing the economic and human 'costs' of adjustment.

13. 'Wirtschaftstheorie–der nächste Schritt' (1959).

14. In *Economics and Sociology*.

15. cf. Robert Heilbroner's 'The problem of value in the constitution of economic thought', *Social Research*, **50** (Summer 1983), where the conclusion is more hopeful concerning embodied abstract labour as a value basis (p. 276).

16. 'Introduction' to Robert L. Heilbroner (ed.), *Economic Means and Social Ends: Essays in Political Economics*, (Englewood Cliffs, NJ: Prentice-Hall, 1969), pp. vii–viii; and quoted by Lowe with full concurrence in 'Is the glass half full or half empty?' with the emphasis added (Essay 8 below).

17. This theme is especially clearly argued by Richard Chase in 'Adolph Lowe's paradigm shift for a scientific economics: an interpretive perspective', *American Journal of Economics and Sociology*, **42** (April 1983).

18. See Norwood R. Hanson, *Patterns of Discovery*, (London: Cambridge University Press, 1958), especially Chapter IV; and the interesting argument developed by Derek Sayer in *Marx's Method: Ideology, Science and Critique in 'Capital'*, (Hassocks, Sussex: Harvester Press, 1979), pp. 110ff.

Part I
Analysing the Structure and Motion of Economic Systems

1 A Structural Model of Production*

It is one sign of the greatness of any achievement, practical or theoretical, scientific or artistic, that its creative stimulus extends far beyond the area for which its author designed it originally. The ultimate intention of Keynes' *General Theory* was certainly practical–political: the aetiology and therapy of capitalist underemployment. It is true, the work abounds with novel scientific tools. But they were forged or, as in the case of the multiplier concept, borrowed for the purpose of illuminating specific problems in applied economics rather than of enriching our tool chest in general. And yet concepts like the consumption function, the marginal efficiency of investment, or the aggregate supply function have become the cornerstone for a general macro-theory of the market, not to mention the strategic role which Keynes' national-income analysis now plays in such diverse fields as economic budgeting and the study of economic change.

The last reference is perhaps the most surprising. It has often been pointed out that Keynes' analytical framework is basically static. Not only are the main data—tastes as well as obstacles—taken as given, but the variables are all related to the same point of time. To be sure, there are notes on the trade cycle and 'occasional digressions', which concern themselves with 'the slow effects of secular progress' (*General Theory*, p. 109). But these passages are too vague to have stimulated more than general speculations on the dynamics of the economic process. In this field the real advances that the Keynesian work has promoted stem from the subsequent 'dynamization' of some of its static concepts. Harrod's synthesis of the multiplier and the accelerator, later refined by Samuelson, Hicks' 'multiplier in a changing economy', and again Harrod's dynamization of the saving–investment identity are cases in point.[1] A book like Hicks' recent study on the trade cycle is hardly

* I wish to express special thanks to Hans Neisser for a number of critical suggestions, pertaining in particular to Section VIII, and to Elizabeth Todd for her creative editorship.

[This Essay was first published in *Social Research*, **19**, 1952. Minor corrections and amendments have been undertaken by the author. — ed.]

conceivable without the building blocks of Keynesian economics. Only on these foundations could he succeed in formalizing his model to such a degree that it can serve as illustration for quite a number of seemingly contradictory theories.

In long-term dynamics, progress along these lines has only started. Of the typical dynamic relations that rule in business cycles, namely lags and derivations, only the latter appear, on *a priori* grounds, to be relevant also in secular change. But, as Harrod and Domar have shown, certain circular mechanisms, like the interaction between multiplier and accelerator, are useful tools also in the study of self-reinforcing growth.

I

The more we learn about the various modes of change and their interaction, the more important it becomes that we form a clear notion of the substratum of such changes. More precisely, our ultimate success in handling dynamic phenomena analytically will depend upon a full grasp not only of the change processes themselves, but also of the strategic variables of the economic system which are exposed to change.

In this respect Keynes' contribution has been even more authoritative, though perhaps, as this paper is to show, less definitive. At any rate, the skeleton of practically all dynamic models designed in recent years is Keynes' national-income identity, or the saving–investment identity derived from it. Thus the basic variables with which modern dynamic analysis operates are aggregate income or output and its components: consumption and saving, or consumption and investment. In the models of secular growth, induced investment is usually distinguished from autonomous investment, and a variable for the capital stock and its depreciation is added. The same specifications are found in certain business-cycle models, some of which take account also of employment, wage and profit rates, and the general price level. More often employment is, in Keynesian fashion, supposed to be uniquely corre- lated with national income, whereas the basic wage rate is treated as a datum, in accord with Keynes' use of the wage unit as the fixed value unit of the system.

The variables enumerated here arc fairly representative of the models devised, for example, by Goodwin, Hansen, Harrod, Hicks, Lange, or Metzler in business-cycle analysis, and by Domar and Harrod in growth analysis.[2] One may wonder whether the choice is wide enough for the study of all dynamic phenomena—wide enough for such problems as the employment and income effects of technical changes, or the peculiar demand and supply conditions affecting the early development stages of so-called backward regions. Nevertheless, our interest here does not centre on possible gaps in the set of variables on which post-Keynesian dynamics builds. What provokes comment is the peculiar manner in which the elements composing the set appear in the various models.

As a rule, all these variables are treated solely as value aggregates or price sums, to the exclusion of the physical–technical properties which attach to them in an industrial system. The implications of this practice can best be shown by considering the one magnitude which even conventional analysis subdivides into physically distinct components: national income, as made up of consumption and investment. There the difference in the technical functions which certain groups of commodities and services perform has been fully recognized, and the integral concepts of income and output have been disaggregated accordingly. But no further reduction, in physical terms, of the component parts themselves—that is, consumption and, above all, investment—is customary. This is quite surprising considering the importance which certain modern business-cycle theories, for example, attach to the physical form taken by investment: fixed capital or working capital, for either additional consumer goods or additional capital goods.[3] Once we treat the law of diminishing returns less cavalierly than has become customary in building long-term dynamic models, we shall have to distinguish between the output of raw materials and that of manufacturing. Still more complicated physical differentiation is required if, in dealing with technical changes, we give up the simple notion of 'neutral' inventions, which are on balance neither labour saving nor capital saving (Harrod). Then it becomes essential to diagnose the precise locus of the technical reorganization: in the sphere of consumer goods or of capital goods, in the stage of finished output or in some earlier stage of production.

Such studies of the physical–technical relationships among the main sectors of the productive structure would by no means have only academic interest. Twice during the last decade a speedy adjustment of American industry to the requirements of defence was impeded by a peculiar physical bottleneck, the lack of machine tools. What stands in the way of an accelerated development of backward regions is not so much general poverty as scarcity of specific commodities, namely capital goods, the physical form of which changes typically with the progress in development.

Still, it is not difficult to understand why the physical aspects of the productive order, and thus the physical conditions for dynamic equilbrium, have received so little attention in both neoclassical and Keynesian economics. Obviously their significance is directly related to the extent to which the dynamic process is exposed to large *internal shifts of specific resources* more or less *fully utilized*. The whole issue can safely be disregarded if resources are by and large non-specific, or if the normal state of the system is one of underemployment. The former condition is assumed in most neoclassical reasoning, whereas the latter proposition is in the centre of Keynesian analysis. Certainly the premise of non-specificity, which was taken over into neoclassical theory from the older classical notion of the 'natural' mobility of the factors of production, has never been realistic, and has become less so with the progress of large-scale industrialization. On the other hand, the Keynesian proposition of underutilization of resources pretty well pictured the facts of the nineteenth and early twentieth centuries, except in boom periods. Such underutilization, though logically contradicting the full-employment framework of neoclassical analysis, made many of the latter's conclusions empirically valid, among them the thesis of the short-run adaptability of the system to large shifts. Most internal adjustments took the form of different rates of growth of the strategic sectors, brought about within a secular process of aggregate expansion. By focusing attention on aggregate changes, Keynesian economics enhanced the traditional belief in the ease with which sectional shifts can be carried out.

As no one realized more clearly than Keynes himself, the practical success of his teaching, brought about through an effective full-employment policy, would make classical theory 'come into its own again'. In the present context this means that in the absence of short-run variations of aggregate employment and output, internal adjustments have to take the Ricardian form of shifting the factors of production among the sectors—but this must now occur under structural conditions in which the Ricardian premise of perfect mobility has been superseded by the specificity of most inputs, not to mention the monopolistic and monopsonistic obstacles to speedy adjustment.

II

If this diagnosis of the adjustment problem under 'regulated' capitalism is correct, the need for a model which takes account of the sectional differentiation of the process of production can hardly be denied. As we have seen, the task is not one of merely adding more variables to the Keynesian set. Nor is it one of disaggregation in general. In the latter case Leontief's input–output table would present the ideal solution.[4] There, in conformance with the Walrasian model of general equilibrium, the physical interrelationships among all the elementary sectors of production, transportation, distribution and consumption have been registered, with their quantitative interdependence described for particular years in the American economy. For the solution of practical problems of comprehensive planning and 'programming', a detailed schema of the Leontief type seems indispensable. But for general analytical purposes its greatest advantage, the high degree of disaggregation, turns into an obstacle.

One reason for this is that it is extremely difficult to trace the dynamic path for such a large number of variables, and to impute their behaviour to specific causes, especially if they are exposed to several stimuli simultaneously. For another thing, a study of the most typical dynamic processes—changes in aggregate demand, in the supply of labour, natural resources, savings and money, and in the technique of production—makes desirable a higher degree of aggregation, in order to throw into clearer relief the pertinent features of the physical structure of production. Certainly, specificity of inputs and outputs creates adjustment problems ultimately for each individual firm. But the ensuing frictions become relevant for the stability of the system only when their size and locus exert a marked effect on the strategic variables, such as aggregate income and its distribution, spending and hoarding, consumption, saving and investment. Thus the task consists in choosing a level of aggregation between those chosen by Keynes and Leontief—high enough to permit analytical manipulation of complex dynamic processes, low enough to reflect those physical properties of an industrial market which affect its general stability.

As a matter of fact, a model of the productive process satisfying these requirements has been available for well over half a century. But it has been stowed away in a place where academic economics, at least its Anglo-American brand, is unlikely to search for conceptual enlightenment. I refer to the schema of production, more precisely of reproduction, which is contained in the second volume of Marx's *Capital*.[5] Inspired by Quesnay's 'tableau économique', Marx's schema is the only comprehensive macroeconomic model of the industrial process of production established before Keynes.

This claim may seem exaggerated in view of the so-called Austrian model of the structure of production, which was first expounded by Eugen von Böhm-Bawerk, only six years after the publication of the second volume of *Capital*.[6] Through the work of Wicksell, and the studies of von Mises and von Hayek on money and business cycles, the Austrian concept has had great influence on Anglo-American economic thinking. But as I shall presently have occasion to point out more precisely, the Austrian schema depicts only a certain segment of the industrial process, a segment, moreover, which Marx discussed at length in the *Theorien über den Mehrwert*, (**I**, pp. 198–231; or *Theories of Surplus Value*, **I**, pp. 107–47). In fairness to Böhm-Bawerk's contribution it should be mentioned, however, that the *Theorien* was published only in 1905, though Marx wrote it, according to Engels' testimony, between 1861 and 1863. In this context a word of acknowledgement is due to John Bates Clark, who as early as 1899 gave a brief description of the flow of production which exhibits in essence all the basic features of Marx's schema.[7] What prevented Clark from drawing the full benefit from his model is the fact that he used it as an expository device rather than as a tool of analysis.

The credit for having synthesized the original ideas of Marx and Böhm-Bawerk in an overall presentation of the problem belongs to F. A. Burchardt.[8] His study corrects some errors in Marx's exposition, in particular his confusion of stocks and flows, and adds all that is valuable in Böhm-Bawerk's version. Though mainly concerned with the static aspects of a schema of production, Burchardt leaves no doubt about its relevance as an instrument for dynamic analysis. In what follows I shall draw heavily on Burchardt's essay, in the original drafting of which I was privileged to participate. I shall concentrate, however, on the positive solution of the problem under investigation, refraining from all polemical digressions. In particular, I shall not go into my reservations regarding the Austrian concept of the structure of production, an extensive critique of which can be found in Burchardt's essay.

III

If at any point of time we were to undertake a census of an industrial community's wealth in physical terms, we would find altogether four different stocks: a stock of labour; a stock of natural resources; a stock of equipment, such as plants, machinery, residential buildings; and a stock of other commodities, which shall presently be discussed specifically.

We would find these stocks distributed among a number of productive units, whose activity consists in converting, through certain technical processes, portions of some or all of the stocks into new commodities. This yields us the most general definition of 'production' in the technical sense of the word—the only sense in which we are interested at the moment.

It will prove useful to subdivide these stocks in four progressive steps, as follows:

First, we can distinguish between 'original' stocks—labour and natural resources, which are the ultimate data of the productive process—and 'manufactured' stocks, represented by the last two types of commodities included in the list.

Secondly, concentrating on the manufactured stocks in particular, we can subdivide them according to the degree of 'completion'. Unfinished and finished commodities are easily distinguished, with the latter defined as those that are 'ready for use'. It is conventional to subdivide the group of unfinished commodities further into raw materials and semimanufactured goods, but there is no easy criterion for this distinction. Since production as a technical process consists of an unbroken chain of operations, any caesura made in order to establish definite 'stages' of completion is arbitrary. This will have to be kept in mind when presently, for reasons of exposition, we devise a 'stage' model. As for transportation and commerce, it is convenient to include these activities in our definition of production, and to regard a commodity as completed only when it has reached its final place and time of use.

Thirdly, narrowing down our field of vision still further, we can classify the group of finished commodities according to their specific use as either consumer goods or equipment goods. The former are used up in the households, whereas the latter are used up during the process of production. (The term 'used up' defines precisely what happens to equipment and consumer goods, in distinction to what happens to the stock of unfinished goods, which are 'used' but not 'used up' during the process of production.) It must be stressed that the physical appearance of a commodity does not always clearly indicate in which group it belongs. The obvious example is coal. It can serve, on the one hand, as a consumer good in the household, on the other hand as an auxiliary material and even as an unfinished commodity (chemical industry) in the productive process. In any concrete case it should be possible, however, to establish the function of a good unambiguously.

Fourthly, our final distinction refers to what figures in the literature as the difference between 'durable' and 'non-durable' commodities. The terminology is not a particularly useful guide to what the distinction is meant to convey. It is true that the number of services a finished commodity is capable of rendering is of great importance for the study of dynamic processes; this is true, for example, of most equipment goods. But some of the essential problems that arise in this connection should be treated from the point of view of 'divisibility' rather than 'durability'. Divisibility as an economic concept depends, however, on the prevailing terms of purchase or hire, no less than on the technical properties of the good in question.

A distinction which takes account of these latter complications is that between goods bought with 'income' and goods bought with 'capital', in the sense of savings funds and business funds.[9] This classification is especially helpful for deciding on certain borderline cases. I refer to residential buildings and a number of other 'durable' and 'semidurable' goods like automobiles which, though intended for use in final consumption, are as a rule financed by means other than current income. They should be treated like equipment goods, and only their services entered on the side of consumption. Also certain auxiliary materials—like coal applied as industrial fuel, or lubricant oils, which are used up in one single act of production—though certainly non-durable in the conventional sense, are, because of their economic functions, preferably classified with productive equipment, which is what our definition does.[10]

Thus far we have dealt with the types of goods and services that make up the physical wealth of a community. It will also be necessary for us to distinguish the productive units in which these goods and services are combined, or from whose productive activity they emanate. In this respect our fundamental distinction is between consumer-goods and equipment-goods industries. Above we have confined the terms 'consumer good' and 'equipment good' to the finished products ready to be 'used up'. In now classifying the two basic industrial groups, it is convenient to extend the meaning of these terms so that they include all stages of production that lead up to the finished goods. In other words, our category of consumer-goods industries includes not only those productive units that actually 'complete' the finished good, but all other units preceding the final stage in the process of completion and thus producing unfinished goods which are to mature into finished consumer goods. The same considerations are valid for our definition of equipment-goods industries.

Since the physical distinction between the goods belonging to the two groups is blurred, it cannot be expected that the respective industries are clearly divided up. On the contrary, certain industries, like coal mining or chemical production, belong to both categories, and it is again only the concrete situation which, revealing the purpose, can tell us where to draw the exact dividing line. Among the equipment-goods industries I propose to distinguish between those that produce equipment to be applied in the production of consumer goods, and others that produce equipment for the equipment-goods industries themselves. Once more it is not postulated that this distinction is always reflected in the actual differentiation of the business units that make up the equipment industry as a whole. But for certain analytical purposes it is important to subdivide at least the output of finished equipment goods according to these two categories.

We now move on from the consideration of stocks to that of the relevant flows. A continuous flow of production requires that the industrial groups, the various stages of completion into which they are subdivided, and the portions of each of the four stocks of goods and services assigned to the individual productive units in every stage of every group, are arranged in a definite order. This order changes, as a rule, with changes in the technique of production. But given a certain technique of production, the relative size and the sequence of the groups and stages are determined.

This has never been contested for the size and sequence of the stages, and there the conceptions of Marx and Böhm-Bawerk coincide. Such an order of stages can easily be described, as shown in the accompanying model, in which N stands for the stock of labour, F for the stock of fixed-capital goods available at each stage (though in Böhm-Bawerk's and Hayek's models F does not appear among the factors of production), and R for the stock of natural resources. Capital letters are used to indicate stocks, irrespective of how much of each stock enters the actual flow of production during any given period of time. Flows are symbolized by lower-case letters. The arrows signify no more than the causal relationship between stocks and inputs on the one hand and outputs on the other hand, and at this stage of our analysis do not express any definite quantitative order. Similarly, the symbol $\cup$ connecting the inputs indicates that for the purpose of production these items are combined in fixed proportions.

Stocks and input flows	Output flows
$N_1 \cup F_1 \cup R_1$	$\rightarrow w_1 = cotton$
$N_2 \cup F_2 \cup R_2 \cup w_1$	$\rightarrow w_2 = yarn$
$N_3 \cup F_3 \cup R_3 \cup w_2$	$\rightarrow w_3 = cloth$
$N_4 \cup F_4 \cup R_4 \cup w_3$	$\rightarrow w_4 = c = dress$

Our stage model contains only one set of flow magnitudes: several items of working-capital goods, denoted by w. In the first stage this symbol appears only once, indicating the output of that stage. In each of the subsequent stages, however, it appears twice, both as an item of input and as an item of output. And at any stage the input w is always of the same kind (though not necessarily of the same quantity) as the output w of the preceding stage. This arrangement manifests the technical meaning of the process of production as the progressive transformation of the 'passive' factor—natural resources—with the help of the 'active' factors—labour and fixed-capital goods. In this process the factor R plays its main role in the first stage, but since every plant has to have a location it cannot be eliminated from the later stages. Working-capital goods are in this sense nothing but partially transformed natural resources, which in the final stage take on the form of the finished good—in our model, a finished consumer good.

To assure continuity of production, two conditions have to be fulfilled. The active factors have to operate in a predetermined sequence on the passive factors, among which we may now count, besides natural resources, also the inputs of working-capital goods. In addition, the stocks of active factors and of natural resources have to be continuously replenished in proportion to what they release into actual production. With regard to the renewal of the stocks of labour and natural resources, economic analysis has nothing to say. Except in a slave economy, in which labour would have to be treated as a fixed-capital good, a continuing supply of labour and natural resources belongs among the 'data' of the economic process.

The case is different with regard to fixed-capital goods, and it is at this point that the models of Marx and Böhm-Bawerk part company. Fixed equipment is as much the result of natural resources, gradually transformed with the help of labour and fixed-capital goods, as are dresses or hats. Therefore by changing the quality of the inputs in our stage model, we can arrive at a sequence of, say, ore–pigiron–steel–machinery, which illustrates the process of production of a fixed-capital good.

But we see at once that this procedure does not solve one basic difficulty. In adding a second-stage model illustrating the output of fixed-capital goods, we tacitly assume the existence of further fixed-capital goods which can function as input factors in the production of such goods, and we seem to be involved in an infinite regress. To avoid this dilemma we might look for a kind of fixed-capital good which is produced with the help of labour and natural resources only. Obviously this would take us back to the beginning of history, when primitive man first picked up a stone to use it as a tool. This not only would teach us little about economic history, but would utterly fail to explain how, on our level of industrial civilization, the existing stock of fixed-capital goods is continuously renewed in the technical sense, not to say expanded, if we assume that the available stock of equipment is fully utilized.

Burchardt (pp. 137–40) has drawn attention to a more elementary situation which poses the same problem. We meet it in agricultural production, even under the most primitive conditions. How can the output of, say, wheat be maintained? Disregarding tools altogether, we require for this purpose labour, land and seed wheat. A constant yield is assured only if part of the final product, wheat, is allotted every year not to consumption but, in the form of seed wheat, to the production of the next crop. And, if the next crop is to be increased over the present one, the ratio of the productive use to the consumptive use of wheat has to be raised.

What makes this example illustrative for our problem, and points the way to its solution, is not the acts of gross saving and net saving as such, but the technical precondition on which they rest. The required shift in use is possible only because wheat and seed wheat are physically identical goods. Thus the primary condition for the economic reproduction of wheat is its physical capacity for self-reproduction.

The lesson is obvious. Only if we succeed in discovering in the realm of fixed-capital goods certain instruments which share with wheat the capacity for physical self-reproduction can our problem be solved. In other words, we have to look for a type of equipment which is technically suited to produce other equipment as well as its own kind. What we find, as a matter of fact, is not one single instrument, but the comprehensive group of instruments which are classified as machine tools. They are for industrial production what seed wheat or the reproductive system in animals represents for agricultural production. They form an indispensable part of input whenever an equipment good, including machine tools themselves, is to be produced. And in the industrial sphere, as is the case in the agricultural sphere, saving and investing rest on a technical foundation: the fact that the existing stock of machine tools can be used for the production of new machine tools.

IV

We have now collected all the basic elements with the help of which the main physical–technical conditions for a continuous flow of industrial production can be described. I propose first to illustrate the resulting schema by a diagram, and then to present in algebraic form certain important relations among the variables. In the accompanying diagram of the schema (Figure 1.1) the essential features are as follows, if we disregard the arabic numbers for the time being.

The order of production has been vertically divided into the two elementary groups, equipment-goods industries and consumer-goods industries, henceforth denoted respectively by the Roman numerals *I* and *II*. To simplify presentation, group *II* is drawn on a smaller scale than I, and is represented by one good only. Group *I*, on the other hand, has been subdivided into *Ia*, which produces the fixed-capital goods applied in group *Ia*, and *Ib* which supplies group *II*. The division

38

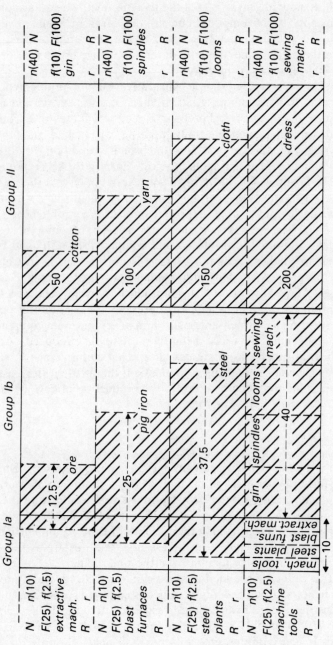

Figure 1.1: Schema of production

is technically relevant only for the last stage, where the productive process in group *I* divides into different types of finished goods.[11] All groups are horizontally divided into four stages, representing the successive maturing of natural resources into finished goods. Again, for the sake of simplicity, the number of stages is made the same in each group.

On both sides of the schema are recorded the active factors—labour, fixed-capital goods and natural resources—the continuous application of which maintains the process of production. In each main group these three factors appear at each stage. Again they are denoted by capital letters (*N*, *F*, *R*), to show that we are dealing with stocks. For the fixed-capital goods the particular physical form in which these goods appear is indicated.

All other magnitudes measure flows—input and output flows—over a certain period of time. The input flows are the specific amounts of the stocks of active factors which enter the productive process at each stage during the given period; these are indicated by the small letters *n*, *f*, and *r* representing, respectively, the hours of labour, the wear and tear on the fixed-capital goods and the amount of natural resources introduced into the process of production over the period. The output flows are represented by the shaded rectangles, which show, in each stage, the outputs produced by the inputs of active factors in combination with the working-capital goods of that stage.

It has already been mentioned that, from the technical point of view, the number of stages and the points of separation between two stages are arbitrary, and this is true also of any attempt to construct a total from a combination of all stages. Certainly such a total must not be mistaken for a measure of the 'flow of working capital' over a given period, a concept that will be examined more closely in the last section of this paper. To be sure, an exact meaning can be attached to the sum total of all stages if we interpret the order of stages as an indicator of business differentiation. Then the total measures the aggregate exchange transactions that occur during the process of transforming natural resources into finished goods. But this magnitude, though of great importance for monetary analysis, has no relevance for the physical–technical aspect of production.

The situation is different with the concept of a stock of working-capital goods. Such a stock must indeed be available continuously if the flow of production is to be continuous. It is not immediately visible in our schema, but it can easily be derived from its elements. To do so we had best start from the moment when the production flow is generated for the first time. To set it in motion, a certain amount of active factors has to be combined with a certain amount of natural resources in the first stage. The resulting output moves to the next stage, to be combined there with another set of active factors, while at the same time a second set of such factors appears in the first stage—and so on until after a certain lapse of time the first quantity of finished output becomes available. From then on, every additional unit of input is matched by a unit of output; but an amount of input equivalent to that accumulated in the various stages during the period of gestation remains permanently in the system so long as production continues in its original dimensions.

It is this amount of output of intermediate goods built up during the gestation period which measures the permanent stock of working-capital goods in a functioning system. This permanent stock depends on what can be called the period of maturation, that is, the average time it takes to transform a unit of natural resources into a finished good, and on the aggregate input of active factors which enter the system during this period. It is not easy to determine the period of maturation statistically; conceptually the term is unambiguous.[12]

V

The purpose of the schema is to represent the process of production as a number of interdependent flows which are themselves related to the basic stocks of the system.

If we concentrate, to begin with, on group *II*, we find there a vertical as well as a horizontal flow. Vertically, natural resources flow in progressive transformation down to the level of finished consumer goods. But the continuity of this vertical flow is assured only by a horizontal flow, from *I* to *II*, of certain amounts of fixed-capital goods—large enough at least to replace the fixed-capital goods used up in every stage during the vertical flow occuring in group *II*.

The vertical flow is the same in group *I*. At first glance there is, however, an important difference with regard to the horizontal flow. In group *I* the currently used-up equipment is replaced from the output of that group itself—more precisely, from the output of *Ia*. Thus the latter horizontal flow—which is as necessary for the continuity of production in *I* as the above-mentioned horizontal flow is in *II*—consists of a portion of the vertical flow which 'turns back'; that is, it is a circular flow.

This apparent difference between *I* and *II* can be resolved by a simple postulate, which has an analogy in the classical definition of 'gross produce'. Just as the output of *I* currently replaces the used-up fixed-capital goods, the output of *II* can be interpreted as the replacement of the input of the labour factor.[13] Then we have, besides the vertical flows, a circular as well as a horizontal flow in each major group. In *II* the horizontal flow replaces the worn-out fixed-capital goods, whereas the circular flow restores the labour stock operating there. Conversely, in *I* the circular flow restores the stock of fixed-capital goods, whereas a horizontal flow from *II* replaces the labour used up in *I*.

Thus understood, any process of production, stationary or dynamic, consists in combining over a certain period a portion of the available stock of original factors (labour and natural resources) with a portion of the available stocks of fixed-capital and working-capital goods. Then all that production can achieve is to increase or decrease or keep constant, with the help of the free gifts of nature, the existing stocks of labour and capital goods. From this point of view the 'purpose' of production can be seen in the maintenance or change of the productive capital of the system—a technological purpose. And this view can be taken with the same logical right with which we customarily establish a sociological purpose—relating to the maintenance or change of the 'human capital'—when we make consumption the final criterion. As a matter of fact, from the point of view of economic accounting, both interpretations are defective, because they obscure the circular nature of the productive process.

It is the failure of most models based on the Austrian concept of the structure of production that they disregard the circular flows, concentrating rather on the linear ones. There is indeed within each group one linear flow, from the first down to the last stage. But to keep industrial production functioning, no less than five circular processes are required, in addition.

Two of these arise from the fact that within each major group one circular flow channels part of the finished output back to the stock of factors employed in that group: in group *II*, consumer goods back to the labour employed; and in group *I*, fixed-capital goods back to the equipment employed.

Two others arise from the fact that between the two groups circular flows channel part of the output of each group into the other: consumer goods flow to the stock of labour employed in *I*; and fixed-capital goods flow to the stock of equipment employed in *II*.

Finally, there is a circular flow within *I*, for which there is no parallel in *II*. More precisely, it concerns *Ia*, where machine tools and the equipment used in *I* are continuously replaced. From the purely technical point of view, as we have seen above, this last circular flow is the most important. It depicts the act of self-reproduction without which a continuous productive process, not to mention its expansion, would be physically impossible. In the labour factor it has its equivalent in the biosociological organization of man—which, however, is part of the schema of production only in a slave economy.

VI

If the schema is to serve as a tool for dynamic analysis, we have now to transform it from an expository device into a set of quantitative relations. Both the linear and the circular processes lend themselves to such transformation. We shall concentrate here on the circular flows, that is, on the interrelations between the finished outputs of the groups and subgroups—and this for two reasons. On the one hand, modern theory, in spite of its stress on the distinction between consumption and investment, has paid little attention to certain intergroup relations which prove requisite for equilibrium, stationary or dynamic. On the other hand, the answers to certain basic problems in business-cycle theory, as well as in the analysis of growth, hinge on an understanding of these very relations.

Our first step will be to consolidate the productive results of our successive stages, thus obtaining aggregates of group outputs. For this purpose we shall focus on the relationship which exists, in each group, between the aggregate output and the aggregate input of active factors in all stages during the period of observation.

In the following algebraic formulations the output of group *Ia* has been designated as *a*, and that of *Ib* as *b*, while for the output of group *II* the letter *z* is used (this choice of letters if intended to emphasize the technical propinquity of the outputs in the subgroups of *I*). The *n*, *f* and *r* notations stand for the aggregate factor inputs (labour, fixed-capital goods and natural resources, respectively) in all stages of the specified group, the relevant group being specified by enclosing its symbol in parentheses; thus $n(a)$ signifies the labour input in group *Ia*, and $f(z)$ the input of fixed-capital goods in group *II*. Successive periods of observation are designated as t' and t''.

In the three expressions numbered (1.1) we start from the most general causal relationship.

$$n(a)_{t'} \cup f(a)_{t'} \cup r(a)_{t'} \rightarrow a_{t'}$$

$$n(b)_{t'} \cup f(b)_{t'} \cup r(b)_{t'} \rightarrow b_{t'} \qquad (1.1)$$

$$n(z)_{t'} \cup f(z)_{t'} \cup r(z)_{t'} \rightarrow z_{t'}$$

The symbols on the left side of the arrows stand for the 'progress in completion' which takes place during the period t' in the production of equipment goods (*a*) intended to make other equipment goods, equipment goods (*b*) intended to make consumer goods, and, finally, consumer goods themselves (*z*). These expressions, however, tell us only that the outputs are the effects of the inputs.

Much more can be said if we postulate continuous production; then *a*, *b* and *z* assume the exclusive meaning of finished ouput in the respective groups, and we have the (1.2) set of equations (here, and in what follows, it is assumed that natural resources are free goods).

$$
\begin{aligned}
a_{t'} &\geq f(a)_{t'} + f(b)_{t'} \\
b_{t'} &\geq f(z)_{t'} \\
z_{t'} &\geq n(a)_{t'} + n(b)_{t'} + n(z)_{t'}
\end{aligned}
\tag{1.2}
$$

These equations mean that the output of finished equipment (*a* and *b*) during one period must, at least, suffice physically to replace the fixed-capital goods worn out during that period; and that, in accordance with our previous interpretation, the same relationship exists between the output of finished consumer goods (*z*) and the current input of labour. The (1.2) equations are strictly valid only over a period which covers the full life of the available stock of fixed-capital goods. During any period shorter than that it is possible, of course, to continue production without actual replacements. We also have to disregard the existence of liquid capital, that is, inventories of fixed-capital goods, working-capital goods and consumer goods.

These qualifications vanish if we postulate stationary equilibrium. Then the finished output of group *Ia*—henceforth called primary machinery—must, in any period, be physically equal to the equipment input in group *I* as a whole during the preceding, as during the subsequent, period. A similar equality has to prevail between the output of group *Ib*—henceforth called secondary machinery—and the equipment input in group *II*, and also between the output of group *II* and the absorption of consumer goods on the part of all income-receiving factors. But—and only this clarifies the physical meaning of the above equations—it is not enough that finished equipment goods and consumer goods are *produced* in amounts sufficient, and in technical forms adequate, to replace the wear and tear on the stock of factors applied in the current period. Parts of the finished output of both groups must, as it were, change places with one another in the order of production. It is a situation analogous to that in foreign trade when each of two countries exports a certain surplus output not required at home. Here, as there, the condition for the 'exchange' is that the physical form of the 'exports' satisfies the requirements of the 'importing' group.

In the present context the first condition for stationary equilibrium is that the current output of secondary machinery must be exchanged for that part of current consumer-goods output which is not retained for the next period's consumption in group *II* itself. In symbolic terms—and using $q(z)$ to denote the ratio of 'domestic' consumption to total consumption—we can say that $b_{t'}$—which is equal to $f(z)_{t''}$—must be exchanged for $z_{t'} - q(z)z_{t'}$. And analogously, that part of the output of primary machinery which is not required for the continuation of production in group *Ia* has to replace the wear and tear of equipment goods in group *Ib*—though here the goods 'given in exchange' do not consist of the output of group *Ib* itself. As we know, this output, consisting of secondary machinery, has to be wholly transferred to group *II*. The goods given 'in payment' from *Ib* to *Ia* consist of consumer goods intended to satisfy the income receivers in *Ia*, and they are acquired by *Ib* from *II* through the exchange process just described. Group *Ib* retains what is necessary to satisfy income receivers there, and exchanges the rest with Group Ia for primary machinery. For this process the symbolic expression is that $[a - q(a)a]_{t''} = f(b)_{t''}$ exchanges for $z_{t'} - [q(b) + q(z)]z_{t'}$.

Thus the 'balance of trade' is established for *Ia* by the exchange of primary machinery for consumer goods, and for *II* by the exchange of consumer goods for secondary machinery. Group *Ib* first balances its trade with group *II* by exporting secondary machinery for consumer goods, and afterwards uses part of its imports for 're-export' to *Ia*.

Thus far we have concentrated exclusively on the physical–technical aspects of the group relations. But it is obvious that we cannot speak of 'exchange' between aggregates of goods unless there exists, apart from their physical compatibility, an equality in value terms. To repeat once more, a purely physical–technical schema of production can yield very important insights into the qualitative interdependence and direction of a number of sectional input–output flows—insights to which there is no access in the dimension of values alone. The fact remains, however, that the size of the flows in question, and their equality or inequality in economic terms, cannot be determined unless we make physically heterogeneous quantities comparable in terms of prices.

The arabic numbers attached to our original model are an attempt at such a translation of the physical magnitudes into a value schema. They describe, as a basis for dynamic analysis, a stationary flow. As period for the measurement of the flows, the calendar year has been chosen, to which an average depreciation rate of 10 per cent has been applied. Moreover, it is assumed that in each group each of the two priced factors—labour and equipment—makes the same contribution in each stage. Finally, the system is a closed one. Needless to say, the schema is in principle capable of reproducing a much more highly differentiated order of production, especially in the consumer-goods group, and of including also a government sector and interrelations with other systems.

The order of the annual production flow can now be represented by the equations in sets (1.3) and (1.4), and the two 'exchanges' noted above take the form of the equations in sets (1.5) and (1.6).

$$n(a)_{t'}(8) + f(a)_{t'}(2) = a_{t'}(10)$$
$$n(b)_{t'}(32) + f(b)_{t'}(8) = b_{t'}(40) \qquad (1.3)$$
$$\mathrm{n}(z)_{t'}(160) + f(z)_{t'}(40) = z_{t'}(200)$$

$$a_{t'}(10) = f(a)_{t'}(2) + f(b)_{t'}(8)$$
$$b_{t'}(40) = f(z)_{t'}(40) \qquad (1.4)$$
$$z_{t'}(200) = n(a)_{t'}(8) + n(b)_{t'}(32) + n(z)_{t'}(160)$$

$$f(z)_{t'}(40) = b_{t'}(40)$$
$$= z_{t'}(200) - n(z)_{t'}(160) \qquad (1.5)$$
$$= n(a)_{t'}(8) + n(b)_{t'}(32)$$

$$f(b)_{t'}(8) = a_{t'}(10) - f(a)_{t'}(2)$$
$$= z_{t'}(200) - n(b)_{t'}(32) - n(z)_{t'}(160) \qquad (1.6)$$
$$= n(a)_{t'}(8)$$

The (1.3) equations can be called 'group cost–price' relationships, since they express the value relation between aggregate inputs and outputs for the technically relevant groups. The (1.4) equations, establishing the conditions under which production is continuous in the relevant groups, can be labelled 'group reproduction' relationships. The same name may be given to the (1.5) and (1.6) equations, which describe the reproduction process among the groups with reference to both simultaneous and successive relations between priced physical aggregates.

VII

What now is the significance of the schema of production for dynamic analysis? To answer this question we have to supplement for formal exposition of the schema in two directions. On the one hand, we have to demonstrate that our model is capable of reproducing all relevant processes of change in a manner accessible to exact calculation. On the other hand, we have to show that the schema enables us to solve problems which prove refractory under conventional treatment. The present section of this paper is to serve the former purpose. In the concluding section certain specific topics will be discussed which the schema is particularly well adapted to clarify.

The price–cost equations and reproduction equations established above describe stationary equilibrium. An important step is to transform them into a picture of dynamic equilibrium, in which all data vary proportionally; this will be discussed in the next section. Here we focus our attention on dynamic disequilibrium, that is, on disproportional changes in the data and the resulting processes of adjustment. For all conceivable processes of this kind the schema can serve as a *tableau économique*. The data changes themselves, the quantitative variations through which the system adapts itself, and finally the new state toward which the system gravitates—all these can be read in typical changes of the priced physical magnitudes composing the schema.

Looking first at the relations that prevail among the different flows, we can discern the effect of three types of data changes. There are, to begin with, shifts in the quality of demand, following either shifts in taste or such changes in technology as induce the substitution of one kind of machinery for another. These variations are reflected in shifts in factor employment and production flow within either the consumer-goods group or one of the two subgroups of the equipment-goods group. To calculate the effects of such changes we must, of course, disaggregate our group equations into price–cost and reproduction relationships valid for the individual industries in question. We can do so by elaborating on the stage model presented in Section III above. This yields us, for the industries concerned, sets of equations depicting concomitant shifts among those stages of production that are implicated in shifts in demand for the final goods.

The same stage model can serve for the analysis of changes due to depletion of, or decreasing returns from, natural resources. There the shift concerns the transfer of labour and equipment from the later to the earlier stages within a single industry. If we know the size of the original output of final goods in any industry, and the distribution of factors over the different stages of production, we can devise a simple formula with the help of which the fall in output and the new distribution of factors can be calculated for any given fall in returns.

Finally, all technical changes that alter the ratio of the technical coefficients for labour and equipment—movements along, as well as shifts of, a given production function—express themselves as relative changes in factor employment and production flow among the main groups. If the technical coefficients vary in the production of equipment a similar change occurs also among the subgroups of the equipment group as a whole.[14] Since the schema registers, besides the values, also the quantities of the different inputs and outputs, the analysis can be elaborated further. We can calculate, for any given factor distribution, the residual amount of factors which a special change in productivity displaces in one group or subgroup, and which has to be transferred to another group before equilibrium of output and employment can be restored.

The schema, however, is not confined to the reproduction of flows. It also depicts the magnitudes of the basic stocks, and the relations and possible variations among stocks and flows, in terms of both values and quantities. This makes it possible to apply the schema to a step-by-step analysis of the most important dynamic phenomena: changes in labour supply and in saving, and those technical variations that are accompanied by a change in the stock of fixed or working capital. In all these cases a change of some flow magnitude (rate of population increase or of saving, labour input or capital input per unit of output) induces a change in the capital stock or its utilization, via a change in the current output of group *Ia* relative to the output of groups *Ib* and *II*. Unless the initiating change is continuous, a backward shift of factors from group *Ia* to groups *Ib* and *II* has to occur, once the capital stock has been expanded to the new equilibrium size. We know from the discussion of the acceleration principle that this backward shift may lead to the abandonment of part of the newly built capital stock. Analysis with the help of the schema enables us to establish the precise conditions under which such 'waste' occurs, and to calculate its size. If additional assumptions are introduced concerning demand and supply elasticities, we can also take into account the concomitant changes in the relative prices of commodities and factors.

This survey of change processes amenable to schema analysis is not meant to be exhaustive. But a word should perhaps be added concerning so-called endogenous changes, which arise from lags between some of the variables and from variations in such lags, independently of any change in the variables themselves. As was shown above, by the (1.4), (1.5) and (1.6) equation sets, the schema lends itself particularly well to sequence analysis. Moreover, it contains all the variables that have proved relevant in lagged processes, such as receipts, expenditures, inputs and outputs, and in a form which is from the outset 'dated'.

VIII

It is obvious that the actual application of a tool can prove its usefulness more convincingly than the most elaborate methodological considerations are able to do. Therefore I propose in conclusion to employ the schema for a more detailed discussion of a few controversial issues. Of course, all that can be attempted in the framework of an article is an indication of the particular services which the schema can render over and above the contribution of other models. A systematic exposition must be reserved for a more comprehensive presentation.

The selection of the problems will be made with regard for the two main features that distinguish the schema from other economic models, such as the Keynesian national-income identity or the Austrian concept of the structure of production. These features are disaggregation in accordance with certain physical characteristics of the productive process, and the elaboration of the circular flows which, by linking up the basic groups, assure the continuity of reproduction. As we know from our previous considerations, both peculiarities gain importance with the specificity which, under industrial conditions, attaches to equipment as well as to labour. Over the Marshallian long period, and certainly over the secular period, most specificities can be overcome, and therefore the schema appears at first sight most useful for the study of the short-term effects of economic change, in which we have to include business cycles. Even over the secular period, however, a self-propelling system can maintain itself only through the medium of successive short-period adjustments. Hence we shall begin with an example which is to prove the schema's value in solving a problem relevant for both short-run and long-run analysis: the conditions of dynamic equilibrium.

(1) In the late 1930s, when Harrod and Samuelson performed the 'marriage between the multiplier and acceleration theories',[15] a new chapter was opened in economic dynamics. It had been the merit of the older acceleration analysis to show that the dynamic path of the system is greatly influenced by the manner in which the rate of change of some magnitudes affects the level of others. But so long as the causal nexus was treated as one-sided only—the rate of change of demand for consumer goods being the stimulus, and an exogenous one at that—no self-reinforcing process could be derived from acceleration. Only when, through the multiplier concept, the dependence of consumer demand upon investment was taken into account, could true interaction be established, both for the short and for the long run.

Whereas the older 'accelerationists' (Aftalion, J. M. Clark) had been interested mainly in the destabilizing effect exerted on the level of the system's activity by variations in the rate of change of the stimulus, Harrod and, later on, Domar have derived from the interaction analysis an essential condition for dynamic equilibrium.[16] If full utilization of resources is to be maintained through time, the capital stock of the system must grow at such a rate that the current investment necessary for such growth equals current savings provided at full-employment income. Or, what amounts to the same, if the average propensity to save (savings ratio) and the average output—capital ratio for the corresponding investment (investment productivity) are given for any period, investment and output will have to rise over that period by a rate which equals the product of the savings ratio and investment productivity.

The above formulation does not contain any assumption as to the stability of the savings ratio or investment productivity taken in isolation. Either factor may change from period to period so long as their product is constant, and the possibility of such variations only seems to emphasize the importance of the rule. Quite a different problem arises if the coefficients in question not only change autonomously but also adjust themselves to any discrepancy between the rate of output and the rate of capital formation. If potential 'oversaving' causes investment productivity to fall—or, in other words, induces via a fall of the rate of interest a deepening of investment—the above condition of dynamic equilibrium seems to lose its significance. The same is true if any potential 'overinvestment' raises the savings ratio, via a rise of the rate of interest. We are then back at the classical mechanism, which, through short-run adjustments of prices and interest rates, maintains the equilibrium of full utilization against any conceivable distortion.[17]

The empirical validity of the Harrod–Domar condition can easily be defended against the classical proposition. The latter rests on the customary classical assumption of perfect mobility. When production is not conditional on the long-lasting commitment of large private funds, the risks of changes in output and investment productivity are small, and entrepreneurs' expectations will stimulate equilibrating behaviour. But such structural conditions for short-run adjustment do not exist in an industrial system. There the productivity coefficients, in particular, are largely fixed over the short period, and the Harrod–Domar rule becomes indeed a necessary condition for dynamic equilibrium.

Nevertheless—and here we come back to our main subject—the postulate that output and investment *in the aggregate* grow at a rate that equals the savings ratio times investment productivity is not a *sufficient* condition. The absence of perfect mobility and the difficulty of short-run adjustment make it imperative that not only the product of the savings ratio and investment productivity but also the values of each one of these two variables remain constant.

This additional condition can be read in the reproduction equations of dynamic equilibrium. They can be derived from the (1.5) and (1.6) equation sets which refer to stationary equilibrium. In order to serve as conditions for dynamic equilibrium they have to be reformulated to take care of saving and net investment as shown in the accompanying sets numbered (1.5a) and (1.6a), in which $\sigma(a)$, $\sigma(b)$ and $\sigma(z)$ stand for the savings made and invested in the respective groups and d is the uniform average depreciation rate.[18]

$$f(z)_{t''} = f(z)_{t'} + \sigma(z)_{t'}.d$$
$$= b_{t'} - \sigma(z)_{t'}.(1-d) \qquad (1.5a)$$

$$f(b)_{t''} = f(b)_{t'} + \sigma(b)_{t'}.d$$
$$= a_{t'} - f(a)_{t'} - \sigma(b)_{t'}.(1-d) \qquad (1.6a)$$

In this form the equations implicitly contain the Harrod–Domar postulate, as well as our additional postulate, and therefore represent sufficient as well as necessary conditions for dynamic equilibrium.[19]

(2) Our next example has been chosen from business-cycle analysis. It concerns Hicks's concept of a 'strong' boom and the mechanism through which it is supposed to turn into a downswing.[20]

A strong boom in Hicks's sense is created by such coefficients for both accelerator and multiplier as would, in conjunction with autonomous investment, induce an explosive movement were it not for the approach to full utilization of resources, which sets an external limit. Once it strikes this 'ceiling,' output cannot simply 'creep along the ceiling' but 'must bounce off from it' (p. 98). The reason for this lies in the fact that up to this point it has been an increase in real output that has determined the rate of induced investment. Henceforth output can rise no more, because of lack of resources, and the previous rate of induced investment can no longer be maintained. Thus aggregate investment is bound to decline, and this in turn must depress output and initiate the downward spiral.

This analytical result is actually based on two special premises, one explicitly stated by Hicks, the other implied. Aggregate output is the equivalent of autonomous investment plus induced investment plus consumption, and any fall in induced investment can, in principle, be compensated for by a simultaneous rise in one or both of the other components. Hicks expressly excludes a compensating increase in autonomous investment, and rightly so, if his definition of autonomous investment is accepted (p. 59). From the above conclusion it follows that a similar assumption—that is, a fixed value of the consumption function all through the cycle—underlies his treatment of consumption. This latter assumption, however, can be maintained only if the propensity to consume is as little related to the behaviour of induced investment as is autonomous investment. But it can easily be shown that under normal conditions a systematic relationship exists between these two factors. The connecting link is the behaviour of the wage rate, which makes the multiplier move inversely with the accelerator.

To clarify this point we must first ascertain the principal cause of the ceiling; that is, we have to identify the particular resource which, for systematic reasons, grows scarce under the conditions described by Hicks. When he first introduces the concept of the ceiling he describes it, referring to Keynes, as one of 'full employment' (p. 83). Subsequent references, among them one expressly mentioning population (p. 96), confirm the impression that the critical locus is the labour market. Later on, however, when Hicks inspects the ceiling in detail, he first defines it as 'full employment or full-capacity output' (p. 124), and thereafter refers exclusively to 'scarce resources' in general (Chapter X, *passim*).

As we shall see presently, a precise definition of the type of resource which establishes the ceiling is of more than semantic importance. We know from our previous considerations that, apart from labour, this role can be performed only by equipment, more precisely by primary machinery, and it is indeed in this direction that the reference to 'full-capacity output' seems to point. I propose to comment on both alternatives, but it should be stated in advance that neither of them is a safe basis for Hicks's analytical conclusions. If scarcity of labour creates the ceiling, Hicks's theory of the downturn needs drastic revision. That theory might fare better if scarcity of primary machinery were the obstacle to further expansion. But it will be shown that primary machinery—leaving aside accidental bottlenecks, which may occur also during a weak boom—cannot be scarce on systematic grounds so long as full employment has not been attained.

Our first proposition is based on the claim that the approach to full employment tends to stabilize rather than to destabilize the system. This can be demonstrated as follows. When the supply of labour grows inelastic all around, money wages are bound to rise. Hicks admits this fact, but all he derives from it is wage inflation, that is, a general rise in prices proportionate to the rise in wages (p. 126), disregarding all secondary effects of the wage rise on the structure of demand and the composition of output. In other words, he neglects the consequences of the change in income distribution which the general shift from profits to wages initiates. It is true that such a change in income distribution will affect the structure of expenditure and output only if the wage earners' marginal propensity to consume differs from that of the receivers of profit. But on commonsense grounds it is precisely a change of this kind, and thus a rise in the ratio of aggregate consumption to aggregate savings, which we have to expect.[21]

Once this is admitted it follows that the system need not 'rebound' from the full-employment ceiling. What happens to output is a shift in its composition rather than a change in its aggregate. The combined cost and demand effects of the wage rise will promote a transfer of resources from the investment sphere to the consumption sphere. In the former demand must fall, as a result of the fall in aggregate savings—and this in the face of rising costs. In the latter, given a high marginal propensity to consume, the rise in demand which emanates from wage earners in all groups of production exceeds the rise in costs, and thus stimulates expansion of employment. If the transfer of resources can be achieved promptly—we shall return to this point presently—there does not seem to be any systematic reason why the trend toward full employment should be reversed. And if from there on aggregate savings keep in line with aggregate investment, as determined by autonomous forces and the natural growth of the system, the 'moving ceiling' becomes the path of a dynamic equilibrium.[22]

We have obtained our result by paying regard to the systematic shifts among the groups of production, whereas Hicks, in Keynesian fashion, concentrates on the forces that affect aggregate output so long as no shifts occur. In other words, we deal here with a problem that can be fully explored only with the help of a partly disaggregated model like the schema. Hicks must have felt this himself, as in his 'Further inspection of the ceiling' (Chapter X) he devotes an extensive discussion to the differential behaviour of prices and output in the investment-goods and consumption-goods industries respectively. But by lumping together groups *Ia* and *Ib* in the traditional manner, he not only fails to realize the locus of possible shifts, but even is caught in an apparent contradiction. In one context (p. 134) a *spurt* of demand for consumer goods is supposed to stimulate the production of investment goods, whereas at another place it is higher profits, due to the wage lag—that is, a *lag* of demand for consumer goods—which is to promote investment (p. 127).

The difficulty disappears as soon as we subdivide investment into primary and secondary machinery. During the upswing the demand effect of the wage lag keeps the output of consumer goods and of secondary machinery within definite limits. Its cost effect, on the other hand, stimulates investment in primary machinery. Here a terminological problem arises. Hicks agrees in the passage referred to

(p. 127) that 'the higher profits, which are a necessary consequence of the wage-lag, will stimulate investment'. But can we regard such investment as the 'induced' type? If response to a preceding rise in output is the sole criterion, we must not do so. On the other hand, as Alexander has shown (*op. cit.* p. 869), there are good reasons for including in the concept the effects brought about 'indirectly via profit, price, and credit movements'.

Whether we wish to call such investment induced or autonomous, what matters is its behaviour during the boom. Then the wage lag disappears, and demand for secondary machinery rises in proportion to the additional spending of wage earners. At this stage investment, far from contracting in the aggregate, shifts from primary to secondary machinery, and maintains its previous level until the backlog of the demand for the latter is worked off.

This discussion has implicitly shown that, so long as unemployment persists, equipment and primary machinery in particular, cannot be generally scarce, and therefore cannot create an obstructive ceiling. So long as labour is plentiful, the ratio between wages and profits, and therefore between consumption and savings, is such as to assure a current output of primary machinery which exceeds the current needs for replacement and expansion of secondary machinery.[23] This 'lop-sided' growth of group *Ia* stops only, and indeed reverses itself, when full employment is realized, that is, at the moment when the rate of expansion slows down and the ceiling coincides with the equilibrium level.

Incidentally the schema provides us with an additional argument for the stabilization of a Hicksian strong boom. In telling us that the first systematic shift at the height of the boom is from primary to secondary machinery, it makes us realize that for once adjustment is not impeded by any specificities, as this shift amounts to no more than a different application of the same factors: primary machinery, and the labour force operating it. From the previous task of producing additional primary machinery they shift to the production of secondary machinery. Not until the final stage, when part of the labour force in group *I* has to move to group *II*, in order to operate the newly produced secondary machinery, will any technical rigidities come into play. Whether at that moment such rigidities will by themselves be strong enough to disturb the otherwise equilibrating tendencies is at least open to doubt. It rather appears that after due qualification Hicks's hypothesis, like all other variants of the 'overinvestment' theory of the crisis, indicates at best a spark for the critical explosion, whereas the truly dangerous powder keg has to be looked for elsewhere.[24]

(3) Our third and final example is an issue which is not directly related

to dynamic problems but has some bearing on their empirical–statistical presentation. It concerns the interpretation of the concept of gross national product. According to present usage, gross national product consists, in addition to the net change of inventories, of the sum total of all finished goods and services made available in a specific period, including those goods which are to compensate for the depreciation and depletion of fixed-capital stocks during that period.

It has again and again been asserted that this definition involves double counting; the reason that is given is that the value of the replacement goods is already contained in the remuneration of those income-receiving factors which produce the replacement goods, and in the equivalent value of goods and services purchased by these factors.[25] One glance at our schema shows, however, that this is not so. If we add up the right sides of our (1.3) equations, we obtain an expression for gross national product in accordance with prevailing usage—that is, the sum of consumer-goods and equipment-goods output. The left sides of the equations tell us that this sum is the equivalent, and no more than the equivalent, of the input of all active factors co-operating in producing output: income-receiving prime factors, and 'amortization-receiving' supplementary factors. To impute the contribution of the latter to the value of the input of the prime factors in group *I*, and to identify the goods value of this contribution with the consumer goods available to these prime factors, would amount to two untenable propositions.

First, it would imply that the value of all primary machinery equals the value of the input of the prime factors employed in their production—the 'Austrian' notion that somewhere in the system goods are produced with labour and natural resources alone. Second, it would disregard the contribution of secondary machinery to the production of consumer goods. It is true that in stationary equilibrium the value of aggregate amortization in group *II equals* the value of the aggregate income of the prime factors in group *I* which is spent on consumption. But these equal values by no means refer to *identical* goods. The goods equivalents—equipment goods to replace the wear and tear in group *II*, and consumer goods to feed the prime factors in group *I*—are not only different but have to emerge from the flow of production simultaneously and side by side. Therefore they must both enter into the calculation of total output.

All difficulties disappear once we look at production in the manner proposed above, that is, as the replacement, and possible expansion or contraction, of the stocks of active factors, rather than as the procurement of a particular kind of output, that is, consumer goods and net investment. The latter view, which leads to the current concept of net national product, is useful for many purposes. But it cannot tell us how much of the stock of active factors has been used up in production, or what its output equivalent is. This total can be ascertained only if we adhere to the conventional definition of gross national product.[26]

Quite a different question might be raised: whether the conventional concept of gross national product is really comprehensive enough to measure all inputs and outputs. As we have seen, it measures the input of all *active* factors of production, that is, labour and equipment. But as was demonstrated in the exposition of the schema, continuous production depends no less on the maintenance and, in a dynamic flow, on the appropriate change of the *passive* stock of working-capital goods—a fact clearly acknowledged also by Kuznets (as quoted in note 26).

The main reason why this technically indispensable 'flow' of working-capital goods is not accounted for in the conventional calculations of aggregate input or output is a practical one: it seems to defy measurement. We have seen that the value sum of all the outputs in successive stages of production cannot serve this purpose. This sum depends on the degree of business differentiation, and varies with it. Except in a fully integrated system it indeed contains duplications in the proper sense of the word, if it is taken as a measure of productive activity. We can expect to arrive at an exact account of all inputs and outputs only if we succeed, at least conceptually, in separating from this value sum of turnovers the indispensable contribution of intermediate goods to the continuance of the productive flow.

Once more the schema yields the clue to the solution. It was shown in Section IV above that we can measure the *stock* of working-capital goods necessary for continuous production if we know the input of active factors over the period under observation and the technically determined average 'period of maturation'. Assuming that the period of maturation equals the period of production over which we measure input and output and again assuming that factor input is equally distributed over the production stages, the value of the stock of working-capital goods is one-half the value of the input of the active factors (see note 12). But this value equals precisely the *flow* of working-capital goods which moves during the period of observation toward completion and is, at the same time, reproduced in the different stages. If the period of maturation is half as long as the period of production, the stock of working-capital goods equals only one-quarter of the value of the input of active factors. But then, during the period of observation, a stock of this size moves twice toward completion, and has to be reproduced twice. We arrive at the plain result that, over a given period, the indispensable contribution of working-capital goods to output always equals half the contribution of the active factors. The grand total of a 'super gross national product' amounts, then, to one and one-half times the value of gross national product in the conventional sense.

NOTES

1. These and subsequent references are meant as random examples of the indirect effect of Keynes upon modern dynamic theory, rather than as a survey of the influences that have shaped the latter. Otherwise pre-Keynesian contributions like those of J. M. Clark, Frisch, Tinbergen, Kalecki, and especially the Swedish school could not be passed over. See in this respect the interesting methodological introduction in William Fellner's 'Employment theory and business cycles', in *A Survey of Contemporary Economics*, Volume 1, edited by Howard S. Ellis (Philadelphia: Blakiston, 1948), pp. 49–98.
2. I am disregarding certain empirical models, like those of Tinbergen or Klein relating to fluctuations in specific economies. These models—which, for example, subdivide income according to sources, and savings and money stocks according to holders, and introduce the government sector as well as foreign economic relations—are much more highly differentiated than the theoretical models referred to above. From what follows it will become clear, however, that the particular proposal for refinement submitted here goes in a different direction.
3. It is obvious that the distinction between induced and autonomous investment is of little help in this respect, since it refers to the dimension of values rather than to that of physical aggregates.
4. *See* Wassily W. Leontief, *The Structure of the American Economy, 1919–39* (Cambridge, Mass: Oxford University Press, 1951). A general outline of an input–output model, though not its empirical–statistical application, was presented earlier by Alfred Kähler, in *Die Theorie der Arbeiterfreisetzung durch die Maschine* (Leipzig: Greifswald, 1933), Chapter IV. For an interesting discussion of the model in relation to other approaches *see* R. Solow, 'On the structure of linear models', in *Econometrica*, **20** (1952), pp. 29–46.
5. Kerr edition (1933) Volume 2, Chapter XX. This chapter, first published in 1885, should be read in conjunction with a section in Marx's *Theorien über den Mehrwert*, Teil I, (Stuttgart: Dietz Verlag, 1905), pp. 164–252; or *Theories of Surplus Value*, Part I, (Moscow: Progress Publishers, 1963), pp. 44–59, 107–47, 308–44. *See also* Paul M. Sweezy, *The Theory of Capitalist Development* (New York: Oxford University Press, 1942), Chapters V and X and Appendix A, and Joan Robinson, 'The model of an expanding economy', in *Economic Journal*, **62** (1952), pp. 42–53.
6. *See* his *The Positive Theory of Capital*, first published in 1891 in Jena, (New York: G. E. Strechert, 1946), Book II, Section IV.
7. John Bates Clark, *The Distribution of Wealth* (New York: Macmillan, 1899), Chapters XVIII–XX; *see also* his *Essentials of Economic Theory* (New York: Macmillan, 1924), Chapters IV, V, XV.

8. F. A. Burchardt, 'Die Schemata des stationären Kreislaufs bei Böhm-Bawerk und Marx', in *Weltwirtschaftliches Archiv*, **34** (1931), pp. 525–64, and **35** (1932), pp. 116–76. In 'The schematic representation of the structure of production', *Review of Economic Studies*, **2** (1935), pp. 232–44, Ragnar Nurkse has delineated certain aspects of Burchardt's work. *See also* David Hawkins, 'Some conditions of macroeconomic stability', in *Econometrica*, **16** (1948), pp. 309–22.

9. I borrow the distinction from Hans Neisser, *Some International Aspects of the Business Cycle* (Phildelphia: University of Pennsylvania Press, 1936), pp. 13–14.

10. See the discussion of this category in Burchardt *op cit*. pp. 122, 127–8, where certain minor problems regarding it are satisfactorily disposed of. I propose to disregard them in the subsequent exposition.

11. The Marxian schema depicts only the two main groups, a procedure to which also Burchardt adheres. As will be shown below, however, the path of many dynamic processes is determined by the relationships which exist between *Ia* and *Ib* and between *Ib* and *II*. I first pointed out the need for a tripartite schema in my paper 'Wie ist Konjunkturtheorie überhaupt möglich?' in *Weltwirtschaftliches Archiv*, **24** (1926), p. 190. It need hardly be stressed that the tripartite schema discussed in the text must not be confused with another tripartite schema, which L. von Bortkiewicz used in his famous critique of the manner in which Marx transformed 'values' into prices. A lucid survey of this discussion is contained in Sweezy *op. cit*. Chapter VII.

12. Denoting by m the period of maturation, by p any period over which we wish to measure output, and by A the aggregate input of active factors during p, we have for the stock of working-capital goods $2Am/p$. The factor 2 enters because the stock of working-capital goods equals the *successive* factor input during the period of maturation, which is half the *simultaneous* factor input that occurs over that period in a continuous flow, provided that the factor input is distributed in equal proportions over the stages of production. The problem has been discussed by D. H. Robertson in his famous analogy with a 'sausage machine' (*Money*, Cambridge, Eng.: Cambridge University Press, 1932, Chapter V, paragraph 7), and was earlier considered by Böhm-Bawerk (*op cit*. Appendix XIV).

13. At this point I should make explicit a simplification which has been introduced into the schema for didactic purposes only. I have confined the number of 'income-receiving' factors to two: labour and natural resources. In what follows I shall go even further and treat natural resources as free gifts. All this, of course, is tenable only for a stationary process, and even there prevailing opinion insists on regarding interest as a positive magnitude. And once we pass on to dynamic conditions, the possible sources of net receipts multiply. The difficulty can be resolved, however, if we redefine the symbol N as standing for all 'income-receiving' factors. The same arrangement makes it possible to dispense with the surplus-value item, which plays such a central role in Marx's formulation of the schema. In a stationary flow, surplus value represents, if its existence can be demonstrated at all, only a specific form of income devoted to the purchase of consumer goods. The manner in which the saving and investing of parts of income affect the schema will be indicated below.

14. In other words, one group 'broadens' whereas another group 'narrows'

proportionally. The notions of 'lengthening' and 'shortening', basic in the Austrian theory of capital, can be reasonably applied only to changes in the period of maturation, that is, to changes in the stock of working-capital goods relative to other stocks of factors—a type of change to which we shall refer presently.

15. For the similarities and differences between the two approaches see Harrod's paper on 'Notes on trade cycle theory', in *Economic Journal*, **61** (1951), pp. 261–75.

16. The briefest exposition of problem and solution is found in Samuelson's 'Dynamic process analysis', in *A Survey of Contemporary Economics*, Volume 1, (cited above, note 1) pp. 361–3.

17. Comparable objections to the condition of dynamic equilibrium were first raised by E. Stern in his polemics against Domar; *see* Stern's 'The problem of capital accumulation', in *American Economic Review*, **39** (1949), pp. 1160–9. That problem has since been reviewed systematically by William Fellner in 'The capital–output ratio in dynamic economics', in *Money, Trade and Economic Growth: In Honor of John Henry Williams* (New York: Macmillan, 1951), pp. 105–34. Fellner also stresses the difference between 'changes' and 'adjustments' of the critical coefficients.

18. *See also* Joan Robinson, 'The model of an expanding economy' (cited above, note 5), p. 46, note 1, and pp. 52–3.

19. The fact that, and the reason why, no aggregate formulation can establish sufficient conditions for dynamic equilibrium have been clearly recognized by Fellner, in his 'Capital–output ratio' essay (cited above, note 17; *see* especially pp. 116–22). But in the absence of a properly disaggregated model he could point only in literary terms to the additional condition: absence of specific scarcities and immobilities, which may distort a process even if the conditions for aggregate equilibrium are temporarily fulfilled. It is precisely this gap in exact analysis which my schema of production is designed to close. The issues referred to gain importance, of course, whenever the rates of saving and investment change, causing either bottlenecks or partial waste of the existing capital stock in group *Ia*.

20. *See* Hicks's *A Contribution to the Theory of the Trade Cycle* (Oxford: Clarendon, 1950), Chapters VIII and X.

21. It can easily be shown that, in a system approaching full employment, monetary expansion cannot, in the long run, affect this shift in relative demand. We need not pursue this line of thought, since Hicks himself emphasizes the fact that, in the situation contemplated, monetary influences have little effect on the action of the real forces.

22. In this connection *see also* S. S. Alexander, 'Issues of business cycle theory', in *American Economic Review*, **41** (1951), pp. 861–78, especially 874–5. Alexander recognizes that 'contrary to Mr. Hicks's argument, a downturn does not necessarily follow an encounter with the ceiling', but he fails to relate this fact to the normal order of the events which make up a strong boom.

23. Hicks has a somewhat cryptic passage (p. 123, note) referring to the effect productive investment must have on the 'movement of the ceiling itself', which may perhaps be interpreted in the above sense. If so, however, it should be clear that, contrary to Hicks's surmise, this effect makes a 'decisive difference to the results obtained'.

24. It can be found only in the realm of autonomous investment, in the

simultaneous onset of the 'Schumpeter effect' when technically superior firms begin to eliminate marginal producers on a large scale. The particular conditions under which this process coincides with the approach to full employment, and other conditions under which it occurs earlier during the upswing, creating a 'weak' boom, require, of course, further elaboration. In this respect *see* my paper on 'The turn of the boom', in Manchester Statistical Society, *Transactions, Group Meetings, 1937–38* (Manchester 1938), pp. 10–15. *See also* Hanns-Joachim Rüstow, *Theorie der Vollbeschäftigung in der freien Marktwirtschaft* (Tübingen: J. C. B. Mohr, 1951), Chapter XI. A similar hypothesis has recently been indicated by Rendigs Fels in 'The theory of business cycles', in *Quarterly Journal of Economics*, **66** (1952), pp. 25–42, especially 37, 41.

25. *See*, for example, Gerhard Colm, 'From estimates of national income to projections of the nation's budget', in *Social Research*, **12** (1945), p. 364. But *see also* S. Kuznets, in National Bureau of Economic Research, *National Income, A Summary of Findings* (New York, 1946), pp. 112–21.

26. Kuznets (*ibid.* pp. 113–16) is fully aware of the postulative nature of any definition of national income or output which is based on the 'goal' of providing goods to households. He expressly states that national income thus conceived 'is not a measure of activity, of how much effort, toil and trouble economic activity represents' (p. 115). He even points out, in accordance with the view I have delineated, that, 'if no ultimate goal is set to economic activity', net national income is reduced to the value of net additions to the stocks of factors (population and its efficiency, fixed-capital and working-capital goods, and foreign claims). Certainly, then, he should not speak of 'duplication' (p. 117) if this net total is supplemented by a gross total in which, besides the 'additions' to the stocks, the efforts necessary to their maintenance are counted.

2 Structural Analysis of Real-Capital Formation*

INTRODUCTION

(1) The following observations are limited in three respects. They concentrate on certain issues of real-capital formation and completely disregard those of 'finance' and 'business organization'. Furthermore, they are concerned with purely analytical problems of 'model-building' and have no direct relationship to statistical and descriptive data. Finally, this paper deals with only one aspect of the theory of capital formation, which I call 'structural'. Since this term has acquired rather diverse meanings in recent writings, I had better explain what it is to signify in the context of this paper.

(2) The course, persistence, or change of economic processes can be studied under two different aspects. On the one hand, there exist certain objective–quantitative relations among the components of the system—say, between effective demand and aggregate employment or between the depreciation of existing equipment and the output of capital goods. On the other hand, there are the motivations and behaviour patterns of householders, firms and productive factors, which shape the prevailing objective relations and are shaped by them. No economic analysis is complete that does not take into account the events occurring in both fields and, in particular, their interaction. But if this requirement of 'total analysis' is in principle admitted, no harm arises from provisionally studying the phenomena in each field separately.

Much of the distinction between these two fields of inquiry is

---

* I wish to express my gratitude to Julius Wyler for a number of critical suggestions, pertaining in particular to the part headed 'The dynamics of once-over changes' below. Moreover, his own work in the field of structural analysis, still unpublished, has provided a valuable check for some of the propositions established below.

[This essay was first presented at a Conference of the Universities – National Bureau Committee for Economic Research held in New York in November 1953. It was subsequently published in M. Abramovitz (ed.), *Capital Formation and Economic Growth*, (Princeton: Princeton University Press, 1955). Some amendments have been made by the author. —ed.]

customarily expressed by the contrast between macroeconomics and microeconomics. But the particular point of difference—namely, between the 'impersonal order' and the 'personal forces'—which is stressed here, has little to do with the degree of aggregation, by which the microeconomic study of firm and industry is traditionally separated from the macroeconomic study of the system as a whole. It is for this reason that I prefer the terms 'structural' and 'functional'. They are neutral to the level of aggregation, and permit the input–output relations among different industries to be considered a 'structural' order, just as Leontief considers them, while the motive–behaviour complex of the Soviet planning authorities appears as a 'functional' problem, even though the ensuing decisions concern the system at large.

(3) Among the structural problems thus defined, those which relate to the money flow (income–expenditure–saving, etc.) can be distinguished from those which relate to the physical flow of goods and services (consumer goods–capital goods; natural resources–intermediate goods–finished goods) occurring in and between different 'sectors' of the economy. Whereas the former structural relations can be fully described in value terms, the latter have, in addition to the value dimension, a physical–technical dimension.

For both types of structural relations another distinction is important. Interest may be directed to the actual relations between effective demand and the level of aggregate employment, or between the output of capital goods and the level of investment, as these magnitudes appear in an empirical system in historical time. Or attention can be focused on a hypothetical order of either the money flow or the physical flow which is *required to attain a postulated state of the system*, such as a certain level of employment or a particular order of distribution, or simply stationary or dynamic equilibrium. According to the viewpoint taken, structural analysis results then either in a number of empirical–statistical relations supplementing the information contained in national income accounts, or in a set of 'consistency conditions'.

This paper deals almost exclusively with the *physical–technical structure* of industrial systems, in so far as it affects the process of capital formation. And it interprets structural analysis in the 'normative' sense, as being concerned with physical–technical *consistency conditions*. These conditions are related, on the one hand, to the sectorial order of stationary and dynamic equilibrium and, on the other hand, to the sectorial adjustment paths required for an industrial system to accomplish, under the impact of economic growth, the formation of real capital in the most 'economical' manner. It hardly needs stressing that structural problems of this nature arise under any form of economic organization, individualist or collectivist. It is mainly for reasons of space that the following observations confine themselves to capital formation in a free-market system. Moreover, the difference in economic organization affects the results of functional rather than of structural analysis.

(4) This line of investigation has been chosen for two reasons. First, the problems encountered in its pursuit touch upon important practical issues pertaining to economic growth in both advanced and backward countries. The specific contribution that 'normative' structural analysis can make to the clarification of such practical issues will be discussed at the end of this paper. Secondly, in contradistinction to its money flows, the physical–technical structure of an industrial economy is still largely unexplored. This is especially true of the manner in which more or less fixed coefficients of production affect the adjustment processes in such a system.

The assumption of fixed technical coefficients is basic for the subsequent exposition. Its practical importance lies in the fact that it reflects the degree of specificity of inputs and outputs. It thus describes the limits set in an industrial system to short-run aggregate expansion as well as to short-run sectorial adjustment. While the former issue is especially relevant in the early stages of industrialization, the latter bears upon the stability of fully industrialized systems. A few cursory remarks must suffice to support this view.

Originally a product of the Industrial Revolution, with its emphasis upon large-scale specialized equipment and differentiated skills, specificity of real capital and labour has varied considerably during the historical stages of industrialization. During the nineteenth century the prevailing tendency was undoubtedly in the direction of increasing specificity. This has somewhat changed during the last generation, and we may well assume that, under purely technical aspects, standardization of equipment parts, further automation and novel methods of labour training will in the future promote greater flexibility of the industrial structure. But a new trend in economic policy seems to counteract this technological tendency. Paradoxically, during the nineteenth century the instability of a rigid structure provided its own cure, by periodically creating large pools of idle resources that facilitated adjustment and growth. An effective full-employment policy is now likely to make for new rigidities. Its very success in stabilizing the structure of money flows may well aggravate the adjustment problems that the physical–technical structure poses. Thus, with all due regard to the dangers arising from insufficient demand, which are now generally admitted, inelasticity of supply owing to technical rigidities stands as another threat to the stability of advanced economic systems. At the same time, in the different 'climate' in which economic development is pursued today, the physical–technical bottlenecks that hamper rapid expansion in backward regions will be felt much more strongly than under the earlier conditions of slow initial growth.

The emphasis placed here upon fixed coefficients of production and the ensuing technical rigidity of the system may not, at first sight, seem appropriate to the main topic of this paper. In the Marshallian tradition, changes in real capital are regarded as a problem for long-period or even secular-period analysis, referring to a time span over which the technical coefficients must be treated as perfectly variable. If this is admitted, are we not going to miss our very problem if we argue on the basis of fixed technical coefficients? Brief reflection will show that this apparent concentration on short-run problems, far from conflicting with the study of long-run economic growth, is an indispensable condition for understanding the latter.

Long-run analysis of economic growth describes a sequence of states of the system, which differ with respect to the quantity and/or quality of real capital. But it must be kept in mind that this sequence, except in the limiting and quite unrealistic case of steady exponential growth, is essentially discontinuous. In analogy with comparative statics it depicts successive levels of capital 'formed' without regard to the intervening processes by which capital is 'being formed'. Now it is precisely these intermediary processes that are in the foreground of this investigation. Their systematic place in the larger context of growth analysis can easily be clarified.

First of all, these adjustment processes, through which capital formation occurs, are indeed of a short-period nature in the strict Marshallian meaning of the term. Through them, additional and possibly qualitatively different real capital is created; but this is done with the help of the initially given quantity and quality of real capital. In other words, given full utilization of the available equipment as a typical modern condition in advanced as well as underdeveloped regions in accord with what was stated above, the prevailing technical coefficients can be varied only by a process of production which is conditioned by the existing coefficients. Secondly, since the technical structure of the given stock of real capital is unalterable in the short period, the degree of its specificity, and of the prevailing factor specificity generally, has a decisive influence upon the path of the adjustment process as well as upon its duration. Finally, while themselves short-run phenomena, these processes of capital formation are the links between successive stages of growth and thus transform the sequence of discontinuous states into a continuous long-run process.

(5) From these considerations one cannot help concluding that the technical structure is a fundamental determinant of the behaviour, and

especially of the mode of change, of any economic system. Therefore, it is rather surprising that, until quite recently, the whole issue received little attention in academic economics. It is to Leontief's lasting credit that he not only devised a theoretical model for the analysis of these structural relations, but also initiated a comprehensive empirical–statistical test for his matrix, which has greatly deepened our insight into the operation of the productive mechanism. Leontief traces his own work back to Walras's model of general equilibrium. As far as the multiplicity of variables is concerned, Walras's parentage is undeniable. But to the extent to which the input–output matrix concentrates upon the interrelationship of 'industries'—that is, aggregates larger than individual firms but smaller than the customary components of macroeconomics—the prototype was established by Marx in his laborious attempts to describe the processes of 'simple' and 'expanded' reproduction by a quantitative schema. Marx's schema is much more highly aggregated than Leontief's matrix; it distinguishes only between one group producing consumer goods and another producing means of production. But, as in modern input–output analysis, Marx's interest was focused upon physical–technical inter-relations in and between these two groups rather than upon the value structure of the total process, which was Walras's ultimate concern.

My further observations will be based upon a modified version of the Marxian schema. In view of the much more extensive disaggregation of the input–output model this decision might, at first sight, be likened to the use of a shovel when a bulldozer is available. And this all the more so since the Leontief model is built upon the same technological assumption of constant input coefficients that has been postulated above. If, nevertheless, the simpler model has been employed, this has been done for two reasons. The first is purely pragmatic. For the practical purpose of planning, one can hardly go too far in disaggregating an interindustry model. But this advantage of Leontief's model in all empirical concerns turns into an obstacle when it is applied to the solution of theoretical problems of a general dynamic nature. It proves just too difficult to trace analytically the path of such a large number of variables, especially if they are exposed to several stimuli simultaneously.

The second reason is substantive and more basic. All subdivisions of the productive structure are not equally important for the study of particular dynamic processes. One can, in principle, conceive of different patterns of disaggregation, each one appropriate to a specific problem. Now, with certain modifications to be explained presently, Marx's schema seems to be suited especially well to the study of real capital formation. There is an *a priori* presumption that the theoretical problems associated with the building up and wearing down of the capital stock, with the relation between capital stock and output flow, with the processes of 'widening' and 'deepening', and with the effects of innovations upon capital formation are basically the same in every industry. But their solution is bound to differ according to whether we study 'capital-producing' or 'capital-using' processes, a distinction which is central for the Marxian schema. I speak of an 'attempt', because in its original form the schema is defective in at least three respects.

The first defect refers to the relation between capital stock and output flow. In spite of his continuous preoccupation with 'capital', the equations that Marx presents in his structural analysis are meaningful only if understood as describing flows. Appropriate stock variables must be added to make the schema an analytical tool for the study of capital formation.

Another defect is that Marx's distinction between two industrial groups focuses upon fixed-capital goods only. If the schema is to apply also to working-capital goods as goods in process, each of the groups must be disaggregated into 'vertical' stages, depicting the process by which natural resources are technically transformed into finished consumer or equipment goods.

Finally, certain essential 'circular' processes can be clearly described only if the equipment-goods group is further disaggregated into one subgroup which produces the equipment for the consumer-goods group, and another subgroup which produces the equipment for both subgroups of the equipment-goods group.

This is, in its most general features, the model I shall use as a tool for the study of real-capital formation under the impact of growth.[1] I shall begin with a brief analysis of the structural conditions that determine stationary equilibrium. Then follows an exposition of certain dynamic relations: first, as they arise under the impact of once-over changes; secondly, as they take shape under continuous change. In the latter category the structural conditions of a constant rate of change, viz. dynamic equilibrium, are distinguished from those of varying rates of change with more complicated adjustment paths, as they emanate, for example, from non-neutral technical changes. During the exposition itself little will be said about the practical relevance for advanced and backward countries of the problems discussed. A brief conclusion will suggest possible applications of this analytical technique.

STRUCTURAL CONDITIONS OF STATIONARY EQUILIBRIUM

Group Model and Stage Model

(6) We start out from an elementary set of relations describing the flow of production over the period t:

$$
\begin{aligned}
(F_a \cdot d_a &\equiv f_{at}) \cup n_{at} \cup r_{at} \rightarrow a_t \\
(F_b \cdot d_b &\equiv f_{bt}) \cup n_{bt} \cup r_{bt} \rightarrow b_t \\
(F_z \cdot d_z &\equiv f_{zt}) \cup n_{zt} \cup r_{zt} \rightarrow z_t
\end{aligned}
\tag{2.1}
$$

At this stage of the argument we deal only with physical magnitudes. Therefore, the relationship between inputs and outputs is expressed as no more than a causal nexus, symbolized by arrows. Similarly, the $\cup$ signs stand for the technical combination of the input factors in fixed proportions.

To the right of the arrows, a signifies the output of a units of equipment goods which are intended to make equipment goods, henceforth called 'primary equipment', whereas b signifies the output of b units of equipment goods intended to make consumer goods, henceforth called 'secondary equipment'; z denotes the aggregate output of z units of consumer goods.[2]

To the left of the arrows are the corresponding inputs for each of the three groups, the relevant group being specified by a subscript. These inputs are subdivided into the basic factors of production: fixed-capital goods, f; labour, n; and natural resources, r. For the input of fixed capital goods two expressions are given: one, denoted by f, is a direct expression of the input flow entering the corresponding output flow; the other expresses the same magnitude in terms of the existing stock of fixed-capital goods, F, multiplied by the prevailing rate of depreciation, d. In principle, similar stock magnitudes could be added to the flow expressions for the other two factors, and they are quite useful for the study of certain dynamic problems. In a study of the dynamics of capital formation they can be disregarded. (Whenever stocks appear in our models and equations, they are symbolized by capital letters, whereas flows are described in lower-case letters.)

(7) In the above form the group relations are the result of a far-reaching aggregation. Each group describes the output of a given period in terms of *finished* goods, ready for use either as means of consumption in the households or as means of production in the firms. These outputs of finished goods are the technical result of the productive process, which transforms natural resources with the help of labour and equipment goods. This process of transformation can, and for the

solution of certain problems must, be disaggregated into a number of 'vertical stages'. A second set of relations describes such a stage model for the group of consumer goods:

$$(F_{z_1} \cdot d_{z_1} \equiv f_{z_1 t}) \cup n_{z_1 t} \cup r_{z_1 t} \to w_{z_1 t}$$

$$(f_{z_2} \cdot d_{z_2} \equiv f_{z_2 t}) \cup n_{z_2 t} \cup r_{z_2 t} \cup w_{z_1 t} \to w_{z_2 t}$$

$$(f_{z_3} \cdot d_{z_3} \equiv f_{z_3 t}) \cup n_{z_3 t} \cup r_{z_3 t} \cup w_{z_2 t} \to w_{z_3 t} \qquad (2.2)$$

$$(f_{z_4} \cdot d_{z_4} \equiv f_{z_4 t}) \cup n_{z_4 t} \cup r_{z_4 t} \cup w_{z_3 t} \to z_t$$

$$(f_z \cdot d_z \equiv f_{zt}) \cup n_{zt} \cup r_{zt} \to z_t$$

This model is based on the assumption, to be examined more closely, that the technical process of production by which the natural resource r_{z_1} is transformed into the finished consumer good z can be subdivided into four stages. The outputs w (working-capital goods) of each stage appear as inputs in the subsequent stage, down to the 'stage of completion', whose output is the finished good. The total for the inputs of each factor in all stages must be equal to the consolidated expression that appears in model (2.1) and is restated at the bottom of model (2.2).

(8) What precise meaning can be attached to the notion of a *technical* sequence of stages of production? There is no doubt that, from the point of view of business organization, a number of successive interfirm exchanges can be distinguished where the buying firm uses its purchases for further manufacturing. Though useful as an indicator of business differentiation and also important for the solution of the 'transaction problems' in the theory of money, from the technical point of view separate stages of production are arbitrary. Only for the first stage, where the 'gifts of nature' are 'seized', and for the last stage, when the finished product is handed over to the prospective user (or speculator), can a definite meaning be attached to such a distinction.

The fact that from a technical point of view the production flow is indivisible has always been recognized in attempts to find a quantitative expression for the stock and the flow or working-capital goods. The total of all 'stage outputs', which can be derived from any given order of business differentiation, cannot be used for this purpose, since it contains unavoidable double counting. Therefore, proper measures for working capital can be established only by referring to factor inputs.[3] But if we are interested in the manner in which a *given* order of business differentiation is affected by vertical shifts of factors—because of, for example, alterations in physical returns or non-neutral technical changes—a stage model of the kind described in model (2.2) is a useful analytical tool. The particular problems of capital formation discussed below refer to fixed capital only, so that the stage model can be disregarded in favour of the consolidated group as formulated in model (2.1) (see, however, Section 19 below).

(9) This conclusion is likely to meet with strong objections from those who conceive of the whole productive process in 'linear' fashion. A schema like that described in model (2.2) underlies the so-called Austrian concept of the structure of production. Originally devised by Eugen v. Böhm-Bawerk, it was introduced into the Anglo-American tool chest by Wicksell and his followers, especially Hayek, eclipsing the much sounder notions of J. B. Clark.[4] The discussion ended in stalemate with the well-known controversy between F. H. Knight and Nicholas Kaldor,[5] to the complete disregard of the work of F. A. Burchardt,[6] in which a happy synthesis between a 'circular' and a 'linear' model had been achieved.

The point at issue is the place of fixed-capital goods in the structure of production. Because they are the result of the productive process, they cannot be treated as data side by side with labour and natural resources. On the other hand, the attempt to 'dissolve' their contribution into inputs of labour and natural resources fails since, to make fixed-capital goods, other fixed-capital goods are needed in addition to labour and natural resources. Therefore it is not possible to treat fixed-capital goods as the output of some intermediary stage in the vertical model, as Böhm-Bawerk and his followers have suggested. In other words, all attempts to describe the process of production in purely linear fashion, tracing all finished goods technically back to nothing but humans and nature, not only are unrealistic but involve an infinite regress.

A solution of this apparent paradox that is in accordance with both facts and logic is possible only if it is recognized, as Marx and J. B. Clark did many decades ago, that fixed-capital goods are replaced and multiplied by a process of physical self-reproduction analogous to the maintenance and increase of the stock of the organic factors of production: humans, animals and plants. Not all fixed-capital goods have this technical capacity. It is the characteristic of a particular group, called machine tools. In conjunction with one another and with labour and natural resources (in the form of special working-capital goods) these tools are capable of making other equipment as well as their own kind. This circular process raises group a to a strategic position in the technical structure of every industrial economy, whatever it social organization. In other words, group a is the bottleneck which any process of rapid expansion must overcome, a problem which a linear concept of the structure of production cannot even locate, let alone study, in substantive terms.

(10) Returning now to the original group schema described in model (2.1), we can transform it into a set of equations by interpreting its variables (with the exception of d) as price-sum magnitudes pertaining to the output of three physically distinct aggregates. Such a 'two-dimensional' determination enables us to establish certain equilibrium conditions of a continuing stationary process, and to express them in marketing terms as well as in physical–technical terms.

For the system to continue in stationary equilibrium, the outputs of period t_1 must become the inputs of period t_2. Thus we have

$$a_{t_1} = f_{at_2} + f_{bt_2}$$
$$b_{t_1} = f_{zt_2} \tag{2.3}$$
$$z_{t_1} = n_{at_2} + n_{bt_2} + n_{zt_2} + r_{at_2} + r_{bt_2} + r_{zt_2}$$

In words, the primary machinery produced during period t_1 re-appears physically in period t_2 as the fixed-capital goods operating in the two equipment-goods groups, whereas the secondary machinery b_{t_1} becomes the fixed-capital goods operating during period t_2 in the consumer-goods group. By this physical application, the outputs of both primary and secondary machinery replace the wear and tear of equipment which occurred in the act of their own production as well as of the simultaneous production of consumer goods. In the same manner, the consumer-goods output during period t_1 can be said to 'replace' the 'wear and tear' of the prime factors N and R—in our context a helpful interpretation of the stationary income claims of their owners—and to serve their maintenance over the period t_2.

To bring about the proper physical 'relocation' the three groups must behave in the manner of countries involved in a triangular exchange relationship. The whole output of secondary machinery of group b moves to group z in exchange for an equivalent amount of consumer goods. Part of these 'imports' into group b are used to feed the prime factors employed there, whereas the rest are 're-exported' to group a for primary equipment required to replace f_{bt_1}. The 'imports' of consumer goods into group a go to the prime factors of this group, whereas the wear and tear of its equipment f_{at_1} is replaced from its own output at_1. In the same manner the prime factors employed in group z are fed out of their own output of consumer goods.

The fact that, as in international trade, these exchanges of non-substitutable goods occur through the marketing actions of individual firms and households in no way reduces the importance of the structural relations among the groups at large. Their significance for macroeconomic analysis is analogous to that of balances of payments in international exchange. The equilibrium conditions of a stationary flow can then be expressed in the following, more comprehensive form:

$$f_{zt_2} = b_{t_1}$$

$$= z_{t_1} - n_{zt_1} - r_{zt_1} \tag{2.4}$$

$$= n_{at_1} + n_{bt_1} + r_{at_1} + r_{bt_1}$$

$$f_{bt_2} = a_{t_1} - f_{at_1}$$

$$= z_{t_1} - n_{bt_1} - n_{zt_1} - r_{bt_1} - r_{zt_1} \tag{2.5}$$

$$= n_{at_1} + r_{at_1}$$

In words, the secondary machinery required per period in group z must equal, physically and in value terms, the output of such equipment produced previously in group b. But it must also equal in value terms a definite amount of consumer goods, namely, the total previous output in group z minus that group's present requirements—a difference which must equal the amount presently demanded by all income receivers in groups a and b. Furthermore, the primary machinery required per period in group b must equal, physically and in value terms, the surplus of such equipment produced previously in group a over and above that group's own present requirements, and must also equal the value of consumer goods at present demanded by the income receivers in group a. In turn it must also equal the total previous output in group z minus the present requirements of consumer goods in both group z and group b.

From these relations a simple inequality can be derived which defines in structural terms the nature of all dynamic processes in the sense of growth or decline of the system. In such a situation there is for any period during which aggregate change occurs:

$$f_z \lessgtr n_a + n_b + r_a + r_b$$

$$f_b \lessgtr n_a + r_a$$

Model (2.1) and equations (2.3) to (2.5) tell us all that is relevant for the group structure in a continuing stationary process. Not only do they describe the physical transformation of inputs into outputs and conversely, but they also express the changing meaning of the corresponding money flows in subsequent periods. In model (2.1) interpreted as equality between input values and output values, the n, r, and f variables must be understood not only as costs to the firms, but also as the money receipts that accrue, in the form of income and amortization, to the holders of the respective stocks. In equations (2.3) to (2.5) the same symbols represent the expenditures on consumer and equipment goods respectively. On the other hand, the a, b and z variables in model (2.1) denote receipts from sales, while they measure aggregates of expenditure in the later equations.

This 'ambiguity' has a parallel in the Keynesian model, which also has a 'supply' as well as a 'demand' meaning. In the first interpretation Keynes deals with aggregate output, consumer-goods output and investment-goods output. His second interpretation refers to aggregate income, divided into one part spent on consumer goods and another part, called savings, which is spent on investment goods. Far from prejudicing analytical clarity, this change of meaning of the basic variables in successive transactions only emphasizes the circular nature of the exchange process.

Stationary Group Relations in Terms of Capital Coefficients

(11) Our next step is to derive some analytical tools, with the help of which the 'group ratios'—that is, the relative size of the three groups and their components in any given state of the system—can be expressed. For this purpose certain concepts relating to a system's capital structure must be defined.

(a) 'Total value productivity' is defined as the unit cost of a given output: $\epsilon = o_v/i_v$ that is, output value over input value. 'Labour productivity' is then consistently defined as $\epsilon_n = o_v/n_v$ that is, output value over payrolls; and 'capital productivity' as $\epsilon_c = o_v/f_v$ that is, output value over replacement value.

For problems other than those discussed in this paper, the relation of input value to output *quantity* is a preferable measure. This is especially true of all investigations having to do with the effect of technical changes on physical productivity, a problem with which we are not concerned here. With technology constant, the two measures are, of course, identical.

(b) Our second concept is 'capital depth' (in the sense in which the term was first used by Hawtrey), or 'capital–output' ratio. This concept we define by the ratio $k = F_v/o_v$ that is, the value of the capital stock over the value of output.[7] The measure has a time dimension and can therefore be applied only to clearly defined periods of observation. As in the definition of productivity, it is possible to relate the quantity, rather than the value, of output to the value of capital stock. Accordingly, 'value capital depth' can be distinguished from 'quantity capital depth'. Throughout this paper k refers to value capital depth.

Combining the measure for capital depth with the rate of depreciation, we have the reciprocal of the measure proposed above for capital productivity: $kd = (F/o).d = (f/do).d = f/o$. This coefficient kd will be a principal tool in the subsequent structural analyses.

(c) Our third concept is 'capital intensity', which is the ratio $c = F_v/n_v$ of the value of the capital stock over the value of payrolls of the workers operating it over a stated period. Having also a time dimension, the measure is formally analogous with capital depth. It proves important in the analysis of labour-displacing and labour-attracting technical changes.

(12) The coefficient kd, the reciprocal of capital productivity, will now be used for a reformulation of the structural relations which prevail among the three strategic groups in a stationary process. To simplify the exposition, I shall from now on drop the variable r from the set of input factors, assuming either that natural resources are 'free gifts' or that the factor n stands for all income-receiving factors. The latter assumption disposes also of any discussion of how to treat interest in a stationary system.

As a first approximation, capital-depth coefficients and depreciation rates are taken to be the same in all groups. The sum of outputs $a + b + z$ over the given period is denoted by o. The total capital stock of the system can then be expressed by ok, and the flow of depreciation over the stated period by okd, to which the condition attaches that $k < 1/d$; okd is equal to $a + b$, that is, the output of equipment goods in the given period. This yields

$$z = o - (a + b) = o(1 - kd)$$

$$b = f_z = F_z.d = o(1 - kd)kd$$

$$a = o - (z + b) = ok^2d^2$$

Therefore,

$$z:b:a = 1:kd:\frac{k^2d^2}{1 - kd} \tag{2.6}$$

which also measures the ratio of the three capital stocks $F_z:F_b:F_a$.

With unequal k's and d's for the three groups, the expression changes to

$$z:b:a = 1:k_zd_z:\frac{k_zd_zk_bd_b}{1 - k_ad_a} \tag{2.7}$$

and identically

$$F_z:F_b:F_a = 1:k_zd_z:\frac{k_zd_zk_bd_b}{1 - k_ad_a} \tag{2.7a}$$

Thus once the capital-depth coefficients and depreciation rates for the respective groups are known, the relative share of the output of the groups in the gross national product and the relative size of net national income, which under stationary conditions coincides with the output of consumer goods, are determined. So is the ratio of the capital stocks, and the distribution of prime and supplementary factors over the groups.

If a stationary process is studied, all capital problems are reduced to replacement problems, that is, to the maintenance of the existing ratios among the three groups. When we turn to the analysis of certain dynamic processes, the notions of both 'group ratios' and 'intergroup equilibrium conditions' will prove useful in dealing with the concomitant problems of capital formation.

THE DYNAMICS OF ONCE-OVER CHANGES

(13) This is not the place to undertake a critical review of all the definitions of economic 'dynamics' that have been put forth in recent years (Frisch, Hicks, Samuelson, Harrod). In what follows the term includes any economic process which is exposed to change, whether bipolar as in the case of a shift in tastes, or aggregate as under conditions of growth or decline of the system as a whole. For the purpose of this paper bipolar changes are disregarded. Among aggregate changes it is convenient to distinguish between once-over and continuous changes.

Harrod defines a once-over change as a single act of change in one or more of the data of the system, such as an increase in labour supply owing to the influx of a certain number of immigrants at a given point of time, or the introduction of a particular technical improvement.[8] After the absorption of such a once-over change the system is supposed to operate again under the previously prevailing (zero or constant) rate of data changes. Unlike Harrod I regard such once-over changes as legitimate problems for dynamic analysis. In the first place, far from dealing with 'trivial matter' 'satisfactorily to be handled by the apparatus of static theory' (*ibid* p. 7), all the practically relevant cases of once-over changes occur in the framework of otherwise continuous change, and the interplay between the two types of change can hardly be studied in terms of comparative statics. Secondly, and more important, a description of the adjustment path that the system pursues under the impact of once-over changes points up particularly well the structural problems of capital formation, which beset all dynamic processes operating under any rate of change other than constant.

I shall concentrate upon one particular type of once-over change, since the basic problems can best be thrown into relief by an isolating analysis. For this purpose a change in labour supply will be selected and the results of the analysis supplemented by a few remarks on 'neutral' changes in productivity.

To highlight the issues relating to capital formation, severely restrictive assumptions have been made. The system is assumed to move initially in stationary equilibrium under conditions of pure competition, with firms of equal size operating in continuous production under minimum average costs. Constant returns are to prevail on all natural resources, which are treated as free goods, and the capital depth coefficients and rates of depreciation are to be equal in all groups.

All these conditions can easily be relaxed. There is also no difficulty in analysing a simultaneous change in labour supply and productivity, as will be indicated below. It is even more important to realize from the outset that the results, though gained within a stationary framework, are fully applicable to a dynamic framework. In other words, changes in a positive rate of change can be analysed by 'superimposing' our results upon a process in dynamic equilibrium with a steady rate of growth.

A Once-Over Change in Labour Supply

(14) Our stationary equilibrium is supposed to be disturbed by an increment α of labour supply, expressing the potential increment Δn_v in the value of labour effort as a fraction of the value of the stationary labour effort n_v per period of observation. Our problem, then, concerns those aggregate changes of, and structural shifts among, the three groups which describe the 'optimal' path for the absorption of the increment or, what amounts to the same thing, restore in the most economical manner stationary equilibrium on a higher level of input and output.

It may be advisable to emphasize once more that the concomitant 'functional' problems—namely, the particular behaviour patterns and motivations of the actors in the market that are the condition for the realization of the structural adjustment—are not discussed in this paper. One fundamental functional assumption referring to savings and investment will be stated below. For the rest little can be said about the functional aspects of dynamic processes before the structural conditions have been clarified.[9]

There are, in principle, two ways in which a labour increment can be absorbed: either by utilizing the existing equipment at more than its optimum intensity—in other words, by expanding output all through the system beyond the point of minimum average costs through a change in factor proportions in favour of labour—or by building new equipment. In accordance with my basic assumption of fixed technical coefficients, I shall concentrate upon the second alternative.[10]

(15) In order to provide the labour increment with working places and real income, the stationary factors must perform a temporary act of net saving and net investment. Its monetary aspect, in which we are not interested here, consists in the transfer of appropriate purchasing power from the stationary income receivers to the entrepreneurs, by an act of voluntary saving, by credit inflation, or even by a general fall in wages resulting from the increased competition in the labour market.[11] Its real aspect, in which alone we are interested, consists in all three cases in the displacement of factors in the consumer-goods group, factors which—given the required mobility—can be transferred to the equipment goods groups for the purpose of expanding the output of equipment. As a first approximation, it is assumed that such mobility exists for labour, so that a weaver can in the very short run be used as, say, a steel worker. However, the whole problem to be studied would be eliminated if the same notion of mobility were applied to fixed capital goods. I therefore assume that the displaced looms cannot be used in steel making, the expansion of which forms part of the process of real-capital formation.

(16) This process of equipment building requires closer examination in accord with what was said above about the technical relationship between primary and secondary machinery. Obviously, once the total labour increment has been finally absorbed, all three groups will have expanded by a rate equal to α under our assumption of unchanged factor proportions. But since under the same assumptions there is no reserve capacity in the field of primary machinery, the addition to secondary machinery presupposes the prior expansion of the output of primary machinery. We saw above that it is the circular nature of production in group a which makes such expansion possible. The fall in output of consumer goods has freed capacity not only in the respective group z, but also in group b, which supplies the replacement of secondary machinery, and in group a itself, which provides the replacement of capacity in group b.

It is this freed capacity in groups a and b[12] which forms the nucleus for the 'self-expansion' of primary machinery and thus for the 'widening' of productive capacity in all three groups. And it is in the gradual self-expansion of group a that the prime factors initially displaced in groups b and z will have to find employment during this first phase of adjustment. The second phase—namely, the process of net absorption—begins when output in group a has risen to a point that permits aggregate employment to rise above the stationary level. This then induces the gradual expansion of groups b and z beyond the level of employment and output to which saving on the part of the stationary factors had reduced them originally, to the new equilibrium level.[13]

This sketchy description of the process of real-capital formation under the conditions assumed forms the background for the structural analysis to follow. More specifically, it will now be our task to formulate, in terms of a minimum number of independent variables, certain strategic relationships which characterize the process of capital formation. They refer to the dynamic group ratios, to the danger of 'overbuilding' the capital stock, and, above all, to the length of the 'period of construction'.

The independent variables, which are to serve as data for our analysis, are four. Two of them—namely, k (capital depth) and d (depreciation)—are directly related to the size of the capital stock. The other two are α, the rate of growth of the labour increment, and s, the ratio of aggregate planned savings to aggregate income in the various phases of the adjustment process. Since in our 'normative' model, planned savings always equal planned investment, s also measures realized savings and investment.

Group Ratios (17) The structural shifts occuring during the process of capital formation can best be read in the variation of the group ratios. Not all the possible variations will be discussed at this point. There is, however, one intermediate phase in the adjustment process that requires closer examination. It concerns that stage of expansion when an amount of prime factors, equal to the amount originally displaced in groups b and z, has found re-employment in group a. Or, as we can also say, it describes the maximum expansion of group a which, with a given savings ratio, can be achieved with the available amount of stationary prime factors. Output at this stage, denoted by the subscript $_{00}$, compares with the stationary magnitudes denoted by $_0$ as follows:

$$z_{00} = z_0(1 - s) = o_0(1 - s)(1 - kd)$$

$$b_{00} = f_{z_{00}} = z_0(1 - s)kd = o_0(1 - s)(1 - kd)kd \qquad (2.8)$$

$$a_{00} = o_0 - (z_{00} + b_{00}) = o_0[1 - (1 - s)(1 - k^2d^2)]$$

Therefore,

$$z_{00}:b_{00}:a_{00} = 1:kd:\frac{k^2d^2(1 - s) + s}{(1 - s)(1 - kd)} \qquad (2.9)$$

It agrees with common sense that group a expands with the size of the savings ratio and the capital-depth coefficient and rate of depreciation of the original capital stock. We saw above that expansion of group a presupposes that savings 'free' part of the available capacity of primary equipment for the purpose of self-reproduction. The variables k and d

determine the potential range within which capacity can be 'freed', and *s* determines the size of capacity actually freed within that range. In this manner it is the savings ratio which fixes, within the limit of the technical variables *k* and *d*, the point of maximum expansion of group *a* in the sense defined, that is, before net absorption starts. In an empirical free market, in which the (*ex ante*) savings ratio is the result of many independent decisions, this may lead to the overbuilding of the capital stock and subsequent waste of part of the addition to primary equipment which is produced during the phase of expansion.

The Overbuilding of Primary Equipment (18)   The problem referred to is customarily dealt with under the heading of the acceleration principle. In particular, the older 'accelerationists' (Aftalion, J. M. Clark) felt troubled about the 'waste' of equipment stock, which seemed to them bound up with any decline in the rate of increase in consumption. Our example of an isolated, once-over change provides a good test for this proposition, since after a single act of expansion the rate of growth of consumption falls back to zero.

The foregoing analysis supplies all the necessary tools for such a test. First of all, it tells exactly where the alleged overbuilding will occur. Since, as the above group ratios show, the demand for secondary equipment always moves in proportion to the demand for consumer goods, the critical sector can only be group *a*, the current output of which, after the expansion, may indeed exceed the final *replacement* demand in both group *a* and group *b*. Secondly, we can calculate in terms of our independent variables the size of the additional primary equipment required in the new state of equilibrium, as well as the size of the actual supply of such equipment at the point of maximum expansion described by equation (2.8).

The first magnitude, primary equipment stock required (StR_{a+b}), can be ascertained in the following manner. *Total* additional investment—that is, the increment of both primary and secondary equipment—must amount to

$$StR_{a+b+z} = \alpha ko \qquad (2.10)$$

Of this addition to total capital stock an amount of

$$StR_{a+b} = \alpha k^2 do \qquad (2.10a)$$

must consist of primary equipment, equivalent to the replacement demand for both primary and secondary equipment.

The second magnitude, net addition to primary equipment stock actually supplied in advance of absorption (StS_a), can be calculated on the basis of equation (2.8). It amounts to the total stock of primary equipment in operation at the maximum point of expansion as defined above, minus the stationary stock of primary equipment. Or in symbolic language:

$$StS_a = (a_{00} + b_{00} - a_0 - b_0)k$$

$$= sk(1 - kd)o \qquad (2.11)$$

Potential waste W of primary equipment built during the process of expansion then amounts to

$$W = StS_a - StR_{a+b}$$

$$= [sk(1 - kd) - \alpha k^2 d]o \qquad (2.12)$$

We can generalize this result by dropping the assumption that the coefficients of capital depth and depreciation valid for the new capital stock are equal to those of the stationary stock. By denoting the new coefficients as k' and d', we obtain

$$W = [sk(1 - kd) - \alpha k'^2 d']o \qquad (2.12a)$$

It is obvious that the expression within the brackets can, but need not, be positive. The result depends on the relative size of the variables s, k, and d on the one hand, and α, k' and d' on the other. A high *ex ante* savings ratio, which under our assumptions is identical with a high 'investment ratio', and a high capital-depth coefficient of the original equipment make for waste, whereas a high rate of growth coupled with a high capital-depth coefficient of the equipment increment counteract it. Depreciation rates for both original and additional capital stock affect waste inversely.

Assuming a savings–investment ratio of 10 per cent, and on both sides capital-depth coefficients of 3 and depreciation rates of 10 per cent, a rate of once-over growth in the neighbourhood of 25 per cent would avoid any waste. This example assumes, in accord with our model, that all planned savings are actually invested in the service of a *change* in the rate of growth. In any empirical market system observed over the last century, a large part of s has always been needed to sustain a positive *constant* rate of growth, and it is hardly surprising that Kuznets and Tinbergen have found little empirical evidence for any investment waste.

This is not the place to dwell upon the flaws which mar the conventional exposition of the process of 'overbuilding'.[14] Apart from faulty notions about the structure of production, which obscure the process of expansion, the pessimistic conclusions arise from the assumption that the entire addition to equipment must be built in one arbitrarily chosen period of construction, an assumption that implies a fantastically high savings ratio. In reality the independent variable is not the construction period, but the savings–investment ratio in conjunction with the coefficients of capital depth and depreciation and the period of maturation of the capital increment (see section 19 below). In other words, in principle the choice is between speedy adjustment by means of a high savings–investment ratio involving the danger of waste, and slow adjustment by a low savings–investment ratio. The latter alternative keeps the building of capital stock in line with subsequent replacement demands, though at the price of making the consumer 'wait' longer for the fruits of investment. Of course, in practice the choice between these two alternatives is open only to a planned system, which can manipulate s in such a manner that, with given k, k', d and d', it just satisfies the requirements of α. In a free-market system, in which none of these variables is subject to overall control, overbuilding, though by no means inevitable, is a possible danger.

The Period of Construction   (19) The assertion that the appearance or non-appearance of waste is related to the size of the savings ratio deserves further investigation, which will also supply us with an exact measure of the minimum period of construction for the capital increment.

Given a system in which labour and equipment are fully utilized, how long will it take to produce an additional unit of a consumer good? Under the assumption of full utilization of the available capital stock, a prior increase in the output of primary and secondary equipment is the condition for an increase in the output of consumer goods. Thus in all three groups some units of natural resources must undergo the process of transformation into a finished good described in our stage schema (model 2.2). The total construction period that must elapse before the additional consumer good is available consists then of the sum of the 'maturation periods', m_a, m_b and m_z, required in the three groups to move the respective natural resources down to the stage of completion.

The notion of a 'period of maturation' was introduced in discussion of the concept of a stock of working capital goods (Section 8). With a given technology, m is an empirical constant which of course differs not only from group to group but from industry to industry. Therefore, if we want to apply this concept to a general process of expansion rather than to the increase in output of a single consumer good, it seems that we must introduce the notion of an 'average' period of maturation, a concept that would be difficult to establish empirically.

In fact, however, what is needed in order to measure the period of construction is the *longest* rather than the *average* period of maturation in each group, because the new equilibrium cannot be attained before the good with the longest period of maturation reaches the state of completion. It does not appear impossible to ascertain empirically such 'maximum' *m*'s.

These considerations seem to yield a measure for the period of construction (*PC*) required to expand the output of consumer goods in a system in which initially all resources are fully utilized. We obtain[15] $PC = m_a max. + m_b max. + m_z max.$ This measure is based entirely upon empirical technical constants without any reference to economic variables such as *s*. However, if examined more closely, the expression is defective in two respects.

First of all, we have so far implicitly assumed that the initial stock of primary equipment necessary to expand such output is fully available from the outset. Our exposition of the expansion process (Section 16) indicated that this is not so. The initial stock of primary equipment must be 'freed', and, as was shown above, the amount 'freed' depends upon the fall in replacement demand, which in its turn is determined by the prevailing savings ratio. Thus under the conditions assumed—with real-capital formation throughout the system—the actual period of maturation in group *a* exceeds m_a max. as defined above. It is a multiple of m_a max., the multiplicand *g* measuring the number of maturation periods required to expand the equipment stock 'freed' (*StF*) to the size of the equipment 'required' for the subsequent over-all increase in output (*StR*).

Secondly, a multiplicand has also to be added to m_b max. Once the required addition to the stock of primary equipment is available, it has to be used for maintaining itself and, above all, for raising the stock of secondary equipment to the required level. The latter aim could be achieved in *one* maturation period only if the size of the additional primary equipment were geared to the continuous *increase* rather than to the current maintenance of the additional secondary equipment. For any size of the additional primary equipment smaller than indicated, a period of $j.m_b$ max. is required to construct the addition to secondary equipment.

The true value for the period of construction is then:

$$PC = g \cdot m_a max. + j \cdot m_b max. + m_z max. \qquad (2.13)$$

and we have now to determine the magnitudes of *g* and *j*.

Whereas the three *m*'s are technical constants, *g* is a variable. To determine it, we need a measure for *StF*, for *StR*, and for the rate of growth of *StF*. It will now be shown that all these variables are related to the independent variables of our system.

Primary equipment freed, *StF*, consists of capacity freed in both group *b* and group *a*. The size of capacity freed in group *b* is determined by the fall of replacement demand on the part of group *z*. The latter being equal to $skdz_0$, the stock of primary equipment freed in group *b* amounts to sk^2dz_0.

On the same principle, an additional stock amounting to $sk^2d^2/(1 - kd)$, z_0 is freed in group *a*.[16] And the total stock of primary equipment freed equals

$$StF_{a+b} = \frac{sk^2d}{1- kd}z_0 = sk^2do_0 \qquad (2.14)$$

StR, the aggregate size of the primary equipment stock *required* (stock freed plus increment) can be determined in accord with equation (2.10a) above: $StR = (s + \alpha)k^2do$.

Finally, the rate of growth of *StF* is a function of *k*. Each unit of stock freed produces an output equal to StF/k, which itself is added to the equipment stock and, allowing for its own depreciation, is ready to produce additional equipment in the next maturation period. Thus the rate of growth of *StF* equals $\dfrac{[k(1 - d) + 1]}{k}$[17] and we obtain

$$StF\left[\frac{k(1 - d) + 1}{k}\right]^g = StR$$

and[18]

$$g = \frac{log\,(s + \alpha)/s}{log[k(1 - d) + 1]/k} \qquad (2.15)$$

We have finally to determine the magnitude of *j*, which measures the number of maturation periods required for the addition to secondary equipment. From equation (2.10a) we can derive the size of the secondary equipment stock required as $StR_z = \alpha k^2d(1 - kd)o_0$. The amount of primary equipment additionally available for the production of secondary equipment (over and above replacement of primary equipment) follows from equation 11 as StS_a for $b = sk(1 - kd)(1 - kd)o_0$ which produces per period of maturation m_b max. an output of secondary equipment

$$\Delta_{o_b} = \frac{[sk(1 - kd)(1 - kd)]}{k}o_0 = s(1 - kd)^2o_0.$$

Therefore,

$$j = \frac{StR_b}{\Delta_{o_0}} = \frac{\alpha k^2 d(1 - kd)}{s(1 - kd)^2} = \frac{\alpha k^2 d}{s(1 - kd)} \qquad (2.15a)$$

The upshot of all this is that, given the three periods of maturation as technical constants, the minimum period of construction of the total additional equipment stock required can be calculated on the basis of our independent variables. As one would expect on common-sense grounds, both g and j, and thus the construction period in its entirety, are directly related to the rate of growth and the depth and depreciation rate of the additional capital stock, and inversely related to the savings ratio and the depth and depreciation rate of the original capital stock.

We saw above that the savings ratio may well prove excessive in view of the goal of optimum utilization of resources. We now have it confirmed by quantitative analysis that the higher the savings ratio the shorter is the minimum period of construction. Thus, as was indicated above, a conflict of goals may arise in a free-market system between 'maximum speed of adjustment' and 'minimum waste of resources'. Considering their low savings ratio, the economies of underdeveloped countries are unlikely to be caught in this dilemma.

Some Remarks on 'Neutral' Changes in Productivity
(20) Besides a change in labour supply it is, above all, a change in technology that may induce a once-over change in capital formation. Since the most important type of technical change—namely, factor-displacing and factor-attracting innovations—will be discussed in the context of continuous change, only 'neutral' changes in productivity will be discussed here. Harrod defines a neutral advance as one that does not alter the coefficients of capital depth.[19] In other words, output rises in the same proportion as capital stock, so that the group ratios in the new equilibrium do not differ from those in the original equilibrium.

As an analogy to the growth rate α of the labour force, a measure for the once-over rise in productivity is needed. This measure, π, is best defined as the difference between the coefficient of total productivity prevailing in the original equilibrium and that prevailing in the final equilibrium: $\pi = \epsilon_1/\epsilon_0 - 1$ where both ϵ's are related to i_0, that is, the unit input of the stationary process (see Section 11). Equations (2.10), (2.10a), (2.12), (2.12a), (2.15), and (2.15a) can then be rewritten by substituting π for α. By inserting $\alpha + \pi$ in the respective terms, we obtain expressions for the required capital stocks, for waste, and for the period of construction under conditions of a simultaneous once-over change in both labour and supply and productivity.

THE DYNAMICS OF CONTINUOUS CHANGE

(21) Turning now to the capital problems related to continuous change, we have first to make a convenient breakdown of this large topic. To explore all structurally relevant cases, from the conditions for dynamic equilibrium to the multitude of dynamic disequilibria and the conditions for re-equilibration, would require a book. Therefore, it seems advisable to subdivide this part according to a formal principle which is applicable to all cases and can serve as a sort of 'cadre', into which the reader may fit those other problems which cannot be discussed in this paper.

The distinction between 'constant' and 'varying' rates of change supplies such a principle. It restates, in a manner, the criterion for distinguishing between a stationary process and a once-over change, but now introducing this criterion into a framework of continuous change. The 'equilibrium norm' of a constant rate of change, which in a stationary process implies a *zero* rate of change, now implies a *positive* rate of change. And, as has already been stated (Section 13), processes involving varying rates of change can then be analysed by the technique applied to once-over changes.

The Dynamics of a Constant Rate of Change (Dynamic Equilibrium)

(22) Certain structural conditions for dynamic equilibrium have received wide attention during the last decade. Considering the Keynesian origin of most of this work, it is not surprising that all the representative formulations (Harrod, Domar, Hicks) are in aggregate terms. Therefore, they describe the conditions which relate to the structure of the income–expenditure flow (Section 3 above) rather than those which concern the physical structure of production. One of our tasks will be to show that, within the frame of reference assumed by the originators, the Harrod–Domar conditions, though necessary, are not sufficient to assure dynamic equilibrium.

For this purpose these conditions themselves must be formulated in terms of our independent variables. Dynamic equilibrium can prevail only if, for any given period, the supply of real capital equals the demand for real capital. Assuming a savings (investment) ratio of s, supply of real capital in terms of aggregate output equals $s(1 - kd)o$. Demand for real capital can be determined with the help of equation (2.10) by interpreting α as a constant rate of growth. Adding to the constant growth in labour supply a constant increase in neutral technical advances, $(\alpha + \pi)ko$ measures the aggregate demand for real capital.

Therefore, in dynamic equilibrium $s(1 - kd) = (\alpha + \pi)k$ or

$$\frac{(\alpha + \pi)k}{1 - kd} = s \tag{2.16}$$

This condition for dynamic equilibrium differs from the 'no waste' condition formulated in equation (2.12) only by the absence of the variable d in the expression for the stock required. The modification indicates what, with respect to capital formation, is the difference between the two types of growth. In 'wasteless' once-over growth, stock building is precisely geared to subsequent replacement demand, whereas in continuous growth the demands of both stock replacement and stock expansion must be satisfied.

It is immediately clear that equation (2.16) is equivalent to both $G_n C_r = s$ (Harrod's Condition) and $\triangle I/I\sigma = s$ (Domar's condition). The terms $\alpha + \pi$ in equation (2.16) have the same meaning as Harrod's G_n ('natural rate of growth') and Domar's addition to investment, $\triangle I/I$, whereas our k is identical with Harrod's C_r ('required capital coefficient') and is the inverse of Domar's σ ('investment productivity'). The only difference is that Harrod and Domar relate s to net output or income, whereas equation (2.16) relates s to gross output.

Thus there is general agreement that dynamic equilibrium cannot persist unless income and investment change at a rate equal to the product of the prevailing savings ratio and Domar's coefficient of investment productivity. But for dynamic equilibrium to be assured in an industrial system with factor specificity, the rate of growth of net output and investment, that is, $\alpha + \pi$, not only must equal the critical product, but must remain constant. Furthermore, given such a constant rate of growth, not only the critical product itself, but also the factors composing it, will have to remain constant. If the rate of growth changes, persistence of dynamic equilibrium will be conditional upon complicated shifts among the groups of production, *even if the product of the savings ratio and the investment productivity ratio spontaneously and simultaneously adjusts itself to the new rate of growth.* Similar shifts will be required if s or $1/k$ change, *even if their product remains constant.* The fact that, and the manner in which, such shifts are likely to destabilize the system will be demonstrated below.[20] In preparation for this discussion the more restrictive conditions, which are both necessary and sufficient for the maintenance of dynamic equilibrium, will now be established.

(23) For this purpose we must, first of all, formulate structural equations of production, equivalent to the set of stationary equations formulated in model (2.1), but now appropriate to dynamic equilibrium:

$$[(1 + \alpha)^{'n} + (1 + \pi)^{'n}][(F_{at_0}d \equiv f_{at_0}) + n_{at_0} + \sigma_{at_0}] = a_{t_n}$$

$$[(1 + \alpha)^{'n} + (1 + \pi)^{'n}][(F_{bt_0}d \equiv f_{bt_0}) + n_{bt_0} + \sigma_{bt_0}] = b_{t_n}$$
$$[(1 + \alpha)^{'n} + (1 + \pi)^{'n}][F_{zt_0}d \equiv f_{zt_0}) + n_{zt_0} + \sigma_{zt_0}] = z_{t_n} \qquad (2.17)$$

The set of equations in (2.17) differs from the stationary equations in two respects. First, the number of input items, contained in the right-hand brackets, is increased by the factor σ, representing savings over the chosen period. Secondly, the left-hand brackets contain a multiplicand, namely the rate of growth by which the system expands from period to period as a result of increase in labour supply and of neutral advances. Therefore, the equations describe the level of *real* output attained in period t_n, expressed as the compounded level of real output in period t_0.

From set (2.17) we can derive the structural conditions of dynamic equilibrium, equivalent to those described for stationary equilibrium in equations (2.4) and (2.5):

$$f_{zt_2} = f_{zt_1} + \sigma_{zt_1}d$$
$$= b_{t_1} - \sigma_{zt_1}(1 - d) \qquad (2.18)$$

$$f_{bt_2} = f_{bt_1} + \sigma_{bt_1}d$$
$$= a_{t_1} - f_{at_1} - \sigma_{at_1} - \sigma_{bt_1}(1 - d) \qquad (2.19)$$

These equilibrium conditions contain implicitly also the condition formulated in equation (2.16), that is, the Harrod–Domar condition for aggregate dynamic equilibrium. But they point up, above all, the physical–technical relations that must persist among certain strategic components of the three groups if today's outputs are to serve as tomorrow's inputs in a steadily expanding process. The underlying principle is that the Harrod–Domar conditions must apply not only to aggregate output and investment, but also to output and investment in each of the three groups.[21]

In this respect a comment is in order with regard to the variable σ. As is the case with all the other variables, σ has a twofold meaning: one monetary, one real (see Section 10 above); that is, it measures both savings and investment. As measures of investment σ_a, σ_b and σ_z express that distribution of total investment over the three groups on which persistence of dynamic equilibrium depends. As measures of savings they express the relative amounts of funds *available* for investment in each group rather than the relative amounts *accumulated* there. In other words, for the maintenance of dynamic equilibrium it does not matter how much of the income of each group is saved by the respective income receivers, so long as the aggregate savings ratio remains constant and the 'oversavings' of one or more groups are transferred to the 'undersaving' group(s) for investment there.

(24) In order to explore fully the structure of dynamic equilibrium, we must now determine the prevailing group ratios. Starting from the group ratios that characterize stationary equilibrium (equation 2.6), it is easy to see that for a given aggregate output, output of consumer goods in dynamic equilibrium (z_{dy}) is reduced below the stationary level by the amount of net savings. Therefore,

$$z_{dy} = z_0(1 - s)$$

$$= (1 - s)(1 - kd)o_0$$

It will be apparent that this expression is identical with the one given in Section 17 for the initial change in output of consumer goods under the impact of a once-over change. The difference is that in dynamic equilibrium with constant money supply, only the *money* expression for z_{dy} lies permanently below the money expression for z_0, but real output rises continuously.

In establishing the size of b_{dy}, a certain complication must be considered. During the first phase of a once-over change, b_{00} simply serves as replacement of $f_{z_{00}}$. In dynamic equilibrium, b_{dy} must fulfil the same function but must also provide for an additional stock of secondary equipment in accord with the prevailing rate of growth. Thus

$$b_{dy} = f_{zdy} + F_{zdy}(\alpha + \pi)$$

$$= [(1 - s)(1 - kd)kd + (1 - s)(1 - kd)k(\alpha + \pi)]o_0$$

From equation (2.16) we know that $s(1 - kd)/k$ can be substituted for $\alpha + \pi$. This yields $b_{dy} = (1 - s)(1 - kd)[kd(1 - s) + s]o_0$.

Finally, $a_{dy} = o_0 - (b_{dy} + z_{dy}) = [kd(1 - s) + s]^2 o_0$ so that

$$z_{dy}:b_{dy}:a_{dy} = 1:kd(1 - s) + s:\frac{[kd(1 - s) + s]^2}{(1 - s)(1 - kd)}$$

$$= F_{zdy}:F_{bdy}:F_{ady} \tag{2.20}$$

Introducing different capital-depth coefficients, different rates of depreciation, and different savings ratios, the three group ratios become

$$z_{dy}:b_{dy}:a_{dy} = 1:(1 - s_z)k_z d_z + s_z$$

$$:\frac{[(1 - s_z)k_z d_z + s_z][(1 - s_b)k_b d_b + s_b]}{(1 - s_a)(1 - k_a d_a)} \tag{2.20a}$$

The ratio $F_{zdy}:F_{bdy}:F_{ady}$ can be obtained by multiplying the members on the right side of equation (2.20a) with k_z, k_b, and k_a, respectively.

(25) It may be appropriate at this point to demonstrate how, with the help of equation (2.20) or (2.20a), the actual structure of the system

can be derived if the values of o, s, k and d are given. The group ratios and capital stock ratios appropriate to the given values of s, k, and d follow from equation (2.20). The absolute values of the group outputs can then be derived by subdividing the value of o accordingly. The absolute values for the capital stocks equal the absolute values of the respective group outputs multiplied by the respective k's. The absolute values of the inputs f_z, f_b, and f_a follow from the respective group outputs multiplied by kd. The income magnitudes $(n + \sigma)$ equal the residual of $o - f$ in each group, and with the help of s we can divide the respective sums of $n + \sigma$ into their components. The equilibrium conditions, equations (2.18) and (2.19), provide a final check.

The Dynamics of a Varying Rate of Change

(26) Once we admit variations in the rate of change, any one of our independent variables, α, π, k, d and s and any combination of these variables can undergo such a change. A complete survey might have to include also shifts in taste, at least to the extent to which the bipolar changes in capital stock bound up with such shifts do not fully balance, and also changes in the supply of natural resources, especially diminishing returns on land.

This discussion will be confined to two examples which illustrate some of the structural problems of capital formation that arise in the context of varying rates of change. One deals with shifts in the demand and supply functions for investment; the other is concerned with non-neutral—that is, factor-displacing—technical changes.

Shifts in the Investment Functions (27) What is at stake here can best be understood in terms of the Harrod–Domar conditions as formulated in equation (2.16): $(\alpha + \pi)k/(1 - kd) = s$. A shift relating to the variables of this equation can mean two things. On the one hand, and this is the usual interpretation, it can refer to a shift of the demand for investment relative to the supply of investment—in popular language, to either undersaving or oversaving. But it can also mean a proportionate change on both sides of the equation by a simultaneous parallel change in the savings ratio and the output of capital goods. This alternative has greater realistic significance than may appear at first sight. It covers, for example, the case of a mature economy in which the community responds to a falling rate of population increase with a rise in the average propensity to consume. Even more important is the case of an over investment boom in Hayek's sense, in which rising real wages cut into savings and enforce a reduction of aggregate investment.

It is interesting to note that Harrod, Domar and all their critics are exclusively concerned with the first alternative, that is, a relative change between the two functions. Parallel shifts do not seem to pose any problems to them, though these are the real test for any equilibrium condition which is formulated in aggregate terms only.[22] The analysis of such shifts will now serve to complete the argument about the conditions of dynamic equilibrium, which was started in Section 22 above.

(28) The case of a parallel shift in the demand and supply functions for investment can be expressed in the following modification of equation (2.16):

$$h\frac{(\alpha + \pi)k}{1 - kd} = hs \qquad (2.16a)$$

where h measures the change in the rate of growth and in the savings ratio as the ratio between the new and the old level of these two magnitudes. If interpreted as an '*ex post*' relationship, the above equation is of course a truism. The problem to which I want to draw attention is posed by the structural shifts within the aggregate, which are enforced by the transition from the state described in equation (2.16) to that described in equation (2.16a).

To follow up these shifts I assume that, with a constant coefficient of capital depth, the rate of population growth falls and that the savings ratio adjusts itself immediately. Even though these shifts are simultaneous, the structure of production is now in disequilibrium. To regain equilibrium, the output of consumer goods and of secondary equipment must rise (in accord with the rise in the average propensity to consume) relative to the output of primary equipment. This change in the output ratio between groups z and b, on the one hand, and group a, on the other hand, depends upon a corresponding reshuffling of factors. Some primary equipment and labour, which under the previous higher rate of absorption produced additional primary machinery, will now have to produce more secondary machinery. This, however, will not keep the total previous stock of primary equipment fully employed. It is true that, as dynamic equilibrium progresses, at some future time the *aggregate* stock of primary and secondary equipment again equals the aggregate stock that would exist had the rate of growth not fallen. But the share of the secondary-equipment stock in this aggregate is now higher, and the share of the primary-equipment stock is reduced correspondingly. This means that, to begin with, some primary equipment must be either scrapped or kept idle until the system grows into the existing capacity, always assuming that, for reasons of specificity, it cannot be used as secondary equipment.

A similar though less drastic friction arises in the labour market. More labour is now needed to mind machines in group z, whereas some labour formerly employed in making machines in group a will be displaced. Labour is never so specialized that gradual transfer cannot take place. But whether and when such adjustment, and with it the approach to a new equilibrium, will occur depends upon what effect capital devaluation and temporary unemployment in group a will have on entrepreneurs' expectations and behaviour.

Here the limits of structural analysis have been reached and functional analysis, the study of behaviour patterns, must take over if the actual stability conditions are to be established. In a general way one may venture the guess that adjustment hangs in the balance, to say the least, if the magnitude of h is considerable and the shift occurs suddenly. The coincidence of both circumstances in a 'strong' boom makes this phase of the cycle highly unstable.[23]

Thus dynamic equilibrium through time is assured only if major shifts among the groups can be excluded. This is equivalent to saying that the Harrod–Domar conditions must be fulfilled for each one of the three groups—the postulate contained in the above formulation of the equilibrium conditions in equations (2.18) and (2.19).

A measure for the waste in primary equipment, which a parallel downward shift of the savings and the investment functions creates, can easily be ascertained by comparing the size of the stock necessary to sustain the higher rate of growth with that required to sustain the lower one. The former equals $St\ A(\text{vailable})_{a+b} = (a_{dy} + b_{dy})k$.

Using equation (2.20), we can transform this into $St\ A_{a+b} = [(1 - s)kd + s]ko$. If the change in the rate of growth, expressed as the ratio between the new and the old rate of growth, equals h, the new stock of primary equipment required equals $St\ R_{a+b} = [(1 - sh)kd + sh]ko$.

Waste, which is equal to the difference between the two expressions, then is

$$W' = sk(1 - h)(1 - kd)o \qquad (2.21)$$

W' varies directly with the size of the capital coefficient and the original savings ratio, and inversely with the change in the rate of growth. If the rate of growth increases waste is 'negative'. Then equation (2.21) measures the additional amount of primary equipment required for the system to adjust to the new rate.

A comment is in order on the relationship between the two kinds of waste, which are determined by equations (2.12) and (2.21) respectively. They refer to quite different phenomena. The term W, waste due to 'overbuilding', indicates that actual investment overshoots the fixed target of required investment. The term W', waste due to a parallel shift in the demand and supply functions for investment, indicates that the investment target itself changes in the downward direction. If it changes in the upward direction, W' is negative. But there is then no positive W either, since no 'overbuilding' can occur so long as the new, higher rate of growth is maintained.

It may well be asked whether the functional obstacles which obstruct adjustment to a falling rate of growth interfere also with adjustment to a rising rate of growth. At the beginning of such a change some secondary equipment and the labour operating it will certainly be displaced. Absolute specificity completely prevents the former from being shifted to group a, and the latter can at best be shifted with some delay. One might argue that the effect of structural frictions upon expectations is less destabilizing in an expanding than in a contracting system. But in the former case an investment decision must be made, while in the latter case output can follow the price signals of a rising consumer demand. Whatever the ultimate conclusion may be, a parallel shift of the savings and investment functions establishes an interesting mechanism. It brings about a change in the income–expenditure structure which as such does not distort the structure itself. This lack of distortion is probably the reason why Harrod and Domar pay no attention to such parallel shifts. However, the change in the income–expenditure structure indirectly causes a distortion of the technical structure. This secondary distortion may in its turn destabilize the income–expenditure structure after all.

(29) The second alternative—namely, a relative change in the investment demand and the investment supply functions—can be expressed by the following inequality: $s \lessgtr (\alpha + \pi)k/(1 - kd)$. The s refers of course to planned savings, whereas the right side defines planned investment. With regard to the effect that such an inequality is likely to have upon the stability of dynamic equilibrium, I have little to add to the insights which the discussion of Harrod's and Domar's work has brought to light during the last few years.[24] Since, as in the previous case, the conclusions must ultimately be derived from behavioural premises, they are again a task for functional rather than for structural analysis. But a brief digression into this area may be of value at this point. It will bring to light the special contribution that structural analysis makes to 'total' analysis. I choose for this purpose the case of potential oversaving, which, in the wake of the Keynesian challenge, was long the centre of attention, and which still forms a subject of controversy between Keynesians and certain neoclassicists.[25] The reader will easily be able to apply the argument to potential undersaving.

According to the traditional neoclassical position, an excess of planned savings over planned investment will be adjusted either by a rise in the average capital depth of the system or by a harmless *numéraire* deflation. The link is the depressing effect which potential oversaving is supposed to exert upon the rate of interest, which in its turn is supposed to induce an increase in the demand for capital goods per unit of labour.

The objections to this harmonistic solution concern both links of the argument. First of all, the rate of interest may not fall at all. The initial excess of planned savings over investment must reduce demand for and prices of consumer goods. This is likely to create elastic price expectations all around and increase the demand for cash. But, even if the rate of interest were to fall, the situation in the consumer-goods market just described would hardly be conducive to an expansion of investment. Thus in either case the result will be a fall in aggregate employment with all the latent dangers of a general 'real' deflation.

So far everybody has won and all must have prizes. But this is so only because the two parties argue at cross-purposes. The neoclassical argument is correct for a state of perfect mobility, where absence of specificity reduces the period of constructing additional capital goods to an insignificant length. In this situation the fall in consumer-goods output can at once be balanced by a rise in the output of producer goods, leaving the elasticity of price expectations unchanged. Far from obstructing adjustment, the fall in consumer-goods output is the very condition for an equilibrating shift of factors from groups z and b to group a. Even if the rate of interest should not fall sufficiently, or the investment elasticity of such a fall should be small, the ensuing general fall of commodity and factor prices (as a result of the 'hoarding' of savings, to use old-fashioned language) need not affect the real magnitudes of the system. When perfect mobility prevails, the downward adjustment of the *numéraire* can take place simultaneously and in the very short run all over the system, leaving expectations again unaffected. The maximum permissible length of this 'short run' can be determined. It must not exceed the shortest of the various income periods in the system (i.e. one week, under present institutional arrangements). If it is longer, factor unemployment cumulates and the monetary deflation deteriorates into a depression.

One has only to spell out its implicit conditions to realize that the neoclassical argument is completely unrealistic in a industrial system. But it is equally clear that it is the lags in the adjustment process due to specificity, especially of equipment goods, and the consequent *longue durée* of the construction period that create cumulative unemployment with its detrimental effect upon the elasticity of price expectations.

Whatever justification there is for the Harrod–Domar pessimism with regard to the stability of dynamic equilibrium—and there is a good deal—it rests ultimately upon the technical rigidity of an industrial order of production.

This result is not accidental. Though the proposition cannot be proved in the context of the present paper, it can be stated as a general rule that, to endanger the stability of the system, distortions of the income–expenditure structure must influence expectations in a particular manner. Whether they do so or not is largely dependent on the length of the potential adjustment period, which in its turn is directly related to the prevailing technical order.[26]

In summarizing this discussion of the consequences that possible changes in the strategic variables can have for the stability of dynamic equilibrium, we can distinguish between three levels of progressively restrictive conditions. The optimistic extreme is represented by the traditional neoclassical approach, which disregards all aspects of specificity. There capital depth is treated as a variable, which changes inversely with a highly sensitive rate of interest. Since any shock arising from a change in either the rate of growth or the savings ratio can be absorbed without delay by a change in k, dynamic equilibrium is stable.

An intermediate position is taken by Harrod and Domar. They treat k as a constant; therefore, changes in the rate of growth relative to the savings ratio cannot be absorbed without frictions and precarious consequences for expectations. But so long as $s/(\alpha + \pi)$ and therefore k remain constant, dynamic equilibrium once existing is stable, though it may shift from one level of activity to another one.

The most restrictive conditions for dynamic equilibrium have been postulated above. Not only the fraction $s/(\alpha + \pi)$ and thus capital depth, but both the numerator and the denominator of the fraction, that is, the savings ratio as well as the rate of growth, must remain constant in order to prevent destabilizing structural shifts among the groups of production.

Non-neutral Technical Changes   (30) The theory of technical change is still a stepchild of economic analysis. The sweeping generalizations of Marx and Schumpeter have not been followed by more detailed macroeconomic investigations. In Keynesian economics technical change figures as no more than one investment variable among others. More recent work, for example the writings of Yale Brozen or William Fellner, has by and large taken a microeconomic turn. Therefore, I shall have to introduce my structural analysis with some more general remarks, to determine, first of all, the context in which macroeconomic problems of capital formation arise when technical changes disturb dynamic equilibrium.

In order to narrow the field, the following observations will be confined to *cost-reducing* technical changes, to the exclusion of *want-creating* innovations, or, to use the customary term, 'new products'. If I read the literature correctly, the latter have so far proved refractory to exact analysis, due mainly to two complications. First, they introduce a simultaneous change in both the supply and the demand function; secondly, since the product is 'new', the new supply function cannot be related to any previously existing supply function—the main difference from cost-reducing changes. Thus what follows refers only to 'technical progress' in the narrower sense.

In contradistinction to what was discussed earlier, in Section 20, here only 'non-neutral' technical changes will be considered. Harrod's definition of neutrality, which was adopted above, refers to a proportional rise of output and capital stock, leaving k unchanged. Harrod is fully aware that this definition implies an assumption about the relative demand for factors in the new state as compared with the old. By a neutral advance 'the productivity of labor embodied in machines is raised in equal measure with that of those engaged in minding machines'.[27] In other words, neutral advances are neither labour displacing nor capital displacing.

These considerations yield a convenient definition of non-neutral technical changes. They comprise all changes that cause at least temporary displacement of one or more factors somewhere in the system, though not necessarily in the industry which introduces the change. It is the kind and size of such displacement, and the manner in which the displaced factors can be re-absorbed (what Continental economists have called the 'compensation' problem), that are in the centre of the structural analysis of non-neutral technical changes so far as capital formation is concerned.

In the conventional manner I distinguish between labour-displacing and capital-displacing changes. Within each of these two subgroups there are three different types, according to whether, per unit of output, units of both factors are displaced or, whether, with units of one factor displaced,[28] the employment of the other remains constant or even increases. All these cases have empirical significance. Because each type can materialize simultaneously in all three groups, or in any two or in only one, because different types can materialize simultaneously in different groups, and furthermore because capital displacement can refer to fixed as well as to working-capital goods, the number of possible models exceeds any manageable range. But in each case the same structural principle is at work, so that the selection of a few simple cases will suffice to formulate the basic problems and to indicate their solution.

I shall concentrate upon pure labour-displacing changes and supplement the results with only brief comments upon labour-displacing and capital-attracting changes, and pure capital-displacing changes. The capital change in both cases will be confined to changes in fixed capital. In accord with the general tenor of this paper, only problems related to capital formation will be discussed, to the exclusion of the productivity effects, private or social, and the distributive effects of technical changes.

(31) As indicated above, structural problems of capital formation arise in two phases of the innovation process: one at the beginning if the introduction of the new device requires a change in the fixed-capital applied; the other when the operation of the new device has displaced some factors of production, the re-absorption of which requires additional real capital. In trying to design models for these problems we are confronted with two alternatives. We can choose as our general frame of reference an economic process in equilibrium, stationary or dynamic, or—an alternative more appropriate for the past history of capitalism—a process in which part of the available resources are idle. Obviously the task of 'capital construction' is greatly facilitated in both phases of adjustment if idle capacity exists in the two equipment-goods groups. On the other hand, such a frame of reference inevitably involves the whole complex of business-cycle analysis. Pursuing this line not only would take us far afield, but would also prevent us from studying the structural issues in isolation. The analysis will therefore be continued within the framework of dynamic equilibrium. Considering the bottlenecks referred to earlier, which nowadays obstruct smooth adjustment to large changes in the rate of change in both developed and underdeveloped countries, the alternative chosen recommends itself also on practical grounds.

These assumptions yield a simple solution of the 'construction' problem. It does not arise in a pure labour-displacing technical change because the value—that is, the claim upon factors though not necessarily the physical form of the equipment stock—remains unchanged by definition. This presupposes, of course, that the change-over to the new technique takes place after the old equipment is fully amortized. On the other hand, a construction problem does arise in capital-attracting changes, as does a problem of capital liquidation in capital-displacing changes. For either case the preceding analysis of once-over changes and of a downward shift of the investment function can be used. What was said, for example, about the 'construction period' (Section 19) and the two types of waste (Sections 18 and 28) is fully applicable here.

The problem of 'compensation' is more complex. There is, above all, no general agreement that compensation is a 'secular-period' problem in the Marshallian sense, or, in other words, that the re-absorption of technologically displaced labour really requires prior capital formation. It is not possible to pursue this question through all its ramifications at this time, and a few remarks must suffice to justify the position taken below.[29]

Starting from a pure labour-displacing device, three short-period solutions of the compensation problem have been suggested since the days when Ricardo deserted the harmonist camp in the chapter 'On machinery'. One points to compensating 'demand', arising either from the profits of the technical pioneer or, if the improvement is generalized over the whole industry, from the rise in consumer real income resulting from the fall in price of the improved output. Whatever one may think about the cogency of this argument,[30] it certainly implies capital formation in those fields towards which the alleged increase in aggregate demand turns.

The second solution hinges upon the variability of factor proportions. In its most extreme version the argument asserts that any amount of idle labour can always be employed on the *existing* capital stock, if only wages adjust to the declining marginal productivity. Now under conditions of factor specificity, as they prevail in an industrial system, the argument cannot refer to the physical form of the existing capital stock, but only to its value. In other words, compensation is then a long-period problem, depending upon the prior transformation of the existing stock of capital goods into a physically different one. Such transformation will not by itself create any friction if the change-over coincides with the moment when the old equipment must be replaced anyhow. But while firms can plan 'construction' in this manner, there is no mechanism which assures such a happy coincidence in the case of compensation. If the two points of time differ, compensation is again conditional upon the formation of new real capital.

The third solution is Ricardo's own: employment of displaced workers in occupations which do not require fixed capital, such as menial services and—happy age!—warfare. The wide range of 'services' offered in any depression is an indication that this solution is not without practical relevance. The general trend of modern industrialism toward 'tertiary' occupations at the expense of 'secondary' ones may indeed provide a safety valve for *secular* technological unemployment of a steady nature. But it is unlikely to absorb the shocks which arise from large discontinuous innovations of a labour-displacing character.

However, the adherents of short-period compensation may point to the fact that many of these discontinuous innovations are at the same time capital attracting. In this case the compensation issue, far from creating an adjustment problem, seems to alleviate the difficulties bound up with the initial construction phase. By creating another need for capital formation, compensation of technological unemployment offers work to the additional stock of primary equipment which had to be built to make the initial capital expansion possible, and may thus preclude 'waste'. The argument certainly deserves consideration. But it is decisive only when the capital depth of the initial investment approximates that of the compensation investment, and even then only over the period during which the compensating equipment must be built. After this second construction period the waste problem again appears, though somewhat mitigated by the need for larger replacements, which have now to maintain two capital stocks.

From all these observations it appears that large, sudden and highly productive innovations of a labour-displacing nature do pose a problem of capital formation (as capital-displacing changes pose a problem of capital liquidation). Therefore, the results obtained above for the length of the construction period and for waste can again be utilized. But they now require an important modification, because non-neutral technical changes alter permanently the relative scarcity of labour and equipment. This is equivalent to saying that the factors have to be reshuffled among the three groups before the new equilibrium can be attained. This new shift in the group ratios is much more complicated than the adjustment to changes in the overall rate of growth, discussed above (Sections 22–9).

(32) Limitations of space permit the detailed exposition of such a shift for only the simplest case, namely, a pure labour-displacing improvement occurring in the consumer-goods group. Given a system in dynamic equilibrium as described in equation (2.20), and also the ratio of workers displaced in group z to workers originally employed there, how will the group ratios, which describe the new equilibrium after compensation, differ from the original? To aid the comparison it is assumed that the supply of money is kept constant, so that output prices adjust to the fall in unit costs which results from the reduction of labour costs.

The principal link between the two equilibria is a systematic rise in the capital depth of the critical group z. This rise in capital depth can be derived from the more obvious rise in capital intensity, which is only another way of saying that less labour is now applied per unit of capital.[31]

The general relationship between capital intensity c (see Section 11) and k can be established as follows: $c = F/n_v = ok/(o - f) = ok/(o - kdo) = k/(1 - kd)$ or $k = c/(1 + cd)$. Denoting the displacement ratio as defined above by δ_z, we have $c_{z_1} = c_{z_0}/(1 - \delta_z)$ where the subscripts 0 and 1 refer to the original and subsequent equilibrium respectively. Therefore,

$$k_{z_1} = \frac{c_{z_0}}{1 - \delta_z + c_{z_0}d_{z_0}} = \frac{k_{z_o}}{1 - \delta_z(1 - k_{z_0}d_{z_0})} \qquad (2.22)$$

Since the technical change is confined to group z, no change in capital depth occurs in groups a and b, so that $k_{b_1} = k_{b_0}$ and $k_{a_1} = k_{a_0}$. By simply substituting k_{z_1} for k_{z_0} in equation (2.20a), the group ratios in the new equilibrium can be established.

It is now possible to determine the capital requirements upon which compensation depends. The new group ratios in combination with the respective capital-depth coefficients yield the new ratios among the capital stocks of the three groups, from which the absolute capital increments can be calculated for any given absolute level of the original output. Our previous investigations supply the tools for determining the length of the construction period required for compensation and the size of capital waste occurring, if any. As a matter of fact, since innovations are the prime cause of uneven changes in the rate of growth, it is in this context that these tools prove their usefulness.

(33) The general principle expounded in the foregoing section is applicable to all cases of factor-displacing innovations. However, in most cases additional considerations must be taken into account, of which two are briefly indicated here.

First, whenever labour-displacing innovations are introduced in one or both equipment-goods groups, technology in the consumer-goods group remaining unchanged, one might expect that the value capital-depth coefficients would change in the innovating groups. In fact this is not so, because the value of the *input* 'equipment' adjusts itself in the new equilibrium to the increased productivity—that is, to the value of its *output*, which itself is equipment. Therefore, both the value of the capital stock and that of output must fall in the same proportion, leaving the quotient k unchanged. On the other hand, the price fall of secondary equipment because of the technical change in group a and/ or group b must affect the value of the capital stock in group z, reducing there the value capital-depth coefficient although the physical–technical combination of the factors has not itself changed.

Secondly, in applying our procedure to capital-displacing improvements, we must remember that such changes *reduce* both value capital intensity and value capital-depth in the innovating groups. Thus the effect is just the opposite of that which arises from labour-displacing changes. This enables us to treat capital-displacing changes as labour-attracting changes. To give an example, for a pure capital-displacing change in the consumer-goods group we have only to substitute $1/(1 - \delta)$ for $1 - \delta$ in equation (2.22). We then obtain the critical coefficient k_z, with the help of which the shift ratio and the new group ratios can be derived in the manner described.

APPLICATION: 'IDEAL' AND 'REAL' MODELS

(34) As stated in the Introduction, this paper is concerned only with the structural part of the theory of dynamic processes. Within this area two main problems have been studied: (1) the minimum capital requirements for various types of economic growth, and (2) the optimum paths that the system must follow in order to readjust the dislocations that different types of growth inflict upon a pre-existing state of stationary or dynamic equilibrium, 'minimum' and 'optimum' to be related to minimum waste of resources and/or maximum speed of adjustment. A final question remains to be answered: Are the results of such structural analysis useful in helping to solve the empirical growth problems which arise in advanced as well as in backward economic systems?

From the outset it is readily admitted that, in an empirical science, the effort spent upon the construction of 'models' can be ultimately justified only by what they contribute to the understanding of real phenomena. In order to pass this test our structural models need elaboration in at least two directions. First, the level of abstraction will have to be reduced below the one chosen in the foregoing exposition, which is appropriate to pure theory only. Secondly, and more important, we have so far been concerned almost exclusively with 'structural' relations and movements, that is, with the impersonal conditions for the absorption of dynamic shocks. But, as was stressed in the beginning, no practical economic problem can even be posed, not to say solved, without due regard to the personal forces as manifested in the motivations and behaviour patterns of the actors. To formulate the general principle in the terminology established above: Only when combined with functional analysis can structural analysis be 'applied'.

However, even when supplemented by a study of the appropriate motivations and behaviour patterns, structural analysis of the type performed above will never yield a 'real' model, that is, a simplified image of any actual growth process. We have to remember that we have not been concerned with the *descriptive* analysis of structural relations and movements as they occur in empirical systems in historical time, but with *normative* analysis, that is, with the structural requirements for the optimal attainment of a postulated goal, say, equilibrating growth. Were we to extend our analysis to the functional conditions required to hold the system to the structurally required path, we should be able to fill the lacunae in our 'ideal' models, but reality, that is, actual behaviour and the real structure that emanates from it, would still escape us.

This gulf between 'ideal' and 'real' models is perhaps less wide in a collectivist system. There the actual dispositions of the planning authority reflect what, under the aspect of the chosen 'holistic' goal, are regarded as required structure and required behaviour. Any deviation of the 'real' from the 'ideal' behaviour is then treated as illegitimate, and as a subject for the penal code rather than for economic study. No such concurrence prevails in a free-market system, where the real order of the whole is not based on holistic decisions but is the result of the independent decisions of the 'particles'. If we want to construct models of the ensuing real processes, we have to study the actual motivations and behaviour patterns that prevail in the actual structure under observation, and to derive from them the actual paths of adjustment to change. Obviously this task is beyond the reach of the purely deductive method with the help of which our 'ideal' models are established; it can be accomplished only with the help of inductive procedures which, in particular, should tell us what the actual behaviour patterns are in a given situation.

Thus our results have, in principle, nothing to contribute to the description of actual growth processes, and even less to the prediction of their future course. However, by establishing what, relative to certain postulated goals, are the most economical forms of growth, they yield the 'efficiency norms' by which the performance of empirical growth processes must be judged. They present an image of 'perfect' growth, and thus point up and locate the structural and functional deficiencies of any empirical system under observation. By disclosing at the same time the structural relations and functional forces most appropriate to optimum performance, our 'ideal' models offer guidance for the improvement of the real processes, and are thus the scientific foundation for economic policy. A few remarks on some practical issues to which our findings can be applied in this manner are to bring these observations to a close.

(35) It is not claimed that the models of once-over and continuous growth described above exhaust the possible range of dynamic processes. Above all, they are concerned only with 'exogenous' shocks, to the exclusion of those endogenous changes which, following Frisch's example, modern econometrics has placed in the centre of its dynamic

investigations. But the number of practically relevant dynamic processes is few, if attention is focused upon the formal properties of rise and fall, continuity and discontinuity, proportionality and disproportionality.

Each of the models discussed above can be associated with one or more characteristic growth phenomena which have appeared during the era of world-wide industrialization. Our 'ideal' model of once-over growth has some sort of empirical replica in the processes by which a 'stationary' pre-industrial system moves off dead centre into 'development'. It is hardly necessary to stress the essential difference between the model underlying the analysis in the part headed 'The dynamics of once-over changes' above and the real structure of any underdeveloped country: the almost complete absence in the latter of groups *b* and *a*. But this very difference emphasizes the strategic position of real capital formation, that is, the nature and duration of the processes by which real capital is built.

How easily this aspect of the developmental process can be lost sight of is apparent in an otherwise most interesting attempt at utilizing structural analysis for practical purposes. I refer to H. W. Singer's essay on 'The mechanics of economic development'.[32] There the Harrod–Domar formula for dynamic equilibrium is used to determine for certain parametric values the relationship between the rate of development, the rate of population increase, capital productivity and savings. On the basis of what he regards as plausible parameters, Singer concludes that autonomous development not supported by capital imports is practically impossible.

I come to the same conclusion, but for different reasons. For Singer the main obstacle lies in the size of the capital-depth coefficient for developmental investment, which he puts at 5. With this assumption, a savings ratio of more than 16 per cent would be required to sustain a population increase of 1.25 per cent per year and an annual increase of real income of 2 per cent. But unless most of the new investment consists of 'social overhead capital' like transportation, irrigation, etc., a capital-depth coefficient of 5 seems much too high. If development were to concentrate on manufacturing projects with an average depth coefficient of slightly under 2, the developmental goal might be reached with a savings ratio of only 6 per cent, which Singer regards as a feasible level. In other words, with this one change in the empirical parameters, autonomous development does not seem to encounter any obstacles.

It is against such optimism that our structural analysis guards. The Harrod–Domar formula (equation 2.16) tells us what rate of growth can be sustained with a given savings ratio, *once the primary real capital necessary for such growth has been formed*. It does not reveal anything about the period of construction, which separates the moment when consumption shrinks because of saving from the moment when real capital has expanded sufficiently for additional consumer goods to reach the market. We saw above that this period of construction is positively correlated with the period of maturation in the field of equipment-goods production, and negatively correlated with the originally available stock of real capital. In both respects the typical underdeveloped country is placed most unfavourably, and the 'waiting period' during which savings depress the standard of living may extend over many years, unless capital imports alleviate the situation. Therefore, a savings ratio that can be regarded as tolerable once development has actually started, may prove far too high to move the system off dead centre.

The next step would then lead to an analysis of the structural consequences of importing real capital from abroad. They obviously differ according to whether the imports consist of primary equipment or secondary equipment. The latter case seems typical for the early stages of industrialization. But there is at least one example—the Soviet Union—in which emphasis was placed from the beginning upon primary equipment. In either case the construction period is drastically reduced. The short-run benefits to the consumer are greatest with imports consisting of secondary equipment. They are pure gains, which do not require even temporary sacrifices in the standard of living, if the real capital can be borrowed under such conditions that the current productivity increase exceeds interest and amortization, and if an equivalent of the current service on the foreign debt is physically adapted to the demand for exports. But even if the equipment imports have to be paid for by consumer-goods exports, foreign trade is a much speedier method of physical transformation than domestic investment.

(36) Scattered remarks about the 'maturity' issue have already pointed to the potential use of our structural models for the secular growth problems of developed countries. As was stated before, whereas capital formation creates a difficult *bottleneck* in the early stages of industrialization, in the later stages it is the need for interindustry *shifts of resources* and the threat of *capital waste* that, in addition to the bottlenecks related to compensation, delay and deflect the 'ideal' adjustment. From this it follows that real growth in developed countries is so closely interrelated with fluctuations that, at least for the past, secular and cyclical problems cannot be studied fruitfully in isolation.

This impression is strengthened by some earlier considerations (Section 28) which suggest that the model of once-over growth, superimposed upon the model of continuous growth, might be usefully applied to the analysis of a 'strong' boom. To build a structural framework for cyclical analysis one must of course go further. The model of a discontinuous change in a positive rate of growth must be refined on the basis of what can be known of models of non-neutral technical changes. An even more complicated superimposition of change processes—introducing analysis of non-compensated factor displacement—seems required for the study of 'weak' booms.

NOTES

1. The model has been described in greater detail in my paper 'A structural model of production', *Social Research*, **19** (1952), pp. 135–76. [See Essay 1 above. –ed.] There reference is also made to the earlier literature on the subject, including a critical comparison between the Marxian concept and the so-called Austrian concept of a 'linear' structure of production that underlies much of modern theoretical reasoning in economic dynamics. In view of the subsequent application of the model to dynamic problems, Hans Neisser's *Some International Aspects of the Business Cycle* (Philadelphia: University of Pennsylvania Press, 1936), Appendix to Chapter 1, deserves special mention.
2. In order to simplify the subsequent exposition the physical distinction among the outputs of the three groups is treated as absolute. This is, of course, not so in reality. Certain products, and the industries producing them, belong in more than one group (e.g. coal, steel, even certain machine tools), though in every concrete instance one can always determine where a specific commodity should be placed. For a more refined exposition *see* my paper *op. cit.* pp. 144–6.
3. Any such measure presupposes a genuine summation of all inputs, which itself is conditional upon the comparability of physically different inputs in a homogeneous value dimension. A simple measure can be devised if we assume that the inputs of fixed-capital goods, labour and natural resources are evenly distributed over all stages as given by the state of business differentiation. Denoting aggregate input of all factors over a stated period by i, the *flow* of working-capital goods which move during that period in the vertical direction toward completion equals $i/2$, since under the conditions assumed half the factor input must serve the replacement of the working capital used in each stage. If the inputs are unevenly distributed over the stages, the fraction $i/2$ changes to iq where $0 < q < 1$. The *stock* of working-capital goods, on the other hand, which has to be maintained in the interest of steady production is then imq/p where p records the period of observation over which we measure i, and m expresses the 'period of maturation', that is, the time it takes with given technology to transform a unit of natural resources into a finished good. In particular, the last concept will prove useful when the process of capital formation is studied more closely. For a generalization of the above results *see* Julius Wyler, 'Working capital and output', *Social Research*, **20** (1953), pp. 91–9.
4. *See* his *Distribution of Wealth* (New York: Macmillan, 1926), Chapters XVIII–XX.

5. Nicholas Kaldor, 'Annual survey of economic theory: the recent controversy on the theory of capital', *Econometrica*, **5** (1937), pp. 201–33; F. H. Knight, 'On the theory of capital: in reply to Mr Kaldor', *Econometrica*, **6** (1938), pp. 63–82; and Nicholas Kaldor, 'On the theory of capital: a rejoinder to Professor Knight', *Econometrica*, **6** (1938), pp. 163–76.

6. 'Die Schemata des stationaeren Kreislaufs bei Boehm-Bawerk und Marx', *Weltwirtschaftliches Archiv*, **34** (1931), pp. 525–64, and **35** (1932), pp. 116–76.

7. If we were to add to the value of the capital stock the value of the *working-*capital stock, the above measure would change to $k_{f+w} = F_v/o_v + W_v/o_v$.

   Since, as shown in note 3 above, $W_v = imq/p$ we obtain by equating the period of observation with the period of maturation $k_{f+w} = k_f + q$.

8. R. F. Harrod, *Toward a Dynamic Economics*, (New York: Macmillan, 1948), Lecture One.

9. The ultimate reason for the dependence of functional analysis upon structural analysis lies in the fact that all dynamic behaviour patterns are shaped by expectations, which in their turn are related to the prevailing structure. For a more detailed exposition *see* my paper 'On the mechanistic approach in economics', *Social Research*, **18** (1951), pp. 403–34.

10. Even if some short-period variability of factor proportions is admitted, the concomitant rise in user costs provides 'a motive for increasing the stock of equipment'. *See* J. R. Hicks, *A Contribution to the Theory of the Trade Cycle*, (Oxford: Clarendon Press, 1950), pp. 39–40. Therefore, for all but very small increments in labour supply the alternative chosen above seems the only realistic one.

11. Whether, and under what conditions, such a decrease in wages frees business funds and thus provides the equivalent of savings, or rather leads to a proportional price fall that leaves real incomes unchanged, is a functional problem whose answer clearly depends on prevailing expectations. The same is true of the effect that such a fall in wages has upon the capital depth of the subsequent investment.

12. Since the physical goods used as primary machinery operate in some instances also as secondary machinery (e.g. extracting machinery and steel mills providing the material for certain household articles or transportation services, and even machine tools 'shaping' the final consumer good), the fall in real consumption also 'frees' some capacity in group z which can be utilized for the expansion of group a. We shall soon see that the size of the freed capacity in groups a and b can be easily determined. To do so for group z presupposes a detailed knowledge of the income elasticities of demand. For this reason the issue is disregarded in what follows, an omission that gives the subsequent conclusions as to 'waste' and as to the length of the construction period a slightly 'pessimistic' bias.

13. To clinch the argument I would have to demonstrate the complementary functional processes in a step-by-step analysis. These processes refer, above all, to the mechanism that transfers aggregate savings to the entrepreneurs in group a; to the consequent attraction of idle prime factors to that group; to the 'multiplier' process by which groups b and z gradually expand, once expansion of group a begins to raise aggregate employment and income above the stationary level; and, last but not least, to the expectational conditions, upon which the postulated behaviour patterns depend.

   Moreover, a definite pattern of saving and investment must be postulated.

The pattern assumed here requires constant (*ex ante*) ratios equal for savings and investment up to the point where the stationary level of employment is again reached; from there on, as absorption proceeds, the savings ratio must fall in proportion to the fall in investment demand, which, with the completion of absorption, reaches zero. It has been stated above that groups *b* and *z* will not expand before employment in group *a* has been increased to the point where aggregate employment equals again the stationary level. This conclusion follows from the premise that the (*ex ante*) savings and investment ratios are equal and constant during the first phase of the adjustment process.

If some of these postulates appear rather unrealistic, the reader should remember that we are not concerned here with the description of empirical processes, but with the analysis of the conditions for 'optimum' adjustment within the framework of a free-market system.

14. *See* e.g. Gottfried Haberler's *Prosperity and Depression*, (New York: Columbia University Press, 1946), Chapter 3, paras. 17–24, especially para. 19.

15. Since small variations of the initially available capacity are in practice possible, the measure yields the upper limit for the construction period necessary to accommodate a *small* rate of growth. For *large* rates of growth the result gives the lower limit.

It may be objected that to increase consumer-goods output, the system need not 'wait' until the last piece of primary and secondary equipment comes from the assembly line. This is certainly true of a partial expansion of group *z*. But such 'staggering' obviously cannot affect the length of the adjustment period for aggregate expansion. We can get *some* consumer goods earlier, but only at the price of having to wait longer for the remainder.

16. The stock freed in group *a* equals *aks*. Since, according to equation (2.6) above, $a = [k^2d^2/(1 - kd)]z$ then $aks = [sk^3d^2/(1 - kd)]z_0$.

17. Since *g* refers to m_a max., all variables such as k, k', d and d', which have a time dimension, must be related to this period.

18. The term *g* measures the number of maturation periods necessary to build the additional stock of primary equipment. Assuming $k = 2$, $d = 1/10$, $s = 1/10$, and $\alpha = 1/5$, equation (2.15) yields $g =$ circa 3.3. How are we to interpret the decimal 0.3? It can mean either that, after the lapse of three maturation periods, the then-available capacity need be employed only over another three-tenths of one period to reach the desired aggregate output, or that only three-tenths of the capacity available after three periods need be utilized for another full period. Since with a given technology the maturation period is fixed, only the second interpretation makes economic sense. From this it follows that *g* must always be rounded upward to the next highest integer before the minimum period of construction can be established.

19. *Op. cit.* p. 23.

20. It is true that both Harrod and Domar regard dynamic equilibrium as described by their equations as extremely unstable. But the initiating shock is always seen in a discrepancy between planned savings and the rate of growth times capital depth, whereas the above propositions include the case of parallel movement and even some cases of constancy of these two rates.

21. It may well be asked whether the above revision of the Harrod–Domar equilibrium conditions goes far enough. Factor specificity is likely to obstruct short-run shifts not only *among* the equipment-goods and consumer-goods groups, but also *within* each one of these groups. From this consideration the ultimate conclusion can be drawn: to assure stability, the structure of demand as well as the rate of growth must remain constant.

    Indeed, this conclusion eliminates large and sudden changes in demand. This, incidentally, is a type of change which as a rule involves also some change in the system's total capital structure, that is, a shift *among* the groups. For small and slow changes in demand the less severe conditions as formulated in equations (2.18) and (2.19) remain valid, since such changes would seem to fall within the range of tolerance for frictions that exists even in an industrial economy.

    For a related problem *see* Robert M. Solow and Paul A. Samuelson, 'Balanced growth under constant returns to scale', *Econometrica*, **21** (1953), pp. 412–24. Hans Neisser's criticism of their paper in *Econometrica*, **22** (1954), pp. 501–3, does not affect the above conclusions, which are based on the assumption of fixed input proportions.

22. 'All that is required for the argument immediately to follow is that any changes in *s*, i.e. savings expressed as a fraction of income, should be small by comparison with experimental changes in G' (Harrod *op. cit.* p. 79). The same position is taken by E. D. Domar, 'The problem of capital accumulation', *American Economic Review*, **38** (1948), p. 779, though the inherent assumption of factor mobility is realized.

23. In this context *see* my critique of Hicks in 'A structural model of production', pp. 168–73. [Essay 1 above, pp. 50–3–ed.] Though I still maintain my objections to Hicks' explanation of the downturn, in the light of the above considerations my own conclusions as stated in the article seem to me now in need of some more 'pessimistic' modification.

24. *See* in particular the writings of Sidney Alexander, W. J. Baumol, Joan Robinson and T. C. Schelling.

25. *See* e.g. the controversy between Domar and E. H. Stern in *American Economic Review*, **39** (1949), pp. 1160–72, and, more recently, Harold Pilvin, 'Full capacity vs. full employment growth', *Quarterly Journal of Economics*, **67** (1953), pp. 545–52, together with R. F. Harrod's 'Comment', *ibid*. pp. 553–9.

26. For a more detailed exposition *see* my paper 'On the mechanistic approach in economics', as cited in note 9 above.

27. Harrod *op cit.* p. 23.

28. If depreciation rates should vary inversely with the change in capital stock, new complications would be introduced. They could be taken care of only by explicit reference to the behaviour of the depreciation rate. In order not to complicate our analysis, I shall, during the subsequent exposition, assume an unchanged rate of depreciation.

29. For a more systematic treatment *see* my paper on 'Technological unemployment reexamined' in G. Eisermann (ed.), *Wirtschaft und Kultursystem: Festschrift fuer Alexander Ruestow*, (Stuttgart und Zuerich: Eugen Rentsch Verlag, 1955), pp. 229–54.

30. The proposition that aggregate demand for commodities rises, in the manner postulated, above aggregate supply and thus raises demand for labour to the equilibrium level is highly dubious. Since the displacement

of workers also initially reduces their demand, a compensating demand of pioneers or consumers seems required to restore equilibrium between supply and demand within the smaller flow of production from which the displaced workers are eliminated.
31. It may be appropriate to stress once more the fact that both capital depth and capital intensity are understood here in value terms.
32. *Indian Economic Review*, **1** (1952), especially pp. 15–18.

3   The Classical Theory of Economic Growth*

One of the most satisfying prospects that the newly awakened interest in economic growth has opened up is the advance in the direction of an integrated social analysis as contrasted with the rigorously circumscribed economic analysis of neoclassical theory. Even in·dealing with a relatively short-term problem like business cycles, one can doubt the wisdom of treating behaviour patterns and the institutional environment as fixed once and for all. Certainly when we turn our attention to growth processes, such as the rise of the industrial system or the secular development of capitalism, systematic mutations in the metaeconomic conditions have to be taken into account as much as changes in the economic field proper.

This is all plain and commonly accepted. Yet when one tries to proceed beyond fine, methodological postulates to the actual work of integration, truly formidable difficulties arise. Not only is the number of metaeconomic variables legion—and they comprise the whole realm of nature and society. But even if the individual sciences—from geology, physics and chemistry, through technology and biology, to psychology, sociology, political science, law and the humanistic sciences of man—could establish a systematic catalogue of these variables as they appear in the context of the respective indigenous field of each science, there would still remain the task of 'translating' their 'meaning' into the conceptual framework of economics.

What this amounts to can best be illustrated by an example. For many centuries the idea of 'monopoly' was known as a sociopolitical concept, pointing toward a certain manner in which power is exercised, with some notion of exploitation thrown in. But neither power nor exploitation is a manageable concept in the framework of traditional market analysis. Only when monopoly was understood as a change in the nature of the price–quantity relationship—compared with the nature of this relationship under fully competitive conditions—did it become a tool in economic analysis. Failure to perform such a translation,

---

* [This essay was first published in *Social Research*, **21** (1954). — ed.]

whenever concepts indigenous to one dimension of science are to be introduced into another dimension, is mainly responsible for the fact that experiments with 'integration' have only rarely carried us beyond description into the realm of genuine causal analysis.

One might expect to find some enlightenment about the problem raised here in the recent writings on economic dynamics. Indeed, a lively discussion is under way, clarifying the nature of processes, the types of change, and the role of time, in their influence on human behaviour.[1] But the time-honoured distinction between dependent and independent variables—that is, between an economic process and the underlying metaeconomic forces which drive it on and change it—is generally maintained. We find an exception to this general approach, however, in what Professor Frisch and his followers have called 'dynamic process analysis'. There certain relations are stressed which may exist between variables at different points of time, and which—because of the prevailing 'lags'—can create self-enforcing processes, even if the variables themselves do not change. Such movements, which may be damped, cyclical, or explosive, are designated as 'endogenous', in contrast with the other type of changes, which arise from 'exogenous' stimuli represented by independent variables.

It is only fair to say that this modern notion of 'endogeneity' is but a dim reflection of a much more ambitious method of analysis that dominated an earlier epoch of theoretical economics. As a matter of fact, upon this issue of endogeneity versus exogeneity, rather than upon conflicting theories of value, hinges the main difference between genuine classical theory and post-Millian economic reasoning, including all versions of neoclassical analysis. The problem and its relevance for the theory of dynamics was probably realized most clearly by the late Joseph Schumpeter, who stated it, a quarter of a century ago, as follows.

After describing economic theory in terms of Marshall's 'tool chest', Schumpeter asserted that it arose from something quite different, namely, from a

theory . . . which claimed to contain the essence of all fundamental knowledge about the economy, and also the solution of its main empirical problems. The practical success as well as the grand defeat of the doctrine of the classical economists . . . are bound up with the fact that they aimed at just this goal, and that to reach it they established, in youthful recklessness, fundamental assertions and postulates without any real basis . . . The characteristic example . . . is the quite uncritical manner in which Ricardo used an alleged connection between wage level and subsistence level as a substitute for a theory of wages . . . Modern theory differs from classical theory not simply in not asserting any longer the existence of that particular relationship, for the reason that it cannot be verified. More important is the fact that modern theory does not establish any such propositions at all. Rather it offers a formal framework, into which any conceivable relationship, e.g., the opposite one, can be inserted *casuistically as a special datum* . . . However no particular relationship as such is indispensable for the validity of the framework itself.[2]

Leaving alone the value judgement expressed in Schumpeter's remarks, we must admit that they do indeed point to a fundamental difference between the classical and the modern approach. What is at stake is no less than the entire possible range of deductive reasoning.

Let us be quite explicit about the disputed region. It concerns the whole natural, social and technical environment of the economic system, that is, the conditions that determine the quality and quantity of demand on the part of consumers and investors, the supply of productive factors, the prevailing technique of production, social distribution, the bargaining behaviour of consumers and producers and, last but not least, the changes in all these elements through time. Modern theory, by treating these conditions once and for all as data, can never give us more than a catalogue of all *possible* movements of the economic system, derived from, and arranged according to, hypothetical sets of data combinations. It does not and cannot claim to tell us which particular set, and consequently which specific movement deduced from it, corresponds to reality. To make deduction applicable to reality, we must in each case first assess, by methods of induction, the order of data ruling in the particular situation. Only then are we in a position to select from our catalogue of hypothetical deductions the one that comes closest to the actual constellation.

This sounds quite trivial to the contemporary economist brought up in the modern tradition. All he may wonder is how one could proceed in any other way. Yet another method was in fact applied for a full century, during which deductive reasoning was not confined to conclusions drawn from sets of data postulated anew whenever analysis took another step. Rather, the explanation of the order and changes of these data itself formed part of the theoretical work of economists.

Of course, every process of deduction must ultimately start from some set of 'synthetic' propositions, which classical economics too could arrive at only by means of induction. But whereas the modern economist is compelled to begin every deductive operation, if it is to have realistic bearing, with another empirical investigation of the relevant data, the classical economist did so only once—namely, when he described the primaeval state of affairs from which the economic process was supposed to have started. Different notions as to the nature of this original reality produced contrasting images of economic evolution in the different classical systems. But for each classical system separately the empirical stage was, at least in principle, set once and for all with these initial assumptions. From there on the economic process could be deduced by an unbroken chain of reasoning. In this sense Ricardo's assertion that the stationary state is the ultimate goal of economic development, or Marx's 'general law of capitalist accumulation', proclaims explicitly what is implicitly contained in all classical systems.

Obviously this classical procedure results in an 'endogenous' dynamics of a much more comprehensive nature than that offered by modern process analysis. Underlying these classical constructions is a belief in the cognitive power of deduction, and a notion of society and history, that seem to contradict all ideas concerning the relationship between science and reality that prevail today. Yet in studying economic growth, at least as it develops under capitalism, the conceptional range of classical theory seems more appropriate than the delimitations of modern theory.

The central problem of capitalism has often been defined as the question of how order rather than chaos ensues from the undirected action of innumerable individuals. We can give this question a time shape by asking what interaction of forces has determined the particular course that capitalist development has taken over the decades. If this development had been 'planned', as may well be the case with the future development of the Western economic system, the problem of an 'endogenous' dynamics would hardly arise. The basic 'data' and their major changes would have been set by conscious decision, and would rightly have to be treated as independent variables of the economic process that has been set in motion by them. But over the last 200 years we have been confronted with a self-propelling secular process, in the course of which not only did the data change 'spontaneously', but in addition these changes displayed striking regularities.

As we look at this secular process in retrospect today, our analysis of it may receive little help from the *substance* of the classical theory of economic development. This does not in itself reflect upon the dynamic *method* which the leading classical economists applied.[3] To realize this, more is required, of course, than a cursory statement of the classical procedure. The latter will have to be elaborated in all its ramifications by the study of some of its most significant protagonists. I begin with the earliest, and in many ways the most lucid example: the theory of economic development as contained in Adam Smith's *Wealth of Nations*. I shall then consider certain modifications that Ricardo and the early 'anti-harmonist' writers introduced into the original model, and shall complete the survey with a detailed examination of Marx. In a concluding section, centred on J. S. Mill, I shall deal briefly with the reasons for the subsequent abandonment of the classical method of growth analysis.

SMITH

I pointed above to the truism that, however far the range of deduction may be extended, it must start from some original set of propositions. In all classical theories of development these propositions are 'historical' that is, they refer to an 'original' order of society from which the economic process is supposed to spring. Smith never defined these original data systematically, but the context of his work leaves no doubt as to what he considered them to be. Division of labour and exchange, allegedly the 'consequence of a certain propensity in human nature',[4] represent the basic pattern of economic behaviour. They operate within the institutional framework of a competitive class society: private property in the means of production, including land, which are unequally distributed after the 'early and rude state of society'[5] has passed, and full mobility of the factors of production, safeguarded by the watchmen of the public interest. As our investigation progresses we shall meet some additional assumptions, which round off the set of historical constants.

Now in order to set the economic process in motion and give it the direction which Smith attributes to actual economic development, these constants have to generate the factors of production in the appropriate quantity and quality: an adequate supply of labour, of natural resources and of capital, and a steady increase in productivity. In contrast with the constants themselves from which they spring, these factors cannot be regarded as given once and for all by nature and history. They are continuously being drained off and replenished according to certain laws of motion.

At this point we encounter the main peculiarity of classical analysis. Again neither the problem at stake nor its solution has been explicitly formulated by Smith. Both have to be inferred from scattered passages, which are found mainly in Chapters 1, 2, 3, 8 and 9 of the first book of *Wealth of Nations*, and in Chapters 3 to 5 of the second book.

First of all, there is a law governing the *supply of labour* (Book 1, Chapter 8). It is based on two complementary hypotheses. On the one hand, forces are at work that tend to reduce, over the secular period, the level of real wages to the subsistence level. The causal nexus is identical with what was later called the 'iron law of wages': variations in the level of real wages evoke counteracting changes in the size of the working population. On the other hand, real wages can and do rise, as long as the natural and technical conditions of a country permit a steady increase in its wealth. Not that the systematic link between the level of real wages and the size of the population is destroyed for good in a progressive society. But demand for labour, as expressed in 'the funds which are destined for the payment of wages', can overtake supply. And with the increase of real wages population grows, since 'the demand for men, like that for any other commodity, necessarily regulates the production of men'.

Thus labour supply is ultimately dominated by the co-operation of two balancing forces: the propensity to procreate, which is seen as a composite of biological urge and a rational calculation of the 'value of children', and the available wage fund. The former is another constant of the socioeconomic process, but one which by itself would cause the system to 'run down' to a constant level of labour supply and thus of real output. This tendency is counteracted by the latter force, which is a variable. What forces rule its changes?

The answer is given by Smith's law of *accumulation*. The funds which govern the variations in labour supply are the result of saving, which itself arises from another alleged human propensity or constant of the social mechanism: 'the desire of bettering our condition' (Book II, Chapter 3). Of course, it is not by the act of saving itself, but by the use they make of their savings, that people fulfil this desire. Accumulation, comprising both saving and investing, 'is the most likely way of augmenting their fortune', provided a 'neat or clear profit' or a rate of interest 'in proportion to the clear profit' can be earned (Book I, Chapter 9).

The level of profit and interest, however, is as precarious a magnitude as the level of wages. 'In a country which had acquired that full complement of riches which the nature of its soil and climate, and situation with respect to other countries allowed it to acquire, which could, therefore, advance no further, and which was not going backwards, both the wages of labour and the profits of stock would, probably, be very low' (Book I, Chapter 9). The reason is seen in the competition among capitalists once a country is 'fully stocked in proportion to all the business it had to transact'. As is the case with wages, 'it is not the actual greatness of national wealth, but its continuous increase' (Book I, Chapter 8) that favours profits. Since the notion of capital deepening lies outside the field of Smith's vision—and for better reasons than the later classical economists can adduce for themselves—only a continuous widening of the capital structure can sustain profits and thus accumulation, and can keep real wages above the subsistence level. Such widening or economic growth, however, can be stimulated only by a rise in productivity, because the other growth factor, population increase, is regarded, as we saw, as a response rather than a stimulus to accumulation. Thus the psychological constant again makes the system 'run down' to a constant level, unless its tendency is counteracted by changes in the variable factor, this time productivity. In this factor we now encounter the strategic variable of the whole system.

If one places side by side the many remarks on productivity and economic progress which are contained in *Wealth of Nations*, one can collect the whole list of factors that Schumpeter classifies as 'innovations': extension and improvement of machinery, increased division of labour, new branches of trade, and territorial expansion. But the emphasis with which these various factors are treated differs markedly. It is technical progress in the narrower sense that is in the centre.

Among the conditions for such improvement of productive power is, first of all, a country's equipment in terms of natural resources and its geographic position. The threat of the exhaustion of natural wealth is regarded as far distant. As to the interim period, Smith is little concerned about decreasing returns, so that for the foreseeable future he can again treat the whole complex of natural conditions as a constant of the dynamic model. The decisive variable is a particular form of technology, namely, 'division of labour'.

It has always been recognized that for Smith division of labour is the true dynamic force. Yet in our context we do well to distinguish between the general phenomenon which, as we have already seen, he traces back to a psychological constant, and the varying forms in which this phenomenon materializes throughout history. The latter comprise for Smith all types of technical progress, in particular the introduction of improved machinery. At the same time, his notion of technical progress is defined by the characteristics of the economies of specialization, as he describes them in his first three chapters. Above all mechanization, like specialization, is supposed to 'facilitate and abridge labour', but not to displace the worker who performs it. Quite to the contrary in the introduction to Book II Smith even asserts that division of labour in this inclusive sense is conditional upon a prior increase in labour supply. The passage is important enough to be quoted in full:

As the division of labour advances, therefore, in order to give constant employment to an equal number of workmen, an equal stock of provisions, and a greater stock of materials and tools than would have been necessary in a ruder state of things, must be accumulated beforehand. But the number of workmen in every branch of business generally increases with the division of labour in that branch, or *rather it is the increase of their number which enables them to class and subdivide themselves in this manner* (italics mine— A. L.).

In other words, the machine is regarded as a complement of labour rather than a substitute for it, a definitely pre-industrial notion of technology. To find such ideas in *Wealth of Nations* is hardly surprising, if we remember the date of publication of the book. They fit well with Smith's distrust of large-scale organization of industry and of long apprenticeship, both of which he evaluates by pre-industrial standards (Book I, Chapter 10).

This identitification of technical progress generally with specialization has far-reaching consequences for Smith's model of economic development. The improvements that determine the rate of economic progress, and thus the rate of profit, do not arise from spontaneous shifts in the production function, catering to the pre-existing level of demand. Their introduction depends rather on the opening of new sources of demand, a proposition that is expressly stated in the title of the famous Chapter 3 of the first book: 'That the Division of Labour is limited by the Extent of the Market'. Far from being an independent variable, technical progress as understood by Smith develops 'in proportion to the riches and populousness' of the country in question, and in proportion to its trade with other countries. It is the rate of increase in aggregate demand that governs the rate of technical progress.

Furthermore, Smith leaves no doubt about where the source of such continuous increase in demand is to be found. It is true that hardly any one before him has put equal emphasis on the advantages of international division of labour, and he sees in foreign commerce the stimulus to most modern improvements in manufacture and even in agriculture. And yet he calls this causal nexus an 'unnatural and retrograde order'. 'According to the natural course of things, therefore, the greater part of the capital of every growing society is first directed to agriculture, afterwards to manufactures, and last of all to foreign commerce' (Book III, Chapter 1). Thus pride of place belongs to the domestic market, that is, to a continuous increase of population, equipped with sufficient buying power. With this our argument has turned a full circle.

Here it may be helpful to restate the sequence of this circular, or rather 'spiral', process, and the strategic points in it where the constants exert their recurring influence. We have to remember that we find ourselves confronted with a process *in development*. Therefore in order to describe the sequence of events we have to break the chain of interdependent links artificially at some point. The most opportune place to do so is the point where the increase of aggregate employment, owing to the preceding 'turn of the spiral', has raised aggregate demand, thus providing new investment opportunities for further division of labour. These opportunities are bound to raise profit expectations and thus demand for money capital, which will keep the level of the rate of interest above the minimum, and, together with the propensity for 'betterment', will stimulate a positive rate of savings. These savings offered for investment represent demand for additional labour and keep real wages above the subsistence level. Under the influence of the propensity to procreate, labour supply responds to the wage stimulus, so that the investment opportunities can actually be realized through increase in employment. At the same time the additional payrolls expand the market beyond the expectations held at the beginning of the spiral turn that is under observation. This creates new investment opportunities, and the next turn begins.

The main centre of interest in this causal chain is the factors of production, on the growth of which the development of the economic process depends. There we must distinguish between the supply of natural resources on one hand, and on the other hand the supply of labour and savings and the changes in the technique of production. The former is treated as a natural constant, at least up to the point when the system has utilized to the full its given stock of resources. The supply of the other factors, and especially all changes in such supply, is a function of the dynamic process itself, together with the operation of certain constants. Labour supply is fully determined by the interaction of a biopsychological constant with the market price of labour, as savings are determined by a psychological constant and the market price of savings. Technological change, finally, is induced by the expansion of what Smith calls 'national wealth' (comparable with what is today called 'national income'), the continual increase of which is the inevitable result of the spiral process.

What is decisive is the fact that this process of development is not distorted by any independent variables. Therefore it is not only open to exact prediction but, in the absence of any possible disturbances from without, it moves in dynamic equilibrium. True, the absence of outside shocks is only a necessary condition for such equilibrium, and is not in itself sufficient to insure it; to clinch the argument in favour of a self-propelling harmonious dynamics, proof had to be given that the spiral chain would never be broken from within. Here lies the systematic significance of the specific form of technology that dominates Smith's dynamic model. Only a technology that is labour attracting insures the steady expansion of the market, and thus the unbroken continuity of the 'upward spiral'.

The so-called 'optimism' of Smith's vision of economic development hinges on his treatment of technical progress. Otherwise, as we saw, all the 'pessimistic' arguments are present which in the hands of his successors turned the expanding secular process into the dismal stationary state. The biopsychological constants, as conceived by Smith, would cause the mechanism to run down, were it not for the counteracting force of technology. But only by linking technical progress strictly with the growth of the system can the mechanism be made to 'run up' steadily, until the full utilization of the natural environment prevents further expansion of aggregate and per capita income.[6]

One element, and only one, in the customary set of data retains in Smith's dynamics the role of an independent variable: consumer tastes. The *bipolar shifts* of the productive factors according to the variations in these tastes exhaust what employment fluctuations the system can undergo, and they are of a sectorial and short-run nature only. The rigid manner in which *aggregate changes* in factor supply are linked with one another in a regular sequence precludes any aggregate fluctuations over the long run, and this for two reasons. Not only are such changes in factor supply always a response to a preceding change in demand, and therefore in the nature of a self-correcting adjustment, but they are also of necessity slow, thus permitting steady absorption. The rhythm of change is ultimately limited by the rearing period of children. Though these periods overlap in a continuous process of growth, making the influx of additional labour into the market a continuous process, they keep the rate of growth slow and steady.

This consideration gives to the hypothesis of 'other things remaining equal', which underlies all classical analysis of short-term processes, a more than methodological significance. In a spiral process of development, as conceived by Smith, all factors other than bipolar changes in taste do in fact remain equal over the short run. Far from assuming the function of controlled experiments, as it does in modern economics, in the context of original classical economics the *ceteris paribus* rule is a pronouncement on reality—at least on the aspired-to reality of perfect competition.

In summary, we can say that Smith's theory of economic development is composed of two kinds of building blocks: a set of natural, psychological and institutional constants, and a circular mechanism that links the changes in the supply data with the course of the economic process in reciprocal causation. This reciprocity of cause and effect over time—though at any given moment cause and effect are clearly separable—raises economic analysis to the level of more comprehensive social analysis, at least so far as the supply conditions of the factors of production reflect the social process. The other social forces, as embodied in the constants, are not drawn into the circular mechanism of causation. We shall see that in this respect at least one later classical system, that of Marx, goes much further in establishing 'laws of interdependence'. But though for Smith the constants only affect the process of development, without themselves being affected by it, their nature as constants prevents them from prejudicing either the stability or the calculability of the economic process. They belong to the 'natural order', in the twofold meaning which this term has in the social philosophy of the Enlightenment. Therefore their mode of operation can be known, and the resulting model of economic dynamics is the image of a fully predictable process of 'natural' development. Social economics was indeed raised by Smith to the formal level of a true science.

RICARDO AND THE EARLY 'ANTI-HARMONISTS'

It is not my intention to present a systematic survey of all the variants that the classical theory of economic development exhibits, or to trace the influence that different writers exerted on one another in formulating their ideas. Our concern with the problem is methodological rather than historical, and for such a purpose a random selection of a few further hypotheses is quite sufficient. The reason for this is that Smith's model has remained the formal pattern for the 'liberal' strand of classical economics, though the later models differ substantially from it and also from one another. The differences arise either from a change in the constants assumed, or from the weakening of the circular mechanism through the introduction of certain independent variables.

The outstanding example in both respects is Ricardo. By substituting the law of diminishing returns on land for Smith's assumption of constant returns, the trend of economic development is radically changed. Ricardo's 'pessimism', as expressed in the first two editions of the *Principles*, is exclusively due to this modification of Smith's model. The idea of an *ultimate* running down of the system is integral to the Smith model also, as we saw above. All that Ricardo did was to move forward into the present the point of time when the stinginess of nature asserts itself. Not only does this place the level of real wages under a constant threat, which can be removed only temporarily by technical progress, but in addition Ricardo presents a new theory of profits, according to which the same tendency threatens their persistence also. It is no longer competition among capitalists, but the rise of money wages—inevitable under the pressure of decreasing returns—that cuts into profits. More and more this strangles accumulation, and thus the whole process of expansion.

Nevertheless, the strictness of the spiral process was in no way affected by this change. A 'downward' spiral was added to the initial 'upward' spiral, and this has important consequences for functional distribution, but the process as such remains fully determinate and calculable.

A much more serious modification was introduced in the third edition of the *Principles*, with the new chapter, 'On machinery'. By taking note of the labour-displacing effects of industrial technology, Ricardo removes the cornerstone of the Smithian structure.[7] As in Smith, profits still depend on technical advance, and even more so when decreasing returns continuously tend to push up money wages. But though the prospects of innovation profits stimulate saving, their investment, which is still taken for granted, no longer assures growing aggregate employment. The displacement effect threatens to diminish the 'gross produce'—that is, the size of the market—and steady growth is no longer assured. Ricardo did not himself draw the far-reaching conclusions regarding the secular process that this new notion of the technical factor suggests. The new insight expressed in the critical Chapter 31—in itself a rare case of self-destructive intellectual honesty—is hardly compatible with the notion of a system which, though 'running down' in terms of real output, is free from any aggregate fluctuations.

It has become customary in recent years to attribute the first genuine insight into the causes of such fluctuations to Malthus. This emphasis is less than fair to some of his forerunners, and more than fair to Malthus's capacity to understand what indeed he saw. On both scores Lord Lauderdale and Sismondi deserve to be reinstated in the position that they held in the history of economic doctrines before Keynes traced to Malthus the introduction into 'respectable circles' of the principle of effective demand.[8]

However this may be, the formal procedure of all these writers is the same. They break the link that—in Smith as well as in Ricardo, and prior to him in Say—had fastened savings firmly to investment. By stressing the 'propensity' element in the creation of savings over and against the circular effect of profit expectations, savings themselves become an independent variable, to which investment may, or may not, adjust itself spontaneously.

With this the stability of economic development is undermined, though not necessarily its upward trend. If Malthus has a claim to originality in this respect, it lies in his demonstration that aggregate fluctuations are compatible with an upward trend of real output and employment. His law of population is much less strict than the hypothesis that underlies Smith's iron law of wages. 'Moral restraint' is capable of breaking the circular chain at the most critical point—where the supply of labour is related to the level of real wages—transforming the latter into an independent variable. This second break in the circular chain may then undo part of the social evils brought about by the first, though it further reduces the determinateness and thus the predictability of the process of development.

MARX

We can say that in order to approximate their models to the complexities of the real world, the early-nineteenth-century writers felt compelled to relax the strictness of the original circular mechanism. Marx's methodological position is unique because, although writing half a century later, he went in the other direction far beyond Smith. He transformed almost all the original constants into dependent variables. For this reason his model is the oustanding case of 'endogenous dynamics', whatever reservations may have to be made about the substance of some of his most essential propositions.

To gain insight into the mechanism of Marx's model, we can best begin by considering those elements for which equivalents can be found in Smith's model. The process of development that Marx tries to formulate in the 'general law of capitalist accumulation'[9] is kept moving, as in Smith, by the interaction of a law of population, a law of accumulation and a law of technical change. But the social forces that replenish the stock of productive factors through these laws are quite different from those postulated by Smith.

To start with the law of population or labour supply, for Marx it is 'relative surplus population' as created by technological displacement, rather than the 'absolute surplus population' due to natural increase, that determines the state of the labour market and the level of real wages (Volume 1, Chapter 25). Since the introduction of labour-displacing technical changes can be geared to the demand for labour, labour supply can be kept at such a level that it is always available at minimum cost, that is, at wages near the subsistence level.[10]

Now the force that makes the capitalist–entrepreneur use the weapon of innovation in this manner operates through the 'special' law of accumulation, the latter term to be understood in the classical sense of saving-plus-investment. But for Marx—in contradistinction to the earlier classical writers—accumulation is not stimulated by an innate propensity, but by the social pressure of a competitive society. Smith's psychological constant is transformed into a dependent variable of the institutional environment, which compels the capitalist 'to keep continuously extending his capital, in order to preserve it' (Volume 1, Chapter 24).

But Marx is in full agreement with both Smith and Ricardo that accumulation alone is not sufficient for the capitalist to survive. This is so, at least, if accumulation takes the form of 'accumulation with constant organic composition of capital'—Marx's term for a 'pure widening' of the capital structure. As will be shown below, in this case profits are threatened from two sides: through price decreases due to the competition of fellow capitalists (Smith's argument), and through wage increases, since in this case the demand for labour rises without a simultaneous increase in supply (Ricardo's argument). Only accumulation with 'rising organic composition of capital'—capital-attracting technical progress, in modern terminology—can sustain the level of profit and with it the process of accumulation and development. And as we shall see presently, even this type of accumulation ultimately defeats its own ends.

Thus in Marx, as in all classical systems, it is technical progress that provides the ultimate dynamic force. But there the resemblance ceases. Before Marx technical progress was regarded as the vehicle of social progress and of market stability. It was supposed to create additional employment and thus to extend the market; to overcome, at least temporarily, the stinginess of nature; to stimulate investment and thus to banish the spectre of oversaving. But to Marx modern technology is a Janus-faced phenomenon. While sustaining accumulation and thus growth, it maintains and even increases mass misery, breaks the stability of the economic process by blocking the extension of the market, and ultimately even jeopardizes profits.

We saw that it was a specific type of technical progress—specialization—that produced the harmonistic effects of the Smithian model. Another peculiar type creates the ambivalent tendencies in Marx's model. Its characteristics are two: it is labour displacing and capital intensifying.

I have already referred to the first characteristic in discussing Marx's law of population. In elaborating the earlier suggestions of Barton and Ricardo, Marx demonstrated that, as a rule, the re-aborption of technological unemployment is, under industrial conditions, not a question of short-run adjustment but of secular growth, conditional on prior formation of real capital. The significance of this proposition for the operation of Marx's model is twofold. On the one hand, by periodically flooding the labour market the industrial reserve army prevents the masses from participating in the benefits that increasing productivity potentially offers. On the other hand, it prevents aggregate consumption from rising in proportion to aggregate output, thus threatening the system with (forced) underconsumption.

The second characteristic of technical progress, as Marx sees it, is progressive capital intensification, that is, an increase in the value of capital relative to the wages paid out over a stated period.[11] On this assumption he builds a supplementary theory of profits, in which the paradoxical effects of technical progress find their climax. This 'law of the falling tendency of the rate of profits' is probably the most controversial of Marx's propositions,[12] although it follows logically from any consistent theory of labour value. If aggregate profits are the difference between the value of output and aggregate payrolls, then the rate of profit (that is, the ratio of aggregate profits to the value of total capital stock) is bound to fall whenever capital intensification raises the value of fixed capital at a higher rate than payrolls—at least so long as it is possible for labour's share in aggregate income to be maintained.[13]

We must ask, of course, why capitalists introduce innovations if the result is a fall rather than a rise of the profit rate. To this Marx has three answers. First, there are a number of counteracting factors that reduce the 'law' to a 'tendency'. The most important of these factors are the reduction of the value of the fixed capital stock (in spite of its physical increase) as a consequence of rising productivity, and the secondary effect of labour displacement on wages, namely, a fall in real wages. But these counteracting forces operate obviously *ex post facto*. Therefore Marx's other two reasons are more convincing from the standpoint of a capitalist who is confronted with the investment decision. On the one hand, Marx is fully aware (Volume 3, Chapters 13 and 15) of the temporary 'pioneer profits' that form the centre of Schumpeter's profit theory; although competition is bound to wipe these out over the long run, until it does so they raise the rate of profit. On the other hand, a fall in the rate of profit is fully compatible with a rise in its volume. This, of course, can be a stimulus only for the borrower, not for the lender, whose remuneration is calculated in terms of the rate. Whenever the rate falls, therefore, especially disturbing effects arise from the behaviour of the capitalist (in the narrower sense), who succumbs to a sort of liquidity preference (Volume 3, Chapter 15).

I have dwelt at some length on this supplementation of the classical theory of profit, since its simple meaning is shrouded in a fog of verbiage spread over it by Marx himself and subsequently by his critics. But again, we are not interested here in the substantive truth of the proposition, but in its significance for the logic of Marx's model.[14] What is new in Marx's law of technical change, compared with the corresponding propositions of his predecessors, is the combination of progressive with regressive tendencies that it describes. Only through its operation can profits, accumulation and employment, and thus economic development, be stimulated—the same phenomena that are also checked by its operation. The result is an endogenous cycle of expansion and contraction, which takes the place of the steady running 'up' or 'down' of the classical mechanism. In this manner Marx's general law of accumulation makes regular fluctuations an inherent property of economic growth.

This modification invests the model with a degree of realism never before attained by any theory of development. But it makes the exposition of the underlying process rather complicated. And this all the more so, since Marx visualizes at least two different types of business cycles. As in many of his propositions, he left his cycle theory as a torso. But Sweezy (*op. cit.* Chapter 10) is probably right in asserting that Marx was fully aware of the two types, which nowadays pass as 'overinvestment' and 'underconsumption' cycles, the action of the falling rate of profit being associated with the latter. And far from playing one off against the other, as has become the modern fashion, he treats them as equivalent forms of the economic process.

We shall not pursue here a detailed examination of the manner in which Marx derives the sequence of cyclical phases for each of the two types. The main methodological significance of his cyclical model of growth lies in the fact that, once the cycle has started, it operates as the law of circular motion, according to which the factors of production are drained off and replenished in calculable fashion.

All that is needed to set the cycle going is an institutional environment, very like the one that figures in Smith's model, and the availability of innovational projects of the type described. The former developed out of the breakdown of mediaeval society, which also provided the original investment funds for what Marx calls the process of 'primitive accumulation' (Volume 1, Chapters 26–32). The latter is a consequence of the industrial revolution. The social pressure of the institutional order assures the appropriate motive force, whereas a continuous stream of inventions is the material for the profit motive to actualize itself through the fundamental economic behaviour: accumulation. No additional channels are required to feed outside forces—biological or psychological—into the economic mechanism. The factors that sustain it, especially labour and capital, are recreated by the mechanism itself.

Again we have to break into a continuous process at an arbitrarily chosen point in order to describe the circular mechanism. We select the point where availability of new projects, together with a large supply of idle labour and capital, induce what is today called 'autonomous investment', thus starting a new revival. What form the ensuing upswing takes, and in what manner it ends, depends on the relative weight, in total investment, of 'pure widening' projects and technical improvements respectively. If the former dominate, the labour pool inherited from the preceding depression will be gradually exhausted and wages will rise. This creates the 'overinvestment' dilemma, resulting in general cut-throat competition.[15] Conversely, a sufficient supply of genuine improvements will, during the upswing, continuously refill the labour pool, thus preventing wage rises. But by this very fact it will drive the system in the end into the underconsumption dilemma.[16] It is characteristic of the end phase of either type of upswing that profits decline. This brings accumulation to a temporary stop, leading to general contraction and the recreation of the large factor pools, which are the condition for a new revival.

When examined from the aspect of determinateness and predictability, Marx's model gains upon Smith's by freeing the circular mechanism from all exogenous biological and psychological constants. As a cycle, the economic process recreates all conditions necessary for its continuation. Up to this point, however, it is difficult to see that the resulting secular process can be anything else but a sequence of cycles, distinguished at best by different types of upswings and crises, but without any specific trend of development. This gap is filled by Marx's most original contribution: the linking up of even the institutional environment with the cyclical process.

The decisive link is the 'capital-intensifying' nature of technical progress, as understood by Marx. First of all, from cycle to cycle it raises the degree of 'concentration'—that is, the average amount of capital per firm, and possibly the average size of the labour force per firm also. Secondly, and even more important for the dynamic process, it promotes 'centralization' of production, namely, an increase in the share of large concerns in capital stock, aggregate output and employment. This transformation is brought about by the periodic downswings, and derives from the greater crisis resistance of the larger and thus the more efficient firms. These retain, even during the depression, a certain volume of profits, whereas the general fall of the rate eliminates the smaller and less efficient firms.

This economic effect of the depression, however, is the cause of much more fundamental social effects. The process of competitive elimination gradually transforms a widely stratified society, originally composed of many independent producers, into two starkly antagonistic groups: a few 'capital magnates', and the large mass of the proletarianized people. But again this process is Janus faced. Misery and exploitation mount, as does underconsumption, making the periodic crises worse and worse. Yet at the same time centralization furthers the rationalization and planning of the productive process and the international unification of markets. It cannot help training the labouring masses in the 'co-operative form' of production, and organizing them in self-defence. 'Centralization of the means of production and socialization of labour at last reach a point where they become incompatible with their capitalist integument. This integument is burst asunder' (Volume 1, Chapter 32). From this point on, the autonomous mechanism of the capitalist process gives way to planned direction.[17]

Thus the trend of socioeconomic development follows from the interaction of two apparently contradictory tendencies. Both are inherent in labour-displacing, capital-intensifying technical change, when applied in a society that has gone through the process of 'primitive accumulation'. A constructive tendency—progressive accumulation, concentration, centralization, proletarian training and self-organization—plays against a destructive tendency—displacement, increasing misery, growing underconsumption and worsening crises. The final catastrophe requires, of course, a 'voluntaristic' stimulus—the 'wrathful indignation' of the proletariat. But even this is traced back to the pressure of the social environment and treated as an inevitable response to it, as is the case with capitalists' profit incentive and its behavioural expression—accumulation. Later Marxists, notably Hilferding, Luxemburg, Sternberg and Sweezy, have extended and refined the argument by applying it to the explanation of monopolistic tendencies and the related behaviour patterns, as well as to the rise of a non-revolutionary working class and a new middle class in the leading capitalistic countries. But the determinateness of the socioeconomic circular mechanism is unimpaired, as long as the effects follow from the operation of the basic variable 'technology' in a historically given, but endogenously changing environment.[18]

For this reason clarity about the logical position of these ultimate 'causes' is crucial for full understanding of the model. The case is simple as far as the environmental factors are concerned. They are the passive element in the process of development. Originally a set of data given by nature and history,they change slowly under the influence of the cyclical process, which they in turn affect through the channel of behaviour. Once the economic process has started, the environment enters into a fully endogenous relationship with it.

The active factor, technology, is a more complex phenomenon. We must distinguish between the scientific–technological process of invention, and innovation as the economic application of invention. The latter is endogenously related to the movements of the cycle, and can be regarded as 'bunched' in reverse proportion to the rate of profit. Invention, on the other hand, seems to be less closely bound up with the socioeconomic process. Certainly modern technology generally is a child of the age and cultural climate in which modern capitalism arose. One might even assert that the constant flow of ever-new inventions is stimulated by the crumbs from the tables of the earners of profit, which fall to the inventor. But this motive can hardly be taken as his sole stimulus, and in any event it operates as a 'carrot' rather than as a 'stick'. Finally and above all, the particular form that the invention has to take in order to direct the dynamic process in the historically ordained direction cannot be attributed to endogenous forces only. That Marx's capitalist should prefer labour-saving to labour-attracting devices agrees with the circular mechanism of the system as well as with the postulated trend of evolution. This is not true of the other characteristic of these devices: their 'capital-intensifying' nature. This feature is indeed indispensable as a causal link in the chain of events, which lead through concentration and centralization to the self-organization of socialism in the 'womb of the old society'. But it cannot be derived with equal cogency from the basic behaviour pattern of the capitalist. His ultimate aim would be served much better by capital-saving devices, which tend—at least in Marx's interpretation—to raise the profit rate. Exactly as in Smith, a very specific technology is an indispensable condition for the evolutionary process taking its postulated course. But again as in Smith, this variable has been introduced into the system from without rather than having been derived from the operation of the circular mechanism.[19]

It is an interesting task to criticize the Marxian model by confronting each one of its 'links' with the actual process of capitalist development. But though the course of history has refuted the prediction of the ultimate catastrophe—at least in the terms conceived by Marx—it has not by this refuted the method by whose help Marx attempted to establish a scientific theory of the development of the industrial market economy. We may well deny every single one of his substantive propositions, and yet regard the methodological lesson of his work as a challenge that no responsible social scientist can afford to evade.

I can vindicate this position by citing a witness who, in view of his earlier pronouncements quoted above, should be accepted as impartial:

there is one truly great achievement to be set against Marx's theoretical misdemeanours . . . the idea of a theory, not merely of an indefinite number of disjointed individual patterns or of the logic of economic quantitites in general, but of the *actual* sequence of these patterns or of the economic process as it goes on under its own steam, in *historic* time, producing at every instant that state which will of itself determine the next one. Thus, the author of so many misconceptions was also the first to visualize what even at the present time is still the economic theory of the future for which we are slowly and laboriously accumulating stone and mortar, statistical facts and functional equations.[20]

THE CLASSICAL THEORY OF GROWTH ABANDONED

It is an open question whether 'theoretical misdemeanours' alone are responsible for the fact that to this day 'respectable circles' have not taken note of Marx's methodological daring, and that men like Silvio Gessell and Major Douglas could crowd him out of the most important treatise written in this generation. The latter fact seems all the more paradoxical since, judged in metholodogical terms, Keynes' *General Theory* is much nearer, if not to Marx himself, at least to his prototype Smith than anything written in academic economics since the days of Mill—a point to which I shall return presently.

But it is true that when *Capital* appeared, the main stream of classical economics had already abandoned not only the original approach to the problem of secular development but even any concern with it at all. The reasons for this were never explicitly stated, and must be inferred from the context of the later classical writings.

An illuminating phase of transition is represented by Book IV of Mill's *Principles*. Chapters 4 to 6 of this Book, dealing with the tendency of profits to fall to a minimum, and with the stationary state, are written much in the old vein, combining the Ricardian 'running down' tendency of the system with the Malthusian alleviations referred to. But these chapters are preceded by the extremely interesting Chapter 3, in which five hypothetical cases of the behaviour of the factors of production are analysed in a thoroughly modern fashion. Changes in factor supply (constant or increasing population combined with constant or increasing capital and constant or increasing productivity) are discussed in a 'catalogue of permutations' that would do honour to any modern text book.

Apparently Mill regarded all these cases as empirically possible, with little to choose between them on *a priori* grounds. This agnostic position follows quite logically from the destruction that had been dealt (by Malthus and by Mill himself) to the 'laws of data changes', especially the iron law of wages and its descendant, the wage-fund theory; to the naive theory of accumulation (by Lauderdale, Sismondi and Wakefield); and to the optimistic interpretation of technical progress (abandoned by Ricardo, and restored by Mill himself only with many qualifications). The existence of business cycles had by Mill's time been fully realized, but no one had succeeded in integrating an explanation of them with the general theory of price and distribution. Even the purely physical tendencies of real output seemed more complex than they had appeared to the optimist Smith or to the pessimist Ricardo. For Mill the outcome depended on a 'conflict between two tendencies' (Book IV, Chapter 2), namely, technical progress and diminishing returns on land, an outcome that he regarded as unpredictable.

In short, the former 'constants'—natural, psychological and technological—had revealed themselves as so many variables. And since Marx's idea of relating them in circular fashion to the institutional environment contradicted what was still left of the original notion of a 'natural order', they could only be regarded as independent variables. This is the manner in which neoclassical economics has treated them ever since, no longer attempting to account for the regular form that the capitalist process has taken during the secular period of 200 years.

I agree with Keirstead (*op. cit.* Chapter 4) that Schumpeter's 'Theory of economic development' is no exception to this rule. What Schumpeter has done is to put forth an explanation of the business cycle on the basis of a theory of innovations. But not only are innovations treated as an independent variable; their effect on the labour market is completely disregarded. Since Shumpteter insists that, in principle at least, every new cycle starts from equilibrium, the economic process as such has no causal function. Of his later works, *Business Cycles* stresses the role of historical causes at the expense of any circular mechanism. By building his model of the secular process on the dubious foundation of Kondratieff's hypothesis, Schumpeter at best *describes* a movement without being able to *explain* it.

His last book, *Capitalism, Socialism and Democracy*, contains a number of highly interesting suggestions about the interaction between the economic process and the social order in late capitalism. But Baumol is certainly right in pointing to the 'somewhat loose and conversational manner which makes it almost impossible to discern the details of the analytical framework'.[21] Thus the man who alone among recent academic economists recognized the meaning, and in the end the lasting importance also, of the Smith–Marx scientific procedure, himself did very little to revive it. The leadership fell to a man who was strangely unaware of the tradition that he followed.

What places Keynes, in spite of his railing against 'classical' economics, squarely within the classical frame of reference is, on the one hand, his return to macroeconomics (in the Quesnay–Marx tradition rather than in the Smith–Ricardo tradition) and, on the other hand, his replacing some of the independent variables of neoclassicism by constants, in the manner of Smith.[22] I refer, of course, to Keynes' revival of specific 'propensities', 'preferences', and 'expectations', with whose help the *actual* course of the economic process is analyzed and predicted, at least for the short run. Certainly the functions that describe the Keynesian system can, in principle, assume any values. To that extent the theory is indeed general and its apparatus purely formal. But when it comes to analysing the actual process of capitalism and its inherent autonomous tendencies, Keynes no longer has recourse to the procedure by which neoclassicism tried to 'apply' its apparatus, namely, by empirically determining the 'data' from case to case. General propositions are put forth about how people at large divide an increment of income between consumption and saving, how movements of the rate of interest affect the demand for cash, and how long–term expectations affect investment. In scattered remarks, which refer to the secular process, a truly Marxian position is taken.[23] And the conclusions drawn regarding an industrial market left to its autonomous devices are hardly more reassuring.

All this, and also the recent attempts to build a more specific and more exact theory of economic growth on Keynesian foundations (Harrod, Hicks), requires detailed discussion beyond the range of this paper. But enough has been said to suggest to the reader that closer study of the classical apparatus, far from having merely historical significance, leads straight into the centre of research in contemporary theoretical economics.

With this we have returned to our starting point: how to construct a verifiable theory of economic growth that adequately combines social with economic analysis. The lesson to be drawn from the foregoing investigation cannot be a call for the return to the 'closed' circular mechanism of classical economics. Rather, the problem consists in establishing the criteria by which those areas where the economic process does indeed interact with its environment can be distinguished from fields where the 'underlying forces' operate as independent variables. In some instances, as in the theory of expectations, elements belonging to both areas may well be active. At this stage we do not possess such criteria, nor does our ability to handle circular mechanisms transcend the rather crude determinism of dynamic process analysis in its modern version.[24] But the growing concern with 'endogeneity' is certainly in accord with sound methodological principles. After all, the limits of endogenous explanation coincide with the limits of our understanding of the social process.

NOTES

1. *See*, for example, Paul A. Samuelson, *Foundations of Economic Analysis* (Cambridge, Mass.: Harvard University Press, 1947), Chapter 11; R. F. Harrod, *Towards a Dynamic Economics* (London: Macmillan, 1948), Lecture I; J. Tinbergen and J. J. Polak, *The Dynamics of Business Cycles* (Chicago: Chicago University Press, 1950), Chapter 9; J. R. Hicks, *A Contribution to the Theory of the Trade Cycle* (Oxford: Clarendon, 1950), p. 10, as well as his earlier *Value and Capital* (Oxford: Clarendon, 1939),

Chapter 9; William J. Baumol, *Economic Dynamics* (New York: Macmillan, 1951), Chapter 1.

2. Joseph A. Schumpeter, 'Deutschland' in *Die Wirtschaftstheorie der Gegenwart* (Vienna: Mayer-Fetter-Reisch, 1927), Volume 1, pp. 6-7. The rather free translation and the italics are mine. — A. L.

3. I first took this position in my *Economics and Sociology* (London: Allen & Unwin, 1935), Chapters 4 and 5. Since then valuable support has been given to this view by B. S. Keirstead in his *Theory of Economic Change* (Toronto: Macmillan, 1948), especially in Parts I and II of that work.

4. Adam Smith, *Wealth of Nations*, ed. by Edwin Cannan (London: Methuen, 1930), Book I, Chapter 2. Subsequent references to Smith are to this edition.

5. *Op. cit* Book I, Chapter 6. This chapter contains the rather naive but methodologically essential hypotheses suggesting how this original state—the basic set of data—was transformed into the civilized state defined by the above conditions.

6. Looking at this axiom of Smith's model from the vantage point of a fully developed industrial system, it is easy to raise the objection that it is unrealistic. But the axiom is an indispensable condition for the twin postulates of 'autonomy' and 'harmony' on which both the theory and the policy recommendations of Smith's economics rest. To have missed this central point is the main defect in Keirstead's otherwise valuable exposition of Smith's dynamics (*see Theory of Economic Change*, cited above, note 3, pp. 69–77). In linking moving equilibrium with a peculiar type of technology, Smith has shown an insight into the operation of the market mechanism that is sadly lacking in the work of most of his classical and all of his neoclassical successors.

7. The fallacies contained in Ricardo's proof of the displacement effect do not alter the systematic consequences of his conclusion.

8. For a balanced treatment of the relative merits of Malthus and Lord Lauderdale *see* A. H. Hansen, *Business Cycles and National Income* (New York: Norton, 1951), Chapter 14. But in concentrating on the notion of 'voluntary' underconsumption or 'oversaving', Hansen disregards the importance of Sismondi in stressing the complementary role, and for the past history of capitalism the more important role, of 'forced' underconsumption due to pressure on the wage level.

9. *Capital* (Chicago: Kerr Edition, 1906, 1909), Volume 1, Chapter 25. Subsequent references to Marx are to this edition.

10. It is a controversial point whether Marx regarded the industrial reserve army as a necessary condition for the pressure on the level of real wages, or merely as a force supplementary to the operation of the law of surplus value. The decision depends on what state of competition, pure or monopsonistic, one attributes to the labour market. Only if one assumes pure competition—hardly Marx's assumption—is the existence of a reserve army a necessary condition. We shall treat it as such, in order not to become involved in Marx's theory of value.

11. In some of Marx's statements, stocks and flows are badly confused. But there is no doubt that the above formulation renders the meaning of what he wanted to express.

12. *See*, for example, the critique of this law contained in P. M. Sweezy, *The Theory of Capitalist Development* (New York: Oxford University Press,

1942), Chapter 6, a book that is certainly sympathetic to the general trend of Marx's ideas.

13. It is quite another question, which has been much discussed in recent years (Sweezy, Joan Robinson), whether real wages, and thus labour's share in aggregate income must not rise under these assumptions. This conclusion would then obviate Marx's whole deduction of the 'catastrophic trend' of capitalist development. Now it is quite true that *per capita* real wages must rise with increasing productivity, unless money wages fall at the same time, which would in turn restore the level of profits. But this need not be true of *aggregate* real wages, unless aggregate employment is maintained. This condition, however, runs counter to Marx's intentions, since he derives an economic crisis from the fall of the profit rate. Whatever may happen to the real wages of the employed, therefore, growing misery of the working class as a whole is quite compatible with such a fall.

14. The substantive conclusion as to the instability of the level of profits can also be derived from the underconsumption effects that labour-displacing innovations exert.

15. The relevant passages (Volume 1, Chapter 25, and Volume 3, Chapter 15), in which a fall in profits, the stoppage of further accumulation, and thus the outbreak of the crisis, are derived from the wage rise, are open to criticism. We know today that overinvestment can arise only to the extent that factor specificity prevents a short-period adjustment of disproportionalities in the structure of production, a line of reasoning that is alien to Marx's thinking.

16. The scattered passages in Marx referring to underconsumption are so vague that this problem has become a fertile field for both text interpretation and controversy; *see* Sweezy (cited above, note 12) Chapter 10. Some neo-Marxists, notably Otto Bauer and Sweezy, have tried to construct from the available building blocks a consistent theory of 'forced underconsumption'. These constructions are defective, because they try to prove with purely 'mechanical' arguments what can be demonstrated only with due regard to 'changes in expectations'.

17. This is true even though under socialism the sphere of material production remains a 'realm of necessity', as Marx maintains (Volume 3, Chapter 48) against some of his more utopian disciples.

18. Luxemburg and Sternberg have added to the institutional factors of the environment the geographical–historical element of a 'non-capitalist space', which is gradually being filled up. Marx's own stand in this respect is not clear.

19. *See also* Lewis S. Feuer, 'Interdeterminacy and economic development', *Philosophy of Science*, **15** (1948), pp. 225–41.

20. Joseph A. Schumpeter, *Capitalism, Socialism and Democracy* (New York: Allen & Unwin, 1942), p. 43, italics mine. — A. L.

21. Baumol, *Economic Dynamics* (cited above, note 1), p. 20, note 2.

22. To realize Keynes' position one must distinguish, of course, first, between classical and neoclassical economics, and second, between the substantive propositions of classical macroeconomics and the method by which they were developed.

23. It is true that the systematic elaboration of what is now called 'maturity' theory is the work of some of Keynes' disciples. But all the elements of this theory are present in the three pages of the *General Theory* that deal

more extensively with economic development (Chapter 21, Section VII). Keynes calls this a question 'for historical generalization rather than for pure theory'. This is precisely the analytical level on which the classical theory of development moves. The apparent difference in generality is exclusively due to the early classical belief in 'natural' parameters, whereas Keynes and his followers are satisfied, like Marx, with generalizing about certain historical periods.

24. *See*, for example, Paul A. Samuelson's contribution in Howard S. Ellis (ed.), *A Survey of Contemporary Economics* (Philadelphia: Blakiston, 1948), pp. 352–81. It remains to be seen whether social scientists will profit from the theory of 'servo-mechanisms' or 'feedback systems', which play an increasingly important role in modern physical research. *See* Richard M. Goodwin's contribution to Alvin H. Hansen, *Business Cycles and National Income* (cited above, note 8), pp. 417–68. That the notion of a 'circular mechanism' is much older than these constructs of modern physics, and is indigenous to social research, should not be doubtful after the foregoing observations.

4   Is Economic Value Still a Problem?*

The formulation of the theme of this paper is intentionally ambiguous. It may indicate that the question it raises has become redundant because there exists a generally accepted solution. This was certainly so during the era of classical economics, and again from the Marginal Revolution until the end of the Second World War. Since then, however, the revival of interest in Ricardian and Marxian economics and, more subtly, in the microfoundations of macroeconomics have disturbed this consensus—so far without any traces of reconciliation among the contestants.

But my question may be interpreted quite differently. Consider the statement with which Paul Samuelson concluded his survey of utility analysis. In trying to show that the subjective theory of value 'is not in a technical sense meaningless', he established two conditions—the nature of which need not concern us here—which would raise the theory above a mere tautology. Still, at the end he wondered 'how much economic theory would be changed if either of the two conditions . . . were found to be empirically untrue. I suspect, very little'.[1] In other words, solution or no solution, the entire problem is seen there as being of little relevance for the major issues in economics.

During my own academic training early in the century, I was fed *ad nauseam* with the controversies between classical and neoclassical value theory. But I confess that I have always shared Samuelson's suspicion. Just imagine Ricardo, Marx, Walras and Marshall assembled in the same room and confronted with some issue of economic policy, such as the effect of a general rise in wages, the introduction of a tariff, or the imposition of a sales tax. I am convinced that they would in most instances arrive at the same correct answer. Where they might disagree—for example, about the role of the rate of interest or of

* I wish to express my sincere thanks to my colleagues Ron Blackwell, Robert L. Heilbroner, Edward J. Nell, and Anwar Shaikh for their critical comments on the first draft of this paper, from which I have greatly benefited.
[This essay was first published in *Social Research*, **48** (1981) — ed.]

flexible factor prices—the reasons would be other than differences in value theory.

In contrast with this sceptical view, Edward Nell has recently taken a radically different position. He insists that the burning issues of our day—inflation, unemployment, population explosion, destruction of the ecological balance, to mention a few—can be truly understood only with the help of the Marxian theory of value and capital.[2] Ironically, Nell combines this exaltation of Marxian theory with a strict denial that the relative inputs of labour quantities determine, directly or indirectly, the ratio of the prices of production—a central postulate of Marx's value theory.

I do not in principle reject the function that Nell assigns to Marxian theory, for which he wisely uses the term 'understanding' in place of 'explaining'. What he has in mind was called by Schumpeter the 'pre-analytic vision' of the economic phenomenon—as a well-ordered or an inharmonious system, as a time-independent or an evolutionary process, as the locus of shared benefits or of exploitation. And there is no doubt that a theory of value can be pressed into the service of such a vision.

However, my interest in raising the question 'whether economic value is still a problem' is much more limited. It is the same that dominated the minds of the classical and neoclassical writers when they inquired whether a theory of value can serve as the basis for the explanation of the cosmos of empirical prices. In other words, I shall be concerned exclusively with the *inner consistency* and the *explanatory power* of the two contestants—the labour theory and the utility theory of value.

I do so for two reasons. On the one hand, if one or even both these theories should prove defective under the aspect of consistency and/or explanatory power, my purpose would be served without entering into the much more intricate problem of the adequacy of the underlying 'vision'. On the other hand, I believe that the gradual purging of utility theory of unessential elements and the re-interpretation of the Marxian enterprise—for example, in the work of Morishima[3]—open the way for a rapprochement of what have hitherto been regarded as irreconcilable positions.

DEFINING THE PROBLEM

In starting out on our undertaking, the first difficulty arises from the danger of a confusion of terms. To give a representative example, let us consider the following statements in Schumpeter's *History of Economic Analysis*. The headline with which he introduces marginal utility reads as follows: 'The revolution in the theory of value and distribution'. To this a footnote is attached stating: 'Instead of using this traditional phrase, I might have used exchange ratios or relative prices'.[4] Now if value and relative prices are one and the same, the former can hardly *explain* the latter. But two pages later Schumpeter correctly states that all of the early marginalists

aimed at the same goal, which was to prove that the principle of marginal utility suffices to *deduce* [my italics — A. L.] the exchange ratios between commodities that will establish themselves in competitive markets . . . In other words, they established what A. Smith, Ricardo and Marx had believed to be impossible, namely, that exchange value can be explained in terms of use value.

In the same context Schumpeter refers also to the rival 'theorem that "prices" of commodities tend to be proportional to the labour quantities embodied in them', indicating that for both schools exchange value results from a more basic determinant–use value in the form of marginal utility, or labour quantity.

It is on this basis that we shall approach the problem by asking whether there is indeed a factor that can serve as an explanation of the ratios of empirical prices (and possibly of the quantities transacted). Or, as the same idea has been formulated more pointedly, *suppose that a universal amnesia were to wipe out the knowledge of all present prices, would there be a rule for re-establishing them?* In other words, what cannot be accepted as valid is an 'historical' solution of the price problem, that is, an explicit or implicit derivation of present prices from past ones. We shall see that this exclusion is of great significance in our further deliberations.

It is trivial to restate that the two conflicting 'causes' of relative prices—labour input and utility—refer to experiences occurring in production or consumption, or that they stand for a technological or a behavioural factor, respectively.[5] Perhaps it is less trivial to stress from the outset that the factor which dominates in classical economics is a measure of the *resistance* with which those who furnish the means of provision have to contend, whereas the neoclassical factor is supposed to measure or otherwise to express the *welfare* that accrues to the beneficiaries of provision. An analogy would be the difference between ohm and volt in electrophysics—an indication that the two approaches may deal with quite different issues and for that reason not be *a priori* incompatible.

In a systematic treatment we would have to review the entire history of the problem from its classical beginnings, even going back to Aristotle and the Church Fathers.[6] For our limited purpose we can confine ourselves to examining only a few salient aspects of the classical and the neoclassical approaches. We shall begin with the latter, for the simple reason that a return to Ricardo or Marx will be justified only if modern theory cannot offer an acceptable solution. Fortunately, we can dispense with a detailed survey of the history of utility theory itself. The features we are interested in are common both to the early 'psychologists' and 'hedonists' among the marginalists and to the purified constructs of Hicks or Debreu. We shall also skirt such time-honoured questions as to whether the utility experienced by a consumer can be directly ascertained or must be inferred from his behaviour, whether utility is measurable in cardinal or only in ordinal terms, and other such issues. What we are concerned with is beyond controversy within the ranks of the marginalists. It is the very foundation on which their theoretical edifice rests.

THE UTILITY THEORY OF VALUE

Some roots of the utility theory of value can be found in certain writings of the classical age, notably in the works of Say and Cournot. Still, the theory arose mainly as an alternative to the classical labour theory of value and its admittedly narrow range of explanatory power. If at all applicable, the classical theory seemed pertinent only to 'natural'—that is, long-period equilibrium—prices, and even to those only under the unrealistic assumption of equal capital-labour ratios throughout the system. Fluctuating market prices, not to say the prices ruling under natural and contractual monopolies, were related to a law of supply and demand whose constituents themselves were left largely unexplained.

Thus it appeared as a big step towards the unification and simplification of analysis when the new theory claimed to be able to explain *all* the variants of the price cosmos by a single principle—*the universal aim of consumers to maximize utility*. Whether understood as a motivational or as a behavioural pattern, this maximization was taken as an expression of free choice among the possible objects of utility, a choice hedged about only by the operation of the so-called Gossen laws, referring to an inverse relationship of marginal utility with the quantities at hand, and to the equalization of marginal utilities when several goods were to be acquired.

It has never been quite clear whether those laws were meant to be facts of experience or postulates of optimizing action. What is clear is that the claim to universality of the principle can be maintained only if the marginal utilities of the consumers determine not only the relative prices of consumer goods but also those of the factors engaged in producing them. To show this is not difficult for the supply prices of the factors themselves. A worker's idea of what his hourly wage should be can be related to the utility he expects to obtain from the consumer goods he is subsequently to buy or to the disutility he experiences in expending effort. But whose utility schedule is to be consulted by the prospective employer in establishing the hourly wage he is to offer?

This is the famous problem of 'imputation' which caused the members of the Austrian school especially a considerable headache. The problem will occupy us later when we examine marginal productivity theory. In the present context it is important to realize that, in all contemporary versions of the doctrine, the utility principle is confined to explaining the behaviour of *householders*, whereas the classical principle of profit (not utility) maximization has been resurrected as an action directive of *firms* when selling commodities or buying productive services.[7] Accepting this, we ask: Will the utility principle at least suffice to determine the price-related behaviour of householders?

LIMITING CONDITIONS

One crucial test is the derivation of an unambiguous *law of demand*. Let us consider the response of the buyer of a consumer good to a fall in price. If his wish to maximize utility is all we know about his aim, we can say no more than that he will raise the quantity demanded or reduce it or leave it as it is. If he raises it, he will indeed respond in accord with the conventional law of demand, according to which a change in price evokes an inverse change in the quantity demanded. But there is no doubt that the other modes of behaviour, though conflicting with the conventional law, can be interpreted equally well as 'utility maximizing'. If demand falls as a response to a price fall, we may deal with the Veblenesque case of ostentatious expenditure, in which expensive goods are valued more highly than cheaper ones. Or the good in question may be regarded by the buyer as what Hicks calls an 'inferior' good on which he spends less when its price falls, to devote the gain in purchasing power to increasing purchases of more highly valued goods. Finally, he may read into the price fall the beginning of a trend indicating a further price fall to follow, so that postponement of purchases to a future date promises still greater satisfaction. And we can interpret such abstention from still other considerations. The buyer may not care at all for the good concerned or, more important, what he acquired in the past may yield him maximum satisfaction—the case of consumer's homeostasis.

In the face of such plain objections, if the protagonists of utility theory still maintain their claim of being able to *predict* consumer behaviour in accord with the conventional law, one suspects that there must be somewhere a limiting assumption in what looks on the surface like a mere tautology. And indeed, closer examination reveals no less than three special conditions that are implied in the conventional proposition. The first concerns the nature of 'things', the utility of which is to be maximized, namely, *priced goods and services*, rather than intangibles such as Veblenesque 'ostentation'. Secondly, and more important, any consumer who tries to maximize utility is supposed to be in a state of *undersatiation*—a state that implies not only the painful experience of a discrepancy between means and ends, but also the desire to attain fuller satisfaction. Thirdly, the time span over which the consumer is supposed to maximize utility is limited to the *immediate future*, thus eliminating the disturbing effect of other than static expectations. In other words, the utility principle is an operational concept only in a *world of undersatiation*[8] *and instantaneous provision*.

Those limiting conditions indeed eliminate the exceptions from the conventional law stated above, exceptions which can all be interpreted as specific states of satiation. But, we must ask, do those exclusions significantly reduce the empirical relevance of the utility principle as an explanation of the behaviour of householders? Is not undersatiation—the psychological reflection of scarcity—man's existential fate? Even if for a fleeting moment he can fully satisfy one or another want, is not the totality of his wants without limit, so that any stock of resources must always appear to him as scarce, making the conventional law of demand the iron rule for his behaviour?

Though it is a cornerstone of modern analysis, the assumption of a transhistorical absolute scarcity of resources is a fiction. Such scarcity prevails only in two historical situations. One is a state of *destitution* in which the available stock of resources does not assure physical survival. At the other end of the scale is a state in which even the largest conceivable stock of resources cannot satisfy all wants because consumers are *insatiable*. However, far from reflecting unalterable natural constraints or intrinsic human propensities, destitution and unlimited appetition are *historical* phenomena, related to particular stages in the technological and cultural evolution of mankind. Stated differently, above the level of destitution scarcity of resources becomes a *relative* notion—relative to the scale of wants that the ruling cultural system sanctions.

Very likely, the natural and social pressures of early capitalism—mass poverty, unbridled competition, and Puritan work ethic—created a climate in which adherence to the conventional law of demand was an imperative for survival.[9] But the affluent marketers of present-day organized capitalism present a different picture. They seem to move somewhere between the two extremes of absolute scarcity, exhibiting growing tendencies toward homeostasis rather than maximization. Maintenance of asset values or of market shares are examples on the supply side; insensitivity to price fluctuations over time or to price differentials for physically homogeneous goods in favour of routinized purchases of branded commodities are examples on the demand side.[10]

Thus at least one of the exceptions to the conventional law of demand—marketers' homeostasis—seems to be far from 'rare and unimportant', as Hicks rightly considers the case of inferior goods.[11] Even more damaging is the assumption of 'timelessness'. It confines the validity of the utility approach to the Marshallian very-short period, restricting it to a static framework. It thus excludes all dynamic phenomena, contrary to the claim on which the marginalists base their superiority over their classical predecessors.

DERIVING PRICES FROM UTILITY

So far we have still been dwelling in the forecourt of the problem, studying the effects of *given* prices and price *changes* on consumers' behaviour. But the central problem is, of course, the derivation from utility considerations of the prices themselves. For this we shall take our bearings from the most sophisticated construct—Walras's theory of the equilibrium of production, refined by Hicks's application of indifference analysis. We can do so without biasing our verdict because the two objections we are going to raise apply to all neoclassical constructs, causal and functional, that try to derive equilibrium price ratios from utility arguments.

To put it in the simplest terms, the theory asserts that, given the marginal rates of substitution of all householders for all commodities, also the quantities of such commodities possessed at the outset by each—what is now often called their initial 'endowment'—together with the production functions and factor supply schedules, we can derive prices and quantities of commodities and factors representing the final market equilibrium.

We shall not raise such much-debated questions as whether the final equilibrium thus attained is 'unique', or whether equality of unknowns and of equations expressing the relationship between knowns and unknowns assures the 'existence' of such an equilibrium. Our objections concern (1) the assumed independence of certain crucial data from prior knowledge of certain prices, and (2) the interpretation of the implied behavioural rule.

As far as the first point is concerned, the critical elements are the initial endowments of each marketer and their effect, on the one hand, on the marginal rates of substitution and, on the other hand, on the factor supply schedules. In fact, the role of those endowments has been called in question before, but the crucial objection has been missed by both opponents and defendants, as shown by the following quotation: 'The taking of these initial endowments as *exogenous* has been criticized and much misunderstood, in particular by Marxist critics. For instance, it is often argued that this makes the distribution of income and wealth exogenous'.[12] Under the aspect of price analysis the objection is the very contrary, namely, the fact that those endowments are *not* exogenous and cannot therefore serve as data or independent variables. Rather, those endowments and their apportioning among the householders are the result of the process of distribution in the preceding period.

The misunderstanding seems to be due to a failure in distinguishing between personal and functional distribution. *Personal* distribution, the manner in which the sources of income and wealth—labour and property—are distributed among the householders, is mainly the result of the ruling political and legal order. As such, it is indeed an exogenous variable and thus a legitimate datum of price determination. Not so *functional* distribution, that is, the relative 'weight' of the components of the householders' aggregate incomes—wages, profit, interest and rent. This weight expresses itself in the *relative factor prices of the preceding period*, and itself depends on the then ruling commodity prices, and so on in an indefinite regress. Since the marginal rates of substitution, as well as the schedules of factor supply, vary with the initial endowments, they partake in this 'historical' nature of the endowment themselves. And in order to establish its 'genesis', we should indeed have to 'start with Neanderthal man',[13] or at least with the era when a general price system was first formed.

Moreover, there is another 'historical' limitation of the Walrasian model of quite a different nature. It concerns its general frame of reference—competitive equilibrium. This confines what validity it possesses to the competitive era of capitalism, excluding from its explanatory range the 'fixprice' structure of contemporary organized capitalism. The writings of Kalecki, Hicks and Morishima have explored the 'abnormal' consequences of fixprices for the operation of market systems. But I know of no attempt to relate fixprices and, in particular, the mark-ups in question to any value theory.

We turn now to our second objection, namely, to ascribing to Walras unreservedly the conventional interpretation of the rule of market behaviour. The problem concerns the *path* over which final equilibrium is to be established or re-established when it has been disturbed. Again, we disregard the well-known objections to Walras's notion of 'crying' prices or to Edgeworth's idea of 'recontracting'. What we are concerned with are the 'tâtonnements' which are supposed to reduce any gap between potential purchases and sales to the point where the market is clear.

From our earlier discussion we know that this path is fully determined and leads in the right direction only under the restrictive assumption of timeless undersatiation. For this reason it is significant that Walras, though stressing in many passages the 'positive' validity of those tâtonnements as a formalization of *actual* behaviour, offers in addition another and quite startling interpretation. In putting forth what he calls the 'law for the establishment of equilibrium prices', he has this to say:

Given several commodities, which are exchanged for one another through the medium of a numéraire, for the market to be in a state of equilibrium or for the price of each and every commodity in terms of the numéraire to be stationary, it is *necessary and sufficient* that at these prices the effective demand for each commodity equal its effective offer. When this equality is absent, the attainment of equilibrium prices *requires* a rise in the prices of those commodities the effective demand for which is greater than the effective offer, and a fall in the prices of those commodities the effective offer of which is greater than the effective demand.[14]

The importance of this passage lies in the fact that here Walras no longer claims that the forces of competition and the utility considerations that impel them will, *in fact*, cause the system to approach general equilibrium. Rather, he establishes certain behavioural *requirements*—requirements that are seen as prerequisites for maintaining equilibrium once it exists, and for establishing it when it is absent. In other words, a *norm* of behaviour is postulated as a means for a specified end—macroequilibrium. Why such an equilibrium should be chosen as the end is not explicitly stated. In now examining more closely its nature, we shall bring to light a possible reason for such choice.

THE THEOREM OF MARGINAL PRODUCTIVITY

An easy access is through the theorem of marginal productivity. As was indicated earlier, the theorem was originally devised as a tool of imputation in functional distribution; that is, as a way of splitting the atom of consumer-good prices into the component elements of factor prices. At first sight it does not seem to be of much interest in the present context if what is to be decomposed—consumer-good prices—can itself be explained only under the extreme and unrealistic conditions set out above. However, once we draw the ultimate consequences from the theorem of marginal productivity—consequences that are usually not drawn—we shall understand those extreme conditions for what they really are.

What is at stake can be most easily explained by using J. B. Clark's analytical tool chest. According to him, a productive factor will be employed to the point at which the addition to output of the last unit equals the cost of that unit. It follows that under perfect competition each factor receives as its remuneration the equivalent of its marginal product. In concentrating on the two basic factors, labour and real capital, Clark establishes a stationary state with positive returns to both factors by placing production in the range of decreasing physical returns.

There is nothing wrong with the logic of this argument if one implicit assumption is accepted, namely, that returns of capital are spent on consumer goods. But is this a realistic assumption in a competitive market? Are we not told that, whatever rules consumers' behaviour, firms aim at the maximization of profits—in the given case, of returns of capital? So we must assume that the returns of capital received in what now appears only as a *pseudostationary* state will be saved and invested. We are reciting here what nowadays is scoffed at as a neoclassical 'parable'. It asserts that, under the stated conditions, a process of accumulation will be initiated that leads to steadily rising capital–labour ratios associated with rising per capita output, rising real wages and falling returns to capital. Where this process will end has been aptly described by Joan Robinson, as follows:

In the special case where the total labour force remains constant . . . if accumulation is going on, a scarcity of labour will sooner or later emerge. A rise in the real wage rate and a fall of accumulation draws labour out of the investment sector. The rate of accumulation falls, but if it is still positive the scarcity of labour will sooner or later emerge again; a further rise in wages will further reduce the rate of accumulation, and so on, until replacement absorbs the whole of gross investment, and the stock of capital ceases to increase. All labour is then employed on producing consumer goods and maintaining capital, wages absorb the whole net product of industry, and the rate of profit is zero. This is . . . properly described . . . as the state of *economic bliss*, since consumption is now at the maximum level which can be permanently maintained in the given technical conditions.[15]

In passing, we must remember that the above proposition must defend itself against objections that have recently been raised under the heading of 'switches of technique' and 'capital reversing'.[16] However, within the limits of a constant supply of labour—one of the assumptions underlying both Joan Robinson's analysis and Clark's pseudostationary state—the steady movement toward economic bliss may be temporarily interrupted but not finally deflected from the state of bliss, so long as accumulation of the returns to capital continues. Temporary blocks to progressive 'mechanization' may arise whenever a more labour-intensive technique promises higher returns. But any such change in technique is bound to increase competition for the constant stock of labour and thus to raise wages, ultimately to the point at which more capital-intensive techniques again yield higher profits.

A more serious objection to the realism of the construction concerns the doubt that, considering the steady fall of returns to capital, accumulation will continue beyond a certain point—Marx's notion of the 'blunting of profits' as a block to further accumulation. In acknowledging this objection, we cannot claim for the state of bliss a *positive* role as describing an empirical phenomenon—it is a *norm* postulating the conditions for maximizing real net output.

In retrospect, the Walrasian model too can be fitted into this interpretation. We remember that its atheoretical, 'historical' nature is due to the effect which functional distribution has on the relative size of the individual endowments. If, as in the foregoing analysis, the number of priced factors is reduced to one, functional distribution will be eliminated and the model will be logically self-contained—though in a form that has no realistic counterpart and, like the Clarkian model, can serve only as a norm.

QUANTITIES AND QUALITIES

We have arrived at an altogether disappointing conclusion. Even within the limited range of competitive capitalism, empirically valid price ratios cannot be derived from utility theory through procedures of self-contained pure theory. We are forced to accept the order of relative prices of the period preceding the one under examination as a datum of analysis—we must implant utility theory in an historical context to achieve testable results. And even within an historical context the conclusions of the theory apply only to a world of undersatiation and even this only over the very short period—thus excluding the empirically important cases of homeostasis and of non-static expectations.

Fortunately, this is not the end of the story. In his famous polemic with Jevons, Marshall opposed to the 'catena' established by Jevons, namely, cost of production determines supply—supply determines final degree of utility—final degree of utility determines value, a catena of his own. It reads: utility determines the *amount* (my italics — A. L.) that has to be supplied—the amount that has to be supplied determines the cost of production—cost of production determines value.[17] The argument is set forth in defence of Ricardo and plays hardly any role in Marshall's substantive discussion of price theory. But it is a useful reminder that, for a full understanding of the market mechanism, we should know not only 'at what price' but also 'what and how much of it at that price'.

It is as an answer to that question that marginal utility in all its versions plays its part. Of course, as the aggregate of commodities demanded depends on income, previously established factor prices enter here too. Still, multidimensional indifference maps quite explicitly show the qualities and quantities demanded at given prices. True, in this way utility has been reduced to a secondary role because it can operate only if the price problem can be solved in some other way. Still, it is a role that has never been claimed by any competitor in the field of value. At the same time it is fully compatible with any solution of the price problem and is itself indispensable for a full understanding of market structures.

LABOUR INPUT AND PRICE

If the foregoing argument is accepted—that is, if the utility approach does not offer a satisfactory, namely, analytical as distinct from historical, answer to the question of what ultimately determines relative prices—the road is open for a re-examination of the classical approach.[18] Once more we are confronted by a long history extending from Cantillon to J. S. Mill and culminating in Marx. The emphasis of the earlier writers was on 'costs of production', that is, on the input of several factors of production, at least whenever 'the supply of a commodity', in Mill's words, 'can be indefinitely increased'.[19] Still, though labour input always played an important role, it was raised to the dominant 'cause' of pricing only by Ricardo and Marx. Both reduced the operative factors of production to two—labour and real capital—and tried to show that the effect of the latter on pricing can be expressed in terms of the former. It was Marx who, by proclaiming 'socially necessary labour time' as the ultimate determinant, seemed to give the clearest expression to a price-independent variable as the source and measure of exchange value.

In what follows we shall concentrate on the Marxian version of the theory. The reason is that the aims which such a theory pursues, as well as the difficulties it encounters, can be examined there most thoroughly. Perhaps it is in order to stress at this point that, whatever else Marx intended to demonstrate in discussing value, no careful reader of *Capital*, Volume 3, Chapter 9, can doubt that one of his major concerns was the relationship of the 'prices of production'—his term for the relative prices prevailing in equilibrium—to the original quantities of labour input.

Before saying more about this, it should be emphasized that a price theory based on the input of socially necessary labour time may, as we shall see, run into serious difficulties. But at first sight it seems to escape the vicious circle of indefinite regress that bedevils all neoclassical price theories when they refer to the real world. Therefore, Samuelson's advice to 'rub out . . . as an unnecessary detour . . . Volume I's analysis of values' may annihilate more than he envisages.[20] Rather, Marx's analysis, resting on an 'objective', physicotechnological, and thus price-independent factor, starts from a basis to whose status as a datum no logical objections can be raised.

THE TRANSFORMATION PROBLEM

Now to begin with, there is no denying that only under the exceptional and unrealistic assumption of equal capital–labour ratios throughout the system will the rate of surplus value in each enterprise coincide with the rate of profit, and thus the ratios of labour inputs be identical with the ratios of the prices of production. Strangely enough, since the days of von Böhm-Bawerk, critics treated this discrepancy as a final refutation of the theory. This would be so only if no *indirect* connection could be established between those deviations and the quantities of embodied labour—the essence of the so-called transformation problem.

In a brilliant paper, Meek has established such a connection by relating Marx's procedure to Sraffa's notion of a 'standard industry'. 'Sraffa is postulating precisely the same relation between the average rate of profit *and the conditions of production* in his "standard" industry as Marx was postulating between the average rate of profit *and the conditions of production in his* industry of "*average organic composition of capital.*"' With one important correction introduced by Sraffa allowing for the effect that a change in wages has on the prices of the means of production, both Marx and Sraffa conclude that 'the average rate of profit, and therefore the deviations of price ratios from embodied labour ratios, are governed by the ratio of direct to indirect labour in the industry whose conditions of production represent a sort of "average" of those prevailing over the economy as a whole'. Thus 'the very deviations of equilibrium price ratios from embodied labour ratios are themselves determined by "quantities of embodied labour"'.[21,22]

But we must now ask: What is the role, if any, of *utility* or *use value* in the classical conception of price determination? Friend and foe seem to agree that Ricardo expressed the classical consensus when he stated on the very first page of the *Principles*: 'Utility . . . is not the measure of exchangeable value, although it is absolutely essential to it. If a commodity were in no way useful . . . it would be destitute of exchangeable value, however scarce it might be, or whatever quantity of labour might be necessary to procure it'.[23]

Such exclusion of utility and thus also of demand from price determination is easily defended when we deal with industries operating at constant costs. It is no longer tenable when we are confronted with rising-cost industries. Even then it can be said that their price ratios coincide with the ratios of the labour input required at the margin of output. Therefore labour input can still serve as a *standard of measurement* of prices. But it is the quantities and qualities demanded that determine *where* on the production scale the margin of output lies. They thus codetermine the quantity of marginal labour input, denying the latter the role of the sole *cause*. In view of the strategic role of natural resources in the process of production, most of which are subject to increasing costs, this modification must not be minimized.[24]

On the other hand, the labour theory of value is not limited by the 'undersatiation' postulate as is the non-tautological utility theory. Even in a homeostatic system, all priced commodities—that is, all commodities the provision of which depends on labour input—exchange in equilibrium at ratios determined by the latter.

THE NON-HOMOGENEITY OF LABOUR

So far the labour theory of value seems to come out with flying colours as a perfect tool of measurement of stationary price ratios and as greatly superior to utility theory in the determination of empirical price ratios—at least to the extent to which equilibrium can be regarded as an approximation to the real world.

Alas, this favourable result will be challenged when we now turn to an examination of what we mean by labour input in view of the great disparity of actual performances. In other words, before resting content we must deal with what critics have defined as the 'non-homogeneity' of labour. In fact, we are confronted with no less than three different types, which we shall label types of 'form', of 'grade', and of 'skill'.

Only if it is possible to reduce all three types to a common denominator does the labour theory of value become operational.

This is not difficult in cases we have denoted as *forms*. By this we refer to labour input of otherwise homogeneous quality in *different occupations*, such as shoemaking or carpentry. There we can accept Ricardo's answer that the proper distribution of forms will be achieved through competition in the labour market, or Marx's equivalent reference to a 'social process that goes on behind the backs of the producers'.[25]

However, as has often been pointed out, this reasoning is not permissible in dealing with differences in grade and skill. Speaking first of *grades*, by which we mean *innate capabilities*—handy as compared to average carpenters—we face a situation comparable to differences in fertility, location and accessibility of natural resources. And the solution lies where Ricardo found it in the latter instance. Because they are able to produce more output per unit of labour time, the higher grades hold a monopoly position that will yield them a 'rent' over and above the wages of the marginal workers. However, as in the Ricardian case, this rent determines neither the costs of production nor consequently the prices of output. As in the case of increasing costs discussed earlier, those prices and thus the rents of skill are determined by the input of marginal—in a preferable formulation, of average grade—labour.

Turning now to different *skills*, that is, *acquired capabilities*, Marx himself has given what looks like the beginning of an answer:

In order to modify the human organism, so it may acquire skill and handiness in a given branch of industry, and become labor-power of a special kind, a special education or training is requisite, and this, on its part, costs an equivalent in commodities of a greater or less amount. . . The expenses of this education . . . enter *pro tanto* into the real value spent in its production[26]

Alas, closer examination of this procedure runs into serious difficulties. Reducing differences in skill to differences in the labour input in education and training is possible only if those relative inputs can themselves be reduced to differences in the training time required. This, in turn, presupposes that different educational labour times can on their part be reduced to a common denominator. In other words, it must be possible to express one hour of skilled labour as a multiple of hours of labour performed with no skill.

In reality all skills are created by the input of *skilled* labour of educators and trainers, an input that is itself the product of the skilled labour of other educators and trainers, and so on, in an indefinite regress. To reach down to the level of unskilled labour as the ultimate creator of skills, one must take into account the entire evolution of civilization from its most primitive stages to the present. Obviously there must have been a gradual evolution of higher from lower skills. This, however, would be another *historical* approach, formally resembling what was said above in the context of a critique of utility theory.

Within the framework of a *given* market order there is no common denominator to which the hierarchy of labour skills could be reduced. Rather, the wide dispersion of such skills must be accepted as an ultimate datum. There may be no objection to this as a practical expedient, but it prevents us from treating the relative prices of commodities produced by different skills as if they represented multiples of some elemental unit. In fact, we have here a perfect analogy to an issue that has come up in the recent debate on capital theory—the irreducibility of different types of real capital to a common denominator.[27]

However, there is another limitation to the empirical validity of the labour theory of value, the practical consequences of which extend far beyond the difficulties created by the irreducibility of labour skills. It is the same limitation that would reduce the applicability of utility theory, even if it were internally consistent. Like the latter, the labour theory presupposes competitive markets and thus cannot account for the conditions of organized capitalism. Nevertheless, if we are to bestow some meaning to it, one that pertains to all market structures, we must again interpret it as a *norm* of pricing by which the performance of real markets can be evaluated.

This has been the very conclusion at which we arrived in analysing the utility approach. In fact, the similarity carries even further. Remembering our discussion of marginal productivity, we saw that in that context true equilibrium of the system coincides with the 'ideal' position where returns to capital fall to zero because the system has reached 'capital saturation' where each worker is equipped with the largest stock of real capital applicable within the prevailing technological horizon.

Now Marx's model of 'simple reproduction', on which his analysis of prices of production is based, is another state of 'pseudoequilibrium', as we labelled the intermediate state which conventional analysis of marginal productivity treats as a state of rest. Though the source of the returns to capital differ in Marx's scheme—being sociopolitical rather than technological—these returns too are supposed to be *consumed*. If we now postulate, as we did for the marginal productivity model, that those returns should be saved and invested—a postulate that is in full accord with the profit-seeking behaviour pattern Marx assumed with regard to firms—we arrive at the same state of *bliss*. That this modification will not yield an empirically applicable result was pointed out before—the approach to bliss being gradually stopped by the 'blunting of profits'. But this does not prevent the terminal state of this process from serving, as in the former case, as a *norm*.[28]

CONCLUSION

We have reached the point at which our results can be summarized in a few general propositions:

(1) Our first and primary problem has been the *derivation of empirical price ratios*. It has turned out that neither the utility theory nor the labour theory of value succeeds in presenting a self-contained analytical solution. Both are inseparable from two kinds of *historical context*. One concerns specific features of the respective theory—the initial endowments in utility theory, the role of different skills in labour theory. The other concerns the evolution of the modern market system, for whatever empirical validity either theory may possess refers only to the competitive stage of capitalism. Recalling our criterion for a 'non-price' determinant of actual price ratios, we must admit that neither approach would permit us to restore the present price cosmos if amnesia were to wipe out our recollection of them, other than by a complex process of trial and error.[29]

These defects common to both approaches must not obscure import- ant differences between them. Within the limitation stated, the labour theory is more comprehensive because it can account for price ratios in a homeostatic as well as a maximizing system. On the other hand, once prices are determined, utility theory can establish the qualities and quantities of the commodities transacted—an issue that the labour theory has never raised.

All in all, the historical nature of both solutions does not come as a surprise to those who have always conceived of economic processes as embedded in a wider sociohistorical context. Lacking the elegance of self-contained pseudomechanical models, the historical frame of reference in which both theories must be understood points to the continuity as well as to the transformation that characterize actual market systems.

(2) The situation changes drastically once we transform the exchange values arising in equilibrium into a *norm*. It is true that, to arrive at an unambiguous standard in this way, we must impose restrictive qualifications that go far beyond the conventional conditions for equilibrium. The normative state then appears as one in which, within

a given technological horizon, the maximum physically possible level of output is attained, with zero profits and the rewards of labour as the only net income. In this ideal state, the two approaches converge.

(3) And yet this is not the last word. We have not yet spelled out the ultimate *criteria* that are to raise this state of bliss and its price order to the rank of a norm.

There is, first, a *technological* criterion. By assuring the maximum net output, such a system operates with maximum technical efficiency. But such a technological maximum satisfies also the *welfare* criterion of maximum provision—a criterion valid so long as the system is exposed to scarcity in the sense of objective destitution, as well as of the subjective experience of undersatiation. Finally, we must accept as a third criterion *equality of provision* in accord with the input of labour skills. In a word, our norm refers to an *egalitarian order of maximum provision under conditions of scarcity*. Now it is essential to realize that none of these criteria has *a priori* validity. Under the economic aspect, the 'relativity' of the technological and the welfare criterion is especially relevant. They lose their validity in homeostatic systems where some limited output suffices to achieve full satiation because the welfare optimum is no longer identical with the technological maximum. We mentioned earlier that, above the level of destitution, a homeostatic economy is today by no means a Utopian data. Moreover, not only a goodly number of primitive societies but the highly civilized communities of the mediaeval town economies resembled such an order as well. Therefore, it is not without interest to ponder the views of a late classical economist as to the prospects of homeostasis in a fully industrialized society.

In his well-known discussion of the stationary state, Mill waxes quite enthusiastic when imagining a society with these features:

A well-paid and affluent body of labourers . . . a much larger body of persons than at present, not only exempt from the coarser toils, but with sufficient leisure, both physical and mental, from mechanical details to cultivate the graces of life . . . There would be as much scope as ever for all kinds of mental culture and moral and social progress; as much room for improving the Art of Living, and much more likelihood of its being improved, when minds ceased to be engrossed by the art of getting.[30]

What Mill depicts as an ideal state is a society in which all strata of the population shift an ever larger part of their energy and time from labour-requiring priced goods to the immaterial 'utilities' of mental culture.

An even more radical transformation, in which labour input loses its power of value creation altogether, was anticipated by Marx himself:

to the degree that large industry develops, the creation of real wealth comes to depend less on labor time and on the amount of labor employed than on the power of the agencies set in motion during labor time, whose 'powerful effectiveness' is itself in turn out of proportion to the direct labor time spent on their production, but depends rather on the general state of science and the progress of technology . . . Real wealth manifests itself . . . in the monstrous disproportion between the labor time applied, and its product, as well as in the qualitative imbalance between labor, reduced to a pure abstraction, and the power of the production process it superintends. Labor no longer appears so much to be included within the production process; rather, the human being comes to relate as watchman and regulator of the production process itself . . . As soon as labor in the direct form has ceased to be the great well-spring of wealth, *labor time ceases and must cease to be its measure*, and hence exchange value [must cease to be the measure] of use value . . . The free development of individualities . . . the general reduction of the necessary labor to a minimum . . . then corresponds to the artistic, scientific, etc. development of the individuals in the time set free . . . *The measure of wealth is then not any longer, in any way, labor time, but rather disposable time.*[31]

What was at the time when Marx wrote (1857) a utopian vision more and more resembles the most recent stage of capitalism with its progressive automation, nowadays stimulated by what has been named the 'microelectronic revolution'.

(4) This raises a final question, on the surface merely a terminological one, but really a paradox for which I have not found a solution. Why has the standard of economic measurement that is supposed to underlie price ratios been associated since the days of Aristotle with the notion of 'value'? Our attempt at moving the concept of exchange value from the empirical to the normative level might be taken as an *ex post* justification of that terminology. However, when we consider the meaning that attaches to the term value in the fields of ethics and aesthetics, not to speak of human relations generally, we should expect optimum welfare—the normative goal—to coincide with the maximization of exchange values.

This is indeed so under the microeconomic aspect when one individual's command over provision is proportional with the exchange value of what he has to offer, though we must not forget that someone else's provision is proportionally reduced. But what about the macroeconomic aspect, when we try to assess optimum aggregate welfare? There the genuine character of exchange value as a measure of *resistance to provision* comes into the open. To see this clearly, we must turn our attention from labour input *ratios* as determinants of price *ratios* to the *absolute* inputs of labour quantities required to achieve a stipulated level of aggregate output. Then it is obvious that the welfare attached to this level of output is inversely related to the absolute labour required—the imaginable optimum being the Garden of Eden where absolute labour input and thus the related value is zero and all goods are free.

In this we only reformulate the essence of what Ricardo has stated in Chapter 20 of his *Principles*, where he contrasts value with 'riches'. He correctly identifies *riches*—the quality and quantity of goods obtainable in exchange—with *utility*, the maximization of which indeed coincides with optimum aggregate welfare, always assuming scarcity. But, as he says, 'value depends not on abundance, but on the difficulty or facility of production'. If this is so, what sort of 'value' is this, the very absence of which would be the condition for economic Utopia to come true?

Now is economic value still a problem? When first raising this question we found that it could be answered from two quite different viewpoints: whether a theoretical solution can be found acceptable to both parties or, solution or no solution, whether the debate is irrelevant at the level of economic practice. Taking the latter viewpoint first, we cannot help admitting that, even if a perfect solution were presented, the discussion of the problem moves at much too high a level of abstraction to matter when we try to explain or predict a concrete event, much less when we try to frame economic policy. For this reason, in practical economics we start quite legitimately from a given historical situation with the prevailing price order as a datum. We then argue from there backward or forward, as the analytical task requires, disregarding the subtler issues that relate to the 'basement' on which the theoretical edifice rests.

The case is different for the pure theorist. If for no other than methodological reasons, he is interested in what goes on in that 'basement'. For him our results are gratifying and disappointing at the same time. They are disappointing because there is no ultimate determinant of empirical prices without abandoning the realm of pure analysis for that of history. It is gratifying because what there is—a normative principle by which we can adjudicate the performance of actual competitive markets—can be derived from either of the two rival approaches. In part their answers are complementary. Thus the psychological underpinning of maximization or the determination of the qualities and quantities transacted are achievements of the utility principle. Mastery of homeostasis and the stress on the 'resistance' character of exchange value go to the credit of the labour principle. For the rest, quite surprisingly their answers turn out to be identical.

NOTES

1. Paul A. Samuelson, *Foundations of Economic Analysis* (Cambridge: Harvard University Press, 1955), pp. 92, 117.
2. Edward J. Nell, 'Value and capital in Marxian economics', *Public Interest*, Special Issue (1980): pp. 174–200, at pp. 194ff.
3. 'I believe that Marx would have accepted the marginal utility theory of consumer's demand if it had become known to him' (Michio Morishima, *Marx's Economics* [Cambridge: Cambridge University Press, 1973], p. 40).
4. Joseph A. Schumpeter, *History of Economic Analysis* (New York: Oxford University Press, 1954), p. 909.
5. Applying the term 'cause' to utility is, of course, correct only for Jevons or Menger and their followers, in contrast to the 'functional' school inaugurated by Walras. For our purposes this difference will prove irrelevant.
6. For a brief sketch of this doctrinal development, *see* my 'The normative basis of economic value', in *Human Values and Economic Policy*, ed. by Sidney Hook (New York: New York University Press, 1967), pp. 170–80.
7. It seems unnecessary to quote examples for this proposition because maximization of utility, together with maximization of profits, is the general standard today for market behaviour in neoclassical theory, although I am not aware of any explicit justification why half of the bargainers should be excluded from the utility rule.
8. The undersatiation condition has been formalized in the convexity postulate of indifference analysis.
9. It is those conditions of the environment which also explain profit maximization as the main action directive of firms. Moreover, even for householders they resolve the apparent clash between maximization of receipts and minimization of expenditure. The former—reflecting the 'dynamics of undersatiation'—is a psychological substructure of the latter.
10. The first to draw attention to the significance of homeostatic tendencies in modern markets was Kenneth E. Boulding in *A Reconstruction of Economics* (New York: Wiley, 1950), Chapter 2.
11. John R. Hicks, *Value and Capital* (Oxford: Clarendon Press, 1939), Chapter 1, Section 6.
12. Frank Hahn, 'General equilibrium theory', *Public Interest*, Special Issue (1980), pp. 123–38, at p. 124, n. 1; my italics — A. L.
13. *ibid.* pp. 124, 127. The gist of the above argument was presented half a century ago in Hans Mayer, 'Der Erkenntniswert der Funktionellen Preistheorien', in *Die Wirtschaftstheorie der Gegenwart*, 4 Volumes (Wien: J. Springer, 1927–32), 2: pp. 147–239, especially p. 196. However, Mayer overlooked the fact that his objection to an indefinite regress was equally valid for the 'causal' theories which Mayer favoured over and above the functional ones.
14. Léon Walras, *Elements of Pure Economics*, translated by William Jaffé (New York: A. M. Kelley, 1954), p. 172; my italics — A. L. An equivalent statement for the case of production appears on pp. 253–4.
15. Joan Robinson, *The Accumulation of Capital* (London: Macmillan, 1956), pp. 81–3. The same reasoning underlies Schumpeter's notion of 'circular flow equilibrium' and Keynes's concept of a 'quasi-stationary community'. *See* Joseph A. Schumpeter, *The Theory of Economic Development*

(Cambridge: Harvard University Press, 1934), Chapters 4–5; John Maynard Keynes, *The General Theory of Employment, Interest and Money* (London: Macmillan, 1936), Chapter 16.

16. *See* G. C. Harcourt, *Some Cambridge Controversies in the Theory of Capital* (Cambridge: Cambridge University Press, 1972).

17. *See* Alfred Marshall, *Principles of Economics*, 8th edn. (London: Macmillan, 1926), pp. 817, 819.

18. An all-inclusive study of the problem would also have to consider the recent contributions of Sraffa and von Neumann. Below we shall briefly refer to their work to the extent to which it touches on the issues of this essay.

19. Where natural or artificial monopolies prevail, price was supposed to be determined by the interplay of 'effectual' demand (Mill) and supply. Effectual demand was seen to depend on 'the wish to possess', as well as on 'the power of purchasing'. Thus the argument is involved in the same historical chain that creates the indefinite regress in utility theory.

20. Paul A. Samuelson, 'Understanding the Marxian notion of exploitation', *Journal of Economic Literature* **9** (1971), pp. 399–431, at p. 421.

21. R. L. Meek, 'Mr Sraffa's rehabilitation of classical economics', in *Economics and Ideology* (London: Chapman & Hall, 1967), pp. 161–78, especially pp. 175–7; his italics.

22. It may be worth noting that even Schumpeter, in the face of other grave objections to Marx's approach, thought it 'possible to hold that the relative prices of commodities, as deduced in the third volume, follow from the labour-quantity theory of the first volume' (Joseph A. Schumpeter, *Capitalism, Socialism, and Democracy* (New York: Harper, 1947), p. 29, n. 9).
Very different is the case of von Neuman. First of all, his 'Model of general economic equilibrium' (*Review of Economic Studies* **13** (1945–6), pp. 1–9) is concerned with *dynamic* equilibrium, more precisely, with balanced growth. It is to this framework that his major innovations apply—a new treatment of fixed capital and its depreciation, and his criterion for the choice of different techniques—*not* to the stationary framework in which Marx discusses the transformation problem. In the latter context, the assumption of a stationary age structure of fixed capital—in any period the quantity of fixed capital produced equals the quantity worn out and thus to be replaced—is not only permissible but indispensable if equilibrium is to persist. When transferred to such a stationary framework, von Neumann's 'inequalities' change back into Marxian equalities.

23. For Marx's formulation of the same idea, *see Capital*, Volume 1, Chapter 1, Section 1. Considering the many editions that are in use, my quotes refer to chapters and sections rather than to the pages of a particular edition of *Capital*.

24. It is noteworthy that, contrary to the categorical denial of any influence of use value and thus of demand on price, as expressed in *Capital*, Volume 1, Marx accepts this modification in Volume 3, Chapter 10, when he writes: 'If demand is so strong that it does not contract when price is regulated by the value of the commodities produced under the most unfavorable conditions, it is these conditions that determine the market value'.

25. Marx, *Capital*, Volume 1, Chapter 2.

26. Marx, *Capital*, Volume 1, Chapter 6.
27. The same conclusion has been drawn by Edward J. Nell in 'Understanding the Marxian notion of exploitation', in George R. Feiwel (ed.), *Samuelson and Classical Economics* (Boston: Kluwer-Nijhoff, 1981). The problem has a long history dating back more than 90 years to von Böhm-Bawerk's *Karl Marx and the Close of His System*, where he sharply criticized the idea that skilled labour could be reduced to simple labour without circular reasoning. On the other hand, an interesting literature in favour of 'reducibility' has recently sprung up in neo-Marxist circles, of which Yilmaz Akyuez, in 'Heterogeneous labour and labour theory of value', *Memorandum from the Institute of Economics* (University of Oslo, 1976) offers a good survey. Morishima, in *Marx's Economics*, pp. 190–3, takes an intermediate position. Though presenting a 'generalization of the labour theory of value' that allows for different kinds of labour, he finds it in conflict with Marx's theory of exploitation.
    I am grateful to my colleagues Robert L. Heilbroner and Anwar Shaikh for helping me to understanding the intricacies of these attempts. They all have one element in common: they attribute from the outset to simple labour a significant role in creating skills—a proposition which seems to me unrealistic at the level of practice and question-begging at the level of theory.
28. Marx's notion of 'simple commodity production' (*Capital*, Volume 3, Chapter 10) resembles the structural features of the state of bliss. It even refers to empirical, though precapitalist states in which farmers and craftsmen own their means of production—an indication that exchange value is not conditional on the presence of 'alienated' labour.
29. The ingenious attempt of Anwar Shaikh, made in an unpublished study, to reduce empirical prices directly to labour values derived from input–output tables, does not refute what is said in the text. Even if his statistical technique goes unchallenged, his original data necessarily reflect what was called above the 'dispersion of skills'. What his study does achieve is to raise doubts about the empirical significance of the transformation problem.
30. John Stuart Mill, *Principles of Political Economy*, Book 4, Chapter 6.
31. Karl Marx, *Grundrisse* (New York: Random House, 1973), pp. 704–8; my italics — A. L.

Part II
The Methodology of Political Economics

5 Toward a Science of Political Economics*

The subsequent pages present the gist of my book *On Economic Knowledge*,[1] in which I originally formulated my ideas on the content and method of a political economics.[2] This condensation of a comprehensive argument to its bare essentials has the advantage of exposing both its strengths and its weaknesses. As far as the latter are concerned, published reviews, private communications, and not least my own further reflections have made me aware of certain shortcomings which, were I to rewrite the book, would cause me to shift certain emphases, soften the tone of some critical comments, and stress even more than I did originally the convergence of my ideas with the trend of current theory and economic policy. Yet my main thesis stands, to my mind, intact, and I will attempt to restate it here, hopefully in terms that will strain neither the patience of the economist nor the understanding of the non-economist.

THE CRITICAL VIEWPOINT OF POLITICAL ECONOMICS[3]

Political Versus Traditional Economics

The dividing line between traditional economics—by which I refer to the standard formulations of economic theory, past and present—and political economics, as I denote my own reformulation of economic theory, can best be approached if we begin from two premises that both procedures share.

The first of these is an emphasis on *theory* rather than on taxonomic or historical description as the essential core of the discipline. Both

---

* [This essay was first presented as the opening position paper at a two-session Symposium on Lowe's work held at the New School for Social Research in February and March of 1968. The Symposium sessions subsequently comprised a series of invited papers by distinguished philosophers and social scientists, with a concluding rejoinder presented by Lowe. This rejoinder is reprinted as Essay 6 below. The proceedings of the Symposium were later published: for details see the opening editorial note to Essay 6 below. — ed.]

traditional economics and political economics, in other words, move from a small number of explanatory principles to a large number of propositions about the facts of economic life. Secondly, both approaches share a common concern with *prediction*. I wish to stress this point from the outset, because the reservations which I have expressed in my book as to the predictive powers of traditional economics have occasionally been misinterpreted as a denial on my part of the possibility—or even the legitimacy—of economic prediction generally. Nothing could be further from my intention. Indeed the major incentive in my search for an alternative to traditional reasoning has been the wish to invest economic theory with the power of prediction that I believe it now lacks.

It does not follow from this that the ability to predict should be regarded as the decisive criterion for scientific economics. As the examples of geology or crystallography show, the capacity to predict is not even a necessary attribute in the physical sciences, and much less so in the social sciences, where historical explanation and structural analysis play such a large role. If, nevertheless, the ability to predict today serves more and more as the touchstone of economic science, the reason is pragmatic. By this I mean not only that the application of economic knowledge is conditional on our capacity to foresee the effect of economic actions, but even more that the adequate functioning of our kind of economic system requires *public action* informed of its consequences. In other words, whether economics is, or is not, capable of prediction is no longer merely a methodological concern but a question of cardinal importance for the organization of economic life.

Thus in the search for explanatory principles from which deductions can be made, and in the focus on prediction as the pragmatic aim of the analytical procedure, traditional and political economics agree. The roads part when we ask: How can we obtain knowledge of the explanatory principles—be they laws or stochastic regularities—from which predictive statements can be derived?

Traditional economics, following the procedure of the 'hard' sciences, tries to derive its laws and stochastic regularities from the observation of *actual* economic processes and of the *actual* behaviour of the elementary units of the economy—buyers and sellers, consumers, investors, etc. Political economics does not reject this procedure once and for all. It recognizes a limited period of economic history—the period of 'classical' capitalism in the decades following the Industrial Revolution—to which the traditional procedure is well adapted. But it finds the predictive usefulness of the so-called 'positive' method on the wane during the later development of industrial capitalism, to the point where, under contemporary conditions, the failures of the method seem to far outweigh the successes. Considering the recent progress in econometric techniques, this trend toward decreasing reliability in economic prediction can hardly be blamed on a lack of refinement of prevailing research methods. Rather it looks as if something had happened to the underlying research object itself to make it progressively more refractory to conventional methods of investigation. The nature of this historical change is, I believe, an ever widening spectrum of behavioural and motivational patterns, with the consequence of increasing 'disorder' in the autonomous processes of modern markets.

If this is true, we are confronted with a grave dilemma. In the interest of the proper functioning of the modern market, this tendency toward disorder must be counteracted by appropriate measures of public policy. But in order to devise suitable policies, we require a theory capable of predicting the effects of the particular measures we employ. However, it seems impossible to construct such a theory if the observable phenomena from which the explanatory principles are to be abstracted lack that minimum degree of orderliness which is the prerequisite of any scientific generalization.

It is from the horns of this dilemma that political economics tries to lift economic analysis. But before showing how this can be done, we should first examine more closely the two presuppositions on which our formulation of the problem rests. One refers to the 'minimum degree of orderliness' on whose presence both the practical functioning of an industrial market and the theoretical explanation and prediction of its movements are said to depend. The other concerns the empirical question of whether the actual movements of contemporary markets do indeed fall short of that 'minimum', and what may be the reasons for such a 'deformation' of mature capitalism.

The Role of 'Order' in Economic Theory and Practice
There is probably agreement that in no field of inquiry can scientific generalizations be derived from the observation of truly 'erratic' phenomena. This does not imply that a continuum of observations that leads from 'perfect order'—meaning invariability of structure and motion—to 'perfect disorder'—namely, full randomization of events—is also a continuum of decreasing scientific tractability. Rather the scientifically inexpedient range lies around the middle of the spectrum, since both extremes and their neighbouring regions are open to deductive or stochastic generalizations.

As frequently as the extreme of randomization seems to occur in the realm of natural phenomena, in the social world it materializes only in exceptional cases when no interrelations exist among the members of a group: for example, in a crowd milling around idly. Nor can we, in view of the spontaneity of the units of social groups, expect the other extreme, invariability of behaviour, to be the rule over any length of time. Hence, for all practical purposes, the relevant region for social occurrences lies somewhere between the extreme of perfect order and the middle range of erratic behaviour, a region in which orderly and disorderly tendencies combine in varying proportions. The critical question for the predictability of autonomous economic phenomena is, then, whether, in a given case, the prevailing degree of orderliness approximates the state of perfect order sufficiently closely to permit the application of a deductive procedure which, taking into account certain disturbance variables, will yield results that fall within a small prediction interval.

There can be legitimate disagreement as to the size of the prediction interval which, in a given case, is still practically useful and thus compatible with orderly structure and motion. Take the problem of a 'reference cycle' for industrial fluctuations. It is one thing to predict—even with a considerable prediction interval—the rates of change of output during an upswing or downswing. It is quite another, however, to predict whether a given economic movement will continue or will turn in a direction contrary to the one in which it is headed at the moment when the prediction is made. In the first case there is no doubt about the direction of the movement; the strategic variables at least have the proper arithmetic sign. In the latter case it is the sign itself and thus the direction that is in doubt.

So, too, in microeconomics, when we predict the effect of a rise in prices on, say, supply. If the situation is orderly enough, we can at least assert that a price rise will bring some increase in supply. But the prediction interval may rise to the point where we may be unable to assert even that much—for instance, if price rises induce a speculative *contraction* in offerings. Therefore, to give some precision to the notion of 'disorder', I shall henceforth define it as any situation in which we cannot unambiguously predict the *direction of economic change*.

In contrast with much modern theorizing, I feel bound to emphasize the singular importance of such 'order' and 'disorder' in microeconomic relations. With Professor Machlup I cannot regard any explanation of macro-processes as complete or any prediction of their future course as safe, unless one can demonstrate the particular micro-processes from whose integration the macro-phenomena result.[4]

Thus, in untangling this problem, the crucial matter of order arises at two levels. On the first level, it is necessary for the *behaviour patterns* of buyers and sellers to form a mutually compatible and consistent chain. However, for this smooth intermeshing of individual actions to occur—and here we reach the second level—the *motivational patterns* underlying the behaviour of individual marketers must themselves be mutually compatible.

These motivational patterns in turn must be understood to result from two separate constituents. One of these constituents represents the strand of purposive intent, of incentives, or, as I call them, *action directives*. Here we have the motives of pecuniary maximization or minimization, maintenance of asset values (Professor Boulding's 'homeostasis'), protection of market positions, etc. But there is a second constituent as well. This is the strand of cognition or interpretation by which a marketer grasps the 'meaning' of the actions of his fellow marketers or anticipates future market events—in particular, the manner in which his fellow marketers will react to his own behaviour—to be subsumed under the concept of *expectations*.

These expectations of the individual actors are of the greatest importance for the construction of a scientific economics because they themselves represent predictions, although they are formed on a 'common-sense' basis from fragmentary experience and information. For only if the state of the market shows a degree of order, in the sense defined above, will the economic actors be able to form correct expectations with a high degree of subjective certainty. And only then will their overt behaviour patterns dovetail in such a way as to sustain the prevailing order, thus enabling the scientific observer to predict macro-events within practically useful limits. It is this common-sense interpretation of the ultimate 'facts'—buyers' and sellers' behaviour—by the actors themselves that so greatly encumbers the work of the economist, a difficulty which the student of molecules and planets, or of cells and organisms, is spared.[5]

However, there is still another complication in the scientific treatment of social processes that must be recognized if the relevance of 'order' for economic theorizing is to be fully grasped. I spoke above several times of the 'adequate functioning' of the market as a task to be achieved by orderly macro-motions and interlocking behavioural and motivational patterns, possibly supported by measures of public policy. This implies that orderly macro- and micro-motion and thus predict-ability, though necessary conditions for constructing an economic theory, are by themselves insufficient ones. Assume, for example, a perfectly periodic business cycle with the same amplitudes and durations of the phases repeated in unbroken sequence, but in which the stagnation phase each time approaches the level of zero output and employment. Although such a process would be fully predictable, it would be rejected as incompatible with another kind of 'order'. This second type of order refers to those macro-states that will accomplish a certain 'purpose' or 'goal'—in the case above, the steady employment of the average member of the economic society in question and his steady provision with goods and services.

There is no logical argument by which we could refute a radical positivism interested only in the explanation and prediction of market movements 'wherever they might lead'. But it can hardly be doubted that some notion of the level of *aggregate* provision that is to arise from the interplay of micro-motions underlies the entire history of economic doctrines, even if it has been conceptualized only recently in the theorems of welfare economics. To put it differently, macroeconomic states and processes have always been interpreted as something more than mere chance aggregations of events. They have been treated as phenomena of 'organization'—whether autonomous organizations such as the self-regulating market, or contrived organizations held together through planned controls.

Therefore, the orderliness of a particular economic event does not consist solely in its regularity and consequent predictability. At the very least the event must also be compatible with the prime purpose of every economic organization—to wit, macro-provision through an appropriate use of available resources. (I intentionally do not speak of 'optimum' provision or of the 'efficient' use of resources. Over and above a socially accepted minimum of subsistence, in principle any level of output produced by a technically suitable segment of the available resources and distributed in socially approved shares may satisfy the goals of a particular economic system.)

At the same time, once this is admitted, there is no denying that the ongoing 'revolution of expectations' in mature as well as developing countries progressively narrows the acceptable range of provision and employment levels. This development is of great importance for the relationship of regularity of motion and predictability to goal adequacy. At first sight these seem to be quite separate aspects of an inclusive definition of economic 'order'. As our earlier example has shown, we can have perfect regularity of motion combined with extreme goal inadequacy. Conversely, so long as low levels of output and employment are accepted as macro-goals, we can conceive of highly irregular and thus unpredictable motions as compatible with goal-adequate states and processes. But since irregular motions are bound to impair allocative as well as productive efficiency, orderliness of motion turns into a prerequisite of goal adequacy once the socially tolerable provision and employment levels rise above a certain threshold. There is little doubt that, in the mature economies of the West, this threshold has reached the point where a degree of motional disorder that in the nineteenth century would have been accepted with animistic fatalism, is no longer compatible with prevailing welfare aspirations. Or to put it differently:

under prevailing conditions, irregular and thus unpredictable economic processes are bound to lead to socially intolerable states of provision.

What Are the Limits of Economic Prediction?

It is the contention of classical and neoclassical economics that, disregarding minor reservations, the decentralized decisions of the marketers, when free of political and contractual constraints, will bring about macro-states and macro-processes that exhibit 'order' in this inclusive sense. All micro-movements are supposed to pursue a fully predictable, self-correcting and self-limiting course, tending toward the establishment of a network of balances conceptualized as 'macro-equilibrium', a state which represents the production–consumption optimum attainable with the given resources under the prevailing order of income distribution. We shall presently examine the implicit sociological and technological assumptions on which this optimistic verdict rests. At this point, however, we are interested in appraising the usefulness of classical and neoclassical models as paradigms for predicting the course of contemporary industrial market processes.

Nothing is simpler than to compile a long list of failures in prediction if the above-stated criterion—accurate forecasting of the *direction* of macro- or micro-movements—is applied to the cyclical changes in the United States over the last two decades. I have dealt with this issue extensively in my book,[6] pointing out there that even the showpiece of recent predictive efforts—the Kennedy tax revision—proves inconclusive, since the upturn in investment preceded the actual tax reduction by a year. And the tug-of-war about the imminence of inflation or deflation that rages while this is being written in December 1966, does not inspire any more confidence in our ability to predict.[7]

In this connection, preliminary results obtained from a forecasting model that postdates the publication of *OEK* teach an even more impressive lesson. I refer to the Quarterly Econometric Model for the United States, developed from Professor Klein's original model by the Office of Business Economics in the Department of Commerce.[8] The model, dealing with the period from 1953 to 1965, has managed to circumvent some of the basic obstacles that usually hamper economic forecasting. It is actually concerned with 'postdiction', because a system of simultaneous equations incorporating what are regarded as the strategic cause–effect relationships is tested *ex post* on statistical material available from observations of the past. This procedure has made it possible to assign to the exogenous variables their actual values. Moreover, the results concern the very period that contained the data to which the model's equations were originally fitted. In spite of these special characteristics, both of which carry a highly favourable bias, the predictions of cyclical turning points have consistently proved to be wrong when made more than two quarters ahead.

Still, in trying to account for these failures, the champions of modern predictive techniques offer some weighty counterarguments. Do we not meet with similar difficulties, they ask, in meteorology—difficulties which the workers in that field are confident of overcoming with the improvement of their research tools? Should we not therefore check our impatience in an enterprise like econometrics that is only two or three decades old? Moreover, is it not true that the observations on which the traditional hypotheses are to be tested reflect an empirical state of affairs in which growing imperfections of competition have removed a prime condition of the traditional model: unconstrained freedom of decision making on the part of the micro-units?

In deference to such apologies I have fallen back in *OEK* on some general methodological considerations that offer certain criteria for the predictability of economic events *independent* of the usefulness of any particular technique. These considerations centre in the fact that economic systems are 'open' systems in a very special sense.

As conventionally understood,[9] an open system is a configuration in which the interplay of the intrasystemic forces—the core process— cannot be insulated from the impact of extrasystemic or environmental factors. Under this aspect the comparison of economics with meteorology seems pertinent, since in both cases the nature of the research object makes it impossible to subject the intrasystemic variables to artificial isolation in the laboratory. And yet the analogy begs a fundamental question. If what we observe are always the results of the 'impure' experiments that nature and history perform for us— experiments in which intra- and extrasystemic variables are inseparably joined—how can we know that there is any independent core process on which a theory can be built?

As a matter of fact, a satisfactory answer to this question can be given as far as meteorology is concerned.[10] There all the forces, however complex their interplay may be, obey the laws of physics and chemistry, laws which themselves have been tested outside the context in which the meteorologist uses them. In other words, the behaviour of the elementary variables is not in doubt, and the true problem of the researcher consists in making the set of such variables inclusive enough to cover all essential influences. This is not an easy task, but it is a technical rather than a theoretical one whose solution is greatly facilitated by modern computers.

Alas, the economist has no such means of testing the elementary laws of motion outside of the economic circuit. And even if he had, he would only run up against another difficulty which his fellow workers in the physical sciences are apparently spared. A simple example will illustrate the salient point. To predict the actual movements of a projectile, the physicist must 'add' to the impact of the intrasystemic forces acting on a body falling freely in a vacuum the retarding effect of the atmosphere, the deflection due to movements of the air and the measurable influence of any other relevant extrasystemic factor. Can we, in analogy with this procedure, predict the effect of a tax reduction on aggregate demand by adding to the current flow of spending a flow equal to the size of the tax relief of business and public, minus an estimated amount of this increment withheld from circulation, plus or minus any monetary flow which other extrasystemic forces may set in motion or shut off?

Suppose that all these latter influences can be strictly calculated. We will still arrive at a confirmable prediction only if, in analogy with the situation in mechanics, the tax reduction and the other extrasystemic changes *will not in turn affect the behavioural forces that govern the current flow of spending*. But is it permissible to transfer the postulate of 'non-interaction' between intra- and extrasystemic forces from physics to economics?

Let us suppose that in 1963 investors and consumers had interpreted the proposed tax cut as a public confession of grave trouble ahead—a response which was in fact feared by some highly experienced governmental experts. The total flow of spending, rather than rising in anticipation of a boom, might then have dropped well below the level prevailing before the tax cut. This is, of course, precisely the manner in which private investment reacted to increased public spending during the New Deal. All this only restates for a specific case what was pointed out in general terms earlier when market expectations were defined as common-sense predictions on the part of the economic actors. For it is just here that all methodological analogies between physics and economics break down. These analogies overlook 'the difference between insensitive particles responding blindly though lawfully to blind stimuli, and purposeful actors who "move" only after they have interpreted their field of action in terms of their goals and their common-sense knowledge'.[11] And in these interpretations the impact of the environmental factors plays a strategic role.

As a matter of fact, the interdependence between the forces of the core process and those emanating from the environment is still closer. Not only are all significant *changes* of the extrasystemic variables bound to affect the intrasystemic ones, but even in a *changeless* environment, behaviour and motivations acquire their strength and direction from the continuous impact which natural, social and technical factors exert on what for purely didactic purposes have been set apart as 'economic' phenomena. For this reason economic systems are 'open' in a more fundamental sense than is true of any physical system including meteorology. Not even ideally can the autonomous economic core processes be treated as closed, and the validity of the results of 'mental experiments' based on the *ceteris paribus* condition cannot be taken for granted beyond the particular set of variables from which they are derived. Rather, theoretical generalizations and, especially, predictions are contingent on what environmental factors do to the core factors of behaviour and motivation from case to case. If their impact creates and maintains 'order' in the inclusive sense defined above, theory and predictability are assured. But when the uncontrolled impact of the environment tends to induce 'disorderly' micro-behaviour, the viability of the industrial market, as well as its theoretical comprehensibility, depends on our ability to devise controls that, in fact and not only by methodological fiction, 'close' the system against disruptive forces.

Disorder in Mature Industrialism

We now arrive at the crucial issue. It is my contention that orderly motion of the *intra*systemic variables—behaviour and motivation—although characteristic of the early phase of industrial capitalism, no longer prevails in the key sectors of contemporary markets. This is equivalent to asserting that the behavioural and motivational premises on which all classical and neoclassical theorizing rests are progressively losing realistic significance.

The premises in question are, at the behavioural level, the appropriate negative-feedback responses that hold all economic motions to an equilibrating course. These responses have been formalized in the so-called 'law of supply and demand', and are supposed to arise as the joint effect of two motivational subpatterns: first, the action directive of maximizing pecuniary receipts and minimizing pecuniary expenditures—what in *OEK* has been defined as the 'extremum principle'—and secondly, what is described in *OEK* as 'stabilizing expectations'—namely, price expectations with less than unit elasticity, the limit being zero elasticity, and quantity expectations with positive elasticity.[12] As a result, a present rise in price will induce buyers, in the interest of minimizing expenditures, to shift purchases from the present to the future—that is, to reduce demand. Sellers on their part will be induced, in the interest of maximizing receipts, to shift sales from the future to the present—that is, to increase supply.[13]

There is no doubt that these premises underlie all traditional economic analyses, including the main body of the Keynesian system, not to mention the bulk of the econometric models employed for prediction. What is more difficult to demonstrate, having become for this reason the target of a good deal of criticism, is my contention that, on the one hand, these premises did depict the actual state of affairs in early capitalism, and on the other hand, they do not do so today.

To the extent to which the 'facts of life' are to give support to these assertions, it is easier to prove the latter thesis, if only because we know so much more about the behaviour and motivation of contemporary marketers. My book enumerates in some detail the many incentives which today contend with the single-valued extremum principle.[14] As the reader can convince himself, this was not meant to deny that a subjective desire to maximize pecuniary receipts is still the dominant action directive of business. *The essential point is that such maximization has itself lost its classical determinacy*, because the time span over which profits are to be maximized can no longer be defined once and for all. In the modern technical and organizational environment, indivisibility of resources, periods of investment and production, the size of financial commitments, etc., vary from branch to branch, possibly from firm to firm, and even in the same firm from time to time. Consequently, *opposite actions, such as an increase or decrease of output, or the raising or lowering of prices, can each be justified as the most promising step for profit maximization.*

The same indeterminacy of the economic time horizon has undermined the stability of expectations, inducing divergent actions even under the rule of the same action directive whenever the evaluation of future market conditions changes. There is, in addition, a disturbing feedback effect from uncertain expectations to action directives, because a lower level of profits that is expected with greater certainty may well become preferable to a higher but less certain one.

Altogether I feel on safe ground in speaking of a wide spectrum of action directives and expectations as prevailing in the modern scene, in stark contrast to the simplistic assumptions of traditional economics. If this is granted, it may appear to be a question of minor importance whether in an earlier stage of industrial capitalism actual behaviour and motivations conformed more closely to the premises of classical and neoclassical economics. This would indeed be so were it not that the thesis offers important clues to the fundamental causes of the present 'disorder' in market behaviour and the resulting impasse in traditional theory.

Briefly, the thesis of a more orderly motion of the processes of early capitalism is derived from the recognition of certain social and technical determinants of marketers' motivations, determinants which tended to bring the latter in conformity with the theoretical postulates of the extremum principle and of stabilizing expectations. Among these determinants were, first, the *automatic pressures* exerted on the action directives of the several social strata by mass poverty, unbridled competition and an intellectual and moral climate favouring the accumulation of wealth, which made the maximization of receipts and minimization of expenditures a condition of economic if not physical survival. A second determinant was the then-prevailing *mobility of resources* that resulted from the smallness and non-specificity of capital equipment and the newly won 'free circulation of labour from one employment to another' (Adam Smith). This mobility very much shortened the time horizon for adjustment to changes in demand and technology—a prime condition for stabilizing expectations in a *laissez-faire* market. A third and supplementary determinant took the form of what in *OEK* is defined as *automatic escapements*, in particular the rising rate of growth through rapid population increase, a steady stream of innovations and the opening of new markets. Through constant stimulation of aggregate demand, these escapements compensated for temporary dislocations and strengthened the stability of expectations by limiting the amplitude and duration of cyclical downswings.

It must be admitted that the empirical data referring to the actual incentives and expectations of that period are much too scanty to serve as a reliable test for the above hypothesis, but they certainly do not contradict it. Moreover, the traditional formulation of the law of supply and demand, in which the classical premises about economic motivations are embodied, dominated the folklore of that age and even today expresses the 'conventional wisdom' with which the average businessman tries to interpret his experience.

That these attempts are not too successful is not surprising in the light of what was said above about the growing indeterminacy of profit maximization, and about the prevailing uncertainty of expectations. Nowadays, rising prices are often accompanied by rising demand, and falling prices, rather than by the 'correct' response of rising demand, by falling demand. What is important is the fact that such divergences of economic motion from the model of classical and neoclassical economics can be easily understood once we take note of the striking historical changes in the original determinants of action directives and expectations. Practically all the social forces that once combined to exert pressure toward extremum motivation have greatly weakened. The consummation of the Industrial Revolution and the democratization of the Western social systems have liberated the masses from the bondage of extreme scarcity; self-organization of producers and interventions of governmental policy culminating in the public controls of the welfare state have mitigated the fierceness of competition, and the earlier system of cultural values extolling acquisitiveness is giving way to what, by the criterion of the classical laws of the market, must be judged as capricious behaviour. At the same time large-scale technology and the long-term financial commitments it demands, coupled with the spread of monopoly in the markets of goods and productive services, are progressively immobilizing the flow of resources, thus extending the time span over which dispositions must be made, as well as reducing the subjective certainty and objective accuracy of business expectations. On the other hand, persistent international tensions and political unrest in many underdeveloped regions hamper the exploitation of vast potential investment opportunities, thus lessening the effectiveness of one of the main escapement mechanisms which had fostered stabilization in an earlier era.

Most of these changes can be taken as symptoms of an affluent society, and as such the inherent 'disorder' of modern industrial markets represents a significant victory of Western man over his environment and a breakthrough into a new realm of freedom. However, we have received ample warning that we must not blindly surrender to this liberation of the behavioural forces. If anything, the Great Depression taught us a lesson about what is likely to happen to an industrial market society that is no longer disciplined by the automatic constraints of the past and, at the same time, lacks an arsenal of compensatory contrived controls. The shock of this experience marks the turning point toward political economics as here understood, both as a new theoretical frame of reference and a new practice of public policy.

THE CONSTRUCTIVE FUNCTION OF POLITICAL ECONOMICS[15]

The Instrumental–Deductive Method

From the outset it was emphasized that political economics, like traditional economics, is a theoretical science. As such it tries to derive a past state of the system (explanation) or a future state (prediction) from the knowledge of a given state (initial conditions) and from some 'law of motion'. The difference between the two approaches lies in the manner in which the law of motion and its more remote determinants are established. In traditional economics either they result from a process of induction—that is, from the generalization of observations concerning, say, actual behavioural and motivational patterns—or they are postulated as heuristic principles independent of any observation, as, for example, the extremum principle is treated in 'positive' economics. Still, whatever their origin, these generalizations or postulates serve as fundamental assumptions or highest-level hypotheses, and as such belong among the knowns of economic reasoning from which the unknown states of the system can be deduced.

As our critical comments have shown, political economics denies that, under the conditions of contemporary capitalism, either observation of actual phenomena or heuristic postulation can come up with highest-level hypotheses capable of functioning as 'once-and-for-all' valid premises from which confirmable predictions can be derived. Rather it insists that the actual forces that rule economic movements and, in particular, bring about a change in their direction, cannot be known *a priori*, but themselves fall in the category of unknowns. Therefore, a major task of political economics consists in devising an analytical technique through which these unknowns can be determined.

In order to understand the precise role of this technique, which I have called *instrumental inference* (or, as now seems to me preferable, instrumental *analysis*), we should compare it with the part played by induction in the traditional procedure of the so-called 'hypothetico-deductive' method. In the practical employment of this method, emphasis rests on deduction: that is, on the 'progressive' inferences that can be drawn from the premisses—the alleged laws of economic behaviour and motivation—to conclusions concerning past or future states of the system. In other words, once these premises have been established, they are taken for granted, and their validity is no longer checked each time a concrete explanation or prediction is to be undertaken. But this concentration on deduction when it comes to the *application* of a theory must not blind us to the fact that in the original act of theory *formation*, the premises of the deductive syllogism, are themselves unknown and must be determined by a 'regressive' procedure from known observations.

In the reasoning of political economics, instrumental analysis is equivalent to this original act of regression in the conventional method. It too searches for explanatory hypotheses which subsequently can serve as premises in a deductive syllogism. And it applies the same procedure, arguing backward from a given phenomenon to its determinants. We shall presently see that such terms as 'given phenomenon' or 'determinant' take on a new meaning in instrumental analysis and that, substantively, we move there in quite another dimension of experience. But awareness of some formal similarity between the hypothetico-deductive method and what is called here the instrumental–deductive method may facilitate the understanding of the latter.

Perhaps the easiest access to the core of instrumental analysis is through the inclusive concept of *order* we established earlier. It will be remembered that this concept combined the 'positive' notion of order of state and motion with the 'normative' notion of the satisfactory functioning of the economy as a 'system'—satisfactory, that is, when judged by criteria such as a stipulated state of resource utilization, aggregate output, income distribution, etc. Now it is a main characteristic of all traditional reasoning before Keynes that in concentrating on the positive study of micro- and macro-motions and the manner in which these individual motions integrated themselves into aggregate states and processes, it treated these states and processes as the more or less inexorable result of unalterable behavioural forces. This did not exclude the *ex post* evaluation of this result under the normative aspect referred to, nor did it rule out attempts to bring the outcome of the autonomous operation of the market in line with accepted welfare goals through measures of public control. But the idea that such goals might serve as *ex ante yardsticks* for the conscious *shaping* of the macro-states and -processes would have been regarded as a collectivist anomaly and as such incompatible with the nature of decentralized decision-making.

It is perhaps the most radical of Keynes's many innovations that he broke with this tradition. The following quote taken from *OEK* expresses what seems to me his decisive turn in the direction of instrumental analysis:

Though [Keynes'] immediate problem is the disequilibria and pseudo-equilibria engendered by lapses of the market from the state of full employment, he does not confine himself to merely explaining and predicting these events which have no place in the orthodox model. By demonstrating that equilibrium and equilibration in the traditional sense are the exceptions rather than the rule in the real world, he has restored awareness of the normative character of these notions. And the entire analytical effort reveals itself as ultimately devoted to the task of determining the requirements for the attainment of a macro-goal—full employment—which is postulated independently of actual experience. Moreover, when the major condition for such attainment turns out to be the substitution, in the sphere of investment, of a novel behavioral force for the traditional decision-making of the micro-units, the realm of instrumental analysis has been entered.[16]

Instrumental analysis is, then, a generalization of Keynes's concern with the requirements for the attainment of full employment; it extends the range of macro-goals, for which the requirements are to be determined, to any conceivable state or process stipulated as desirable. And it systematically analyses these requirements—or, as we shall henceforth call them, *conditions suitable for goal attainment*—into their macro- and micro-components. In doing so, instrumental analysis 'inverts' the theoretical problem by treating some of the knowns of traditional analysis as unknown and, conversely, by treating the major unknowns of traditional analysis—the terminal states and processes—as known. Or to state the same idea in a different form, the traditional procedure of deriving an effect from given causes is transposed into a procedure by which suitable means are derived from given ends. Under this aspect, instrumental analysis can be called the *logic of economic goal seeking*.[17]

In explicating this logical structure we begin with the *unknowns*. They are enumerated here in the sequence in which instrumental analysis tries to determine them, each subsequent step depending on the successful accomplishment of the prior one: (1) the *path* or the succession of macro-states of the system suitable to transform a given initial state into a stipulated terminal state; (2) *patterns of micro-behaviour* appropriate to keeping the system to the suitable path; (3) *micro-motivations* capable of generating suitable behaviour; and (4) *a state of the environment* including, possibly though not necessarily, political controls designed to stimulate suitable motivations.[18]

These unknowns are to be determined with the help of the following *knowns*: (1) the *initial state* of the system under investigation; (2) a *macro-goal* specified as a terminal state, either by stipulating the 'numerical values of the target variables' (Tinbergen) or by stipulating the qualitative interrelations among the target variables in terms of, say, a *Pareto* optimum, full resource utilization, or a steady rate of growth; and (3) certain *laws, rules and empirical generalizations* with whose help the suitability of means for the attainment of ends can be established.

The specific procedure by which the unknowns can be derived from the knowns will be illustrated below in an elementary example. But first a brief comment is due on the role that is assigned here to the macro-goals.

The Terminal State as Datum

The 'inversion' of the analytical procedure referred to above finds one expression in the change of role of the terminal state from the major unknown into a datum. This change is less striking if we compare instrumental analysis, as we should, with its methodological counterpart: inductive rather than deductive inference. Still, there remains an important difference between these two regressive procedures, which concerns the nature of the 'facts' from which they taken their bearings. In the case of induction these facts are *observed* terminal states—namely, the realized effects of causes to be discovered. In sharp contrast, instrumental analysis starts out from a *stipulated* terminal state which (except in the marginal case when the macro-goal is stipulated as preservation of the initial state) is beyond present observation and which, whenever political economics fails to solve its problem, may not even become observable in the future.

This is not to imply that the choice of an economic macro-goal is an arbitrary act. In the concluding section of this paper a few words will be said about this problem. But it is intuitively obvious that such a discussion will carry us beyond the realm of facts and factual relations into the region of value judgements—a region in which discursive thinking, and thus scientific inquiry as the modern mind understands it, cannot by themselves offer final answers. At any rate, the processes by which goals are chosen are not the subject of *economic* studies, and in the latter the macro-goals of instrumental analysis would have to play the role of data, even if reason or revelation—philosophy or theology—were able to present us with 'intersubjectively demonstrable' criteria.[19]

However, there is another issue connected with the choice of macro-goals that poses a genuine scientific problem. It is mentioned in *OEK* as an afterthought,[20] but deserves stronger emphasis as a preparatory stage of instrumental analysis proper. It refers to the implicit assumption that the different aspirations of a goal setter are mutually compatible and can be translated into a consistent and realizable set of targets.

For certain types of goals, such as those that are concerned with a rearrangement of employed or latent resources, these prerequisites are in the nature of the case always fulfilled. This is not so, however, if for example a specific level of output or a certain rate of growth is stipulated, especially if the terminal state is further qualified by optimization criteria, such as the maintenance of a certain level of consumption or of stable prices. In all such cases the search for the suitable means must be preceded by a study of the compatibility of the several goals with one another and with the stock of available resources. Fortunately, the various techniques of mathematical programming are providing us with a growing arsenal of tools with whose help the 'feasibility' of a programme can be established, taking into consideration all encountered and stipulated constraints.

In passing, it should be noted that such complementarity between instrumental analysis and mathematical programming is by no means accidental. Both procedures are goal oriented, even if the analytical interest of mathematical programming, like that of welfare economics, is more limited. This interest is confined to the technical arrangements through which a stipulated bill of goods materializes or some objective function is maximized or minimized, while it disregards the behavioural and motivational forces at work. Under this aspect the complementarity of the two procedures is mutual: mathematical programming provides the ground from which instrumental analysis takes its bearing, and the latter transforms the technocratic insights of the former into genuine socioeconomic knowledge.

What Laws and Rules Link Ends and Means?

No other proposition relating to instrumental analysis has aroused as critical a response as did the alleged contradiction in my asserting, on the one hand, that there are today no reliable laws of economic behaviour on which predictions can be based, and, on the other hand, that it is possible to derive, from the knowledge of an initial and a stipulated terminal state, paths and forces suitable to transform the former into the latter. What else is it but a prediction, the critics ask, if a particular behaviour pattern is selected as suitable to set the system on a path that will lead to a stipulated goal? Or, more concretely, how does one know that a rise in the rate of investment is a suitable means of promoting employment, or that the incentive of receipt maximization coupled with positive elasticities of price and quantity expectations will be suitable to stimulate investment decisions? To make such statements, is it not necessary to appeal to laws and rules that relate specific means to specific ends, and to derive the latter as effects from the former as causes?

Far from denying any of these propositions, I am in full agreement on this point with my critics, as I have pointed out in several passages.[21] At the same time I have insisted that the laws and rules which permit us to predict what means are suitable for the attainment of a given end are of a nature quite different from what passes in traditional economics as laws of economic behaviour, such as the law of supply and demand. At this point let me briefly indicate the nature of these differences, and subsequently discuss the details at greater length.

(1) The relationship between ends and means is a problem of technology in the broadest sense. Applied to the realm of economics, in which the relation of matter as a means to human ends plays a strategic role, the problem is one of material technology. Therefore, once the ends, including their hierarchical order, are stipulated, the suitability of means is determined, first of all, by the currently known rules of engineering.

(2) Knowledge of such engineering rules, and of certain mathematical theorems that permit the determination of suitable quantitative relations, is all that is required to establish both goal-adequate paths and, within a given sociopsychological environment, goal-adequate behaviour. Since the question of whether the goal-adequate path and behaviour actually materialize is *not* posed at this stage, there is no need for any 'laws of behaviour' of the type that states: If behaviour A occurs, then behaviour B will follow. Rather the 'law' implied in these engineering rules states: If behaviour A occurs, the state C will follow.

(3) For the determination of goal-adequate motivations, it is necess-

ary to take into account, in addition to a knowledge of goal-adequate behaviour, a psychological hypothesis that relates specific motivations to specific behaviour. However, if accepted at all, this hypothesis is of such generality that its validity extends far beyond the economic realm.

(4) Only when instrumental analysis regresses to the point where economic motivations are to be related to environmental factors—a step that is necessary if subsequently the deductive part of political economics is to be completed—does a causal problem arise that is formally comparable with, but substantively quite different from, the cause–effect relations formulated in the laws of traditional economics. Now let us consider these four points *in extenso*.

(1) *The role of technology*. In placing the technological aspect of economics in the centre of instrumental analysis, I do not wish to intimate that economics is nothing but technology, or that the investigation of man–matter relations is its only concern. Outside of the methodological fiction of a Crusoe economy, all real economic processes are the combined result of technological and sociological forces, so that the man–matter relationships always operate through the prevailing man–man relationships. But this does not alter the fact that, once we have stipulated a definite state of provision with goods and services—that is, a feasible programme of production and/or distribution—the search for the suitable means is first of all a study of the suitable materials, devices and processes—in a word, a technological problem. From this it follows that the sociopsychological forces that must be called upon for the realization of the stipulated programme are themselves suitable only to the extent to which they are compatible with, and promoters of, the technological prerequisites.[22]

(2) *Engineering rules as instrumental criteria for path and behaviour*. Technological relations, such as those that determine the suitability of specific materials, devices and processes for the realization of a feasible programme of production and distribution, are governed by rules of engineering, understood in the comprehensive sense of physical, chemical and biological manipulations. These rules themselves are derived from the apposite laws of nature, which thus reveal themselves as the ultimate determinants of instrumental relationships. To these determinants the rules governing socioeconomic relations—behavioural and motivational patterns—will have to *adapt* themselves if the stipulated goals are to be attained.

In Chapter 11 of *OEK* I have demonstrated this proposition on three test cases: maintaining a stationary process, stabilizing a market economy in the sense of raising it from a level of underutilization to that of full utilization of resources, and balancing a system undergoing growth by assuring continuous absorption of resource increments and of increases in productivity. In particular, it could be shown that application of the pertinent engineering rules to the creation of characteristic equalities and inequalities among the components of the system is all that is required for the determination of the *path*—that is, a sequence of states of the aggregate suitable for transforming the initial into the terminal configuration. I cannot repeat this demonstration within the limits of this paper. All I can do here is to illustrate it briefly with reference to the simplest—but for that reason least realistic—example: stationary equilibrium. For a discussion that goes beyond an elementary exercise, the reader must consult the original text.

For our purposes stationary equilibrium must be understood, not as a methodological device, but as the structural model of an economic macro-goal. What is singular in this model is the fact that the initial state is structurally identical with the terminal state or, speaking in terms of a process, that the path of the system presents itself as a steady sequence of identical states.

Since by assumption we deal with an industrial system in which all productive processes are supposed to require the employment of real capital as an input, the stationary structure of production can be conceived as a three-sectoral model. Disregarding the input of natural resources, we can say that in each sector certain quantities of labour and fixed capital or equipment goods combine to produce specific outputs, the sum of all sector inputs exhausting the available supply of resources so that full utilization is continually maintained. We also disregard the 'vertical' order of the stages in which, in each sector, natural resources are gradually transformed into finished goods. The outputs are then all finished goods, which consist of three physical types: primary-equipment goods issuing in sector I and capable of producing equipment goods, secondary-equipment goods issuing in sector II and capable of producing consumer goods, and, finally, consumer goods issuing in sector III. For simplicity it is assumed that the specificity of the three types of output is absolute.

At first sight one might suspect that all that can be said about the path suitable for maintaining such a stationary process is that there must be continuity of the processes of production in the three sectors. Such continuity—the maintenance of well-circumscribed engineering processes—is certainly a necessary condition, but it is by no means sufficient. Continuity of outputs presupposes continuity of inputs. As far as labour input is concerned, we may conceive of it as a metaeconomic issue, treating the steady 'replacement' of 'worn-out' labour as a datum. We certainly cannot do so with regard to equipment.

Rather the assumed tripartite structure of production is a consequence of the technological fact that the provision of equipment is an intraeconomic problem, equipment being not only an input but also an output. In other words, continuous output of consumer goods in sector III is conditional on the steady replacement of worn-out secondary equipment through the steady output of such equipment in sector II. In turn, such output of secondary equipment depends on the condition that the primary equipment, which produces secondary equipment in sector II, is steadily replaced from the output in sector I. But sector I can provide such replacement only if its own equipment stock is steadily maintained. This amounts to the further condition that the aggregate output in sector I must be large enough steadily to replace the worn-out equipment in both sectors I and II.

From these elementary observations it follows that, to maintain steady production in the system, not only must each sector produce its respective output but parts of this output must be 'moved' by other engineering processes from the producing sector into some 'utilizing' sector. The same is obviously true of the output consisting of consumer goods, whose aggregate must be distributed among the workers of all three sectors. Were we to adopt the classical position which, in some fashion, interprets the output of consumer goods as the 'fuel' that rekindles the working energy of labour, the conception of the path as an engineering process would be further strengthened.

In these physical processes in which inputs are transformed and outputs are shifted, definite quantitative relations must be maintained between inputs and outputs within each sector, between the outputs of the three sectors, and between that part of each sector's output which is applied 'at home' and that part which is 'exported' to other sectors. We can indeed conceive of the stationary path in analogy with a system of triangular trade relations for which zero surplus balances are stipulated. Obviously the size and proportions of the exchanges that bring about such zero trade balances can be determined without prior knowledge of the 'forces'—centralized or decentralized decision making and the respective behaviour patterns—through which such balances are established and maintained. In the same manner, the course of the *suitable* stationary path can be derived without any knowledge of the *actual* behaviour of the productive agents, on which, of course, the realization of such a path depends. Rather the instrumental dependence is reversed: not until we know the technologically determined path are we able to 'select' the behaviour patterns that are suitable to keep the system to that path.[23]

Thus the suitable behaviour of human agents, whether they are productive factors offering their services, managers combining these services according to productive requirements, or distributive agents moving the outputs toward their final destination as objects of consumption or replacement, is nothing but a mode of application of the pertinent engineering rules. It throws some light on the merely 'subsidiary' role which these human actions play that there is, at least in principle, an alternative means of realizing the engineering requirements: automation. I am using the term here in the general sense of all mechanical, thermal and chemical manipulations which at earlier levels of technological developments were performed by human actors. For our present purposes it is convenient to imagine complete automation of all processes of production and distribution to the point where human decision making is limited to goal setting—that is, to decisions that concern the content of the output menu and the specific techniques to be applied, and to the acts of programming the computers. Whatever probability we may want to assign to the eventual advent of such a regime, its image offers an intuitive confirmation of the fundamental thesis that, once the goal is set, the structure of the path and the operation of the active 'forces' suitable for goal attainment—human or subhuman—can be derived from the knowledge of engineering rules alone.

This is not to say that, as long as human decisions participate in the application of these rules, we can disregard the social setting in which economic processes occur when we try to establish path-adequate behaviour patterns. To take the two extremes of economic organization—monolithic collectivism and a *laissez-faire* market—it is evident that the behaviour patterns appropriate to centralized command and subordinate execution differ drastically from the anonymous price–quantity manipulations through which the market operates. One can interpret the respective behavioural patterns as elements of a vast information system and thus establish the basis for another analogy with the cybernetics of a fully automated economy. But this must not blind us to the fact that, at least in the present state of our knowledge, the 'sensorium' through which human agents communicate, the manner in which their 'responses' are elicited and the secondary responses ('sanctions') which the primary responses draw, seem radically different from the mechanical or electronic stimulus–response relations in an automated system.

In order to translate the input–output configurations that represent the path into a suitable chain of co-ordinated actions, we must know the nature of the prevailing signal system and the social rules according to which information is communicated and specific action solicited. But it must be realized that the meaning of the signals through which information is conveyed is by no means intrinsically fixed. In principle, a market is operable just as well under the rule that rising prices indicate excess supply, as under the conventional rule according to which they indicate excess demand. All that is necessary to insure an interlocking of behaviour patterns is consistency in the use of the informative symbols.

At the same time it cannot be stated often enough that even such consistency in interpretation can only tell us what action *if taken* will agree with the pre-established path; it cannot assure us that these actions *will be taken in fact*. It is true that even in a fully automated system, goal realization is threatened by mechanical or electronical failures. But the possibility of goal-*in*adequate responses is inherent in a system that must rely for its driving force on spontaneous human behaviour.

(3) *The nexus between behaviour and motivation.* This indeterminacy at the level of behavioural responses is the reason why instrumental analysis cannot stop short at the study of behaviour, but must pursue its regressive course to the level of motivation. In other words, we must inquire what motivations are suitable to induce goal-adequate behaviour. Naturally, this step leads beyond the territory where engineering rules dominate, into the realm of functional or dynamic psychology. This is not the place to embark upon a systematic discussion of the relationship between behaviour and motivation, and I certainly lack professional competence for such a task. Fortunately, all we need for our purposes is the acceptance of the hypothesis that, in the absence of external constraints, overt economic behaviour can be predicted if the underlying action directive and expectations are known. This then makes it possible to infer regressively from a known behaviour one or more motivational compounds that are suitable to induce that behaviour.

To illustrate this proposition by our previous example, we start out from a behavioural rule formulated in accord with the guidelines given above. Once the stationary path has been established (its establishment is a dynamic process with its own rules), suitable behaviour to maintain it consists in routinized repetition of the actions that achieve the physical transformations and shifts prescribed by the pertinent engineering rules. Now we ask what compounds of motivations are suitable for the establishment of such behavioural routine. Focusing on a market system, we come up with alternative answers: either the extremum incentive as action directive coupled with zero elasticity of price and quantity expectations, or homeostatic action directives coupled with the same type of expectations.

For a proof we assume—along the lines of modern stability analysis, of which our discussion is an amplification—that, accidentally, managers in the consumer-goods sector raise their demand for secondary equipment beyond their current replacement needs, and possibly, even offer higher unit prices. If the price and quantity expectations of the producers of secondary equipment are positive, the extremum incentive will induce them to expand output. Contrariwise, while striving for maintenance of asset values—a homeostatic incentive—the same expectations will induce them to contract output. Either response, instead of eliminating the accidental distortion, tends to perpetuate it. Only zero elasticity of expectations—namely, disregard of present changes in demand and price—will in either case maintain the stationary relations among the sectoral outputs, and thus assure the stability of the system.

In discussing growth processes, I have come up against a number of quite varied motivational compounds as suitable conditions for behaviour in successive stages leading to balanced growth.[24] But once the behaviour patterns themselves have been regressively derived from the engineering rules governing the path, it is, in principle, always possible to infer suitable motivational substructures.

(4) *The link between motivation and control*. Before carrying our regressive procedure to completion, we had better review what instrumental analysis has proved capable of achieving up to this point. It is meant to serve as an alternative to the traditional procedure by which the intrasystemic forces either are derived by induction or are postulated as heuristic principles. Instead, instrumental analysis derives these patterns by regressively relating a stipulated terminal state to an observable initial state. Furthermore, it does so without recourse to any 'laws of economic behaviour', but by invoking pertinent 'laws of subhuman nature' and engineering rules derived from them.

These claims appear as fully vindicated. Once we know the apposite engineering rules and the social organization that sustains the economic processes under examination (a datum which is included in the knowledge of the initial state), and once we accept the hypothesis that specific behaviour can be derived from specific motivational compounds, we indeed arrive at a precise definition of the paths and the underlying behavioural and motivational patterns that connect the initial and terminal states.

But now suppose that we were to employ the patterns thus derived as highest-level hypotheses in a deductive model, Could we expect the conclusions to yield confirmable predictions about the terminal state toward which the system in question will actually tend? The answer is obviously in the negative, since all we can assert with confidence is that the instrumentally valid intrasystemic forces will lead to the stipulated end, *provided that these forces are actually set in motion*. If, however, the forces at work at the time of observation differ from the goal-adequate ones, not only instrumental analysis but any theoretical procedure imaginable is by itself powerless to set 'capricious reality' right. Only the *practical act* of altering the autonomous course of the real economic processes by changing the underlying motivational and behavioural patterns can make reality converge toward a state of goal adequacy.

Even if this statement were to imply no more than the idea that instrumental knowledge is a useful guide for the framing of economic policy, its analytical technique would be vindicated. But much more is at stake. *Prior re-organization of economic reality in line with the instrumental findings is now a precondition for establishing a viable economic theory.* To be specific, once measures of economic policy have succeeded in changing the existing behavioural and motivational patterns into goal-adequate ones, we can indeed apply our instrumental findings in the deductive part of political economics. Thus *analysis and political practice appear as inseparately connected steps in the acquisition of economic knowledge*; this is the rationale for the use of the term 'political economics'. The instrumental–deductive method of political economics now reveals itself as a *three-stage procedure*: (1) 'resolutive' discovery of what is goal adequate; (2) 'compositive' prediction of what will happen once goal-adequate forces are active; (3) the linking together of these two theoretical stages by an intermediate practical stage in which political control makes the actual forces coincide with the goal-adequate ones.

With these comments we have implicitly answered another question: to wit, how to test the theorems resulting from the instrumental–deductive procedure. Since these theorems will be empirically true—and not merely logically consistent—only to the extent to which control succeeds in transforming real states into goal-adequate ones, testing can only be 'indirect' through confrontation of the theorems of political economics with manipulated experience. But now the objects of experience are no longer 'passively observed' as is the case in the traditional procedure. The theorems to be tested will prove true to the extent to which political action succeeds in *making* them true.

If anything, it is this linkage of theoretical analysis and political practice that sets political economics apart not only from traditional economics, but from all conventional theory formation. It introduces an engineering element into the procedure by which knowledge is generated. The methodological implications for other fields of the social sciences and perhaps even for some of the natural sciences are obvious, but cannot be explored here.

In the foregoing remarks we have linked the actualization of goal-adequate motivations to public control. But in doing so we have skipped a problem whose answer is needed to forge this link. What are the specific measures of public control which, in a given situation, are capable of transforming actual action directives and expectations into suitable ones? Though the application of such measures is a political task, the discovery of what measures are suitable for the purpose is certainly a scientific one. And we realize that the work of instrumental analysis is not completed until we have succeeded in regressing from goal-adequate motivations to suitable measures of control.

To tackle this problem, we must first place it in a wider context. When surveying the procedure of traditional economics, I advanced the hypothesis that its predictive success during the classical period of capitalism was due to a combination of exceptional environmental circumstances—automatic pressures, resource mobility, escapements —that influenced economic motivations in the direction of extremum incentives and stabilizing expectations. Such a hypothesis implies that it is, in principle, possible to trace a causal nexus from specific environmental conditions to specific economic motivations. Thus the search for an instrumental link between 'contrived pressures' of public control on the one hand and goal-adequate action directives and expectations on the other hand reveals itself as a special case of the wider problem of 'social causation': that is, the manner in which behaviour and motivation generally can be related to the 'forces' of the environment, and the strength of this relationship.

Here we are referred to another field of psychology, unfortunately one in which little progress has been made since J. S. Mill pondered the prospects of an 'ethology or science of character'.[25] There are at least three limitations to the efficacy of external influences on economic motivations. One is the multiplicity of such influences; even a highly intervention-minded public authority can subject only a limited number of them to conscious control. Another limitation consists of the 'internal influences' arising from the psychosomatic structure of the individuals concerned, which may successfully compete with the pressures from without. Third, and most important, there is the ineradicable spontaneity of human decision making, which renders compliance with the prescripts of control conditional on affirmation by the one controlled. Such affirmation in turn presupposes that the intentions of the controllers are rightly understood and, if so, that both the ends and the measures taken are approved.

In the circumstances, it is not surprising that psychology has not yet presented us with any 'laws of social causation' on which instrumental analysis could be safely based. However, this does not exclude a few empirical generalizations or rules of thumb that permit us to form an estimate of the probable effect of certain types of control on economic motivations. Thus it seems safe to presume that the effect of control will be determinate and predictable whenever (1) the macro-goal at which control aims and the specific measures it takes coincide with the 'freely chosen' micro-goals of the controlled, and/or (2) the sanctions imposed for non-compliance are severe and inescapable.

We shall presently see that these rules impose some limits on the choice of macro-goals. At this point it is worth noting that the impact which controls are likely to have on expectations is more easily predicted than the impact on action directives.

In a regime guided by political economics, *control of expectations* has two functions. The first is to spread information about the future course of economic processes among the marketers, thereby rectifying their own independent guesses and reducing uncertainty of expectations below the critical threshold. Secondly, the content of such public information—that is, the course of events predicted by the public authority—must coincide with a goal-adequate path if the new expectations are themselves to be goal adequate.

Judged by rule 1 above, there is every likelihood that such control through information will be highly effective. To quote from *OEK*:[26] '. . . every marketer is interested in improving his commonsense knowledge about his present and future field of action. Therefore . . . he can be supposed to accept gladly any public information capable of correcting the content of his expectations and reducing the uncertainty of their coming true.'

Nor is there any doubt that public information thus broadcast can be made to conform to the practical requirements. Thus, continuing the above quote from *OEK*:

Once it has established the macro-goal and the optimization criteria, the controlling authority can acquire by a process of instrumental inference precise knowledge of the adjustment processes through which the system is to move toward the postulated terminal state. Thus the successive market constellations—the future field of action of the marketers—are known at the moment when the decision about the goal is taken, and can be communicated to the prospective actors as the body of facts on which correct expectations can be built.

No such prestabilized harmony exists for the *control of action directives*. In the short run, the controllers will have to accept the prevailing incentives as data, trying to neutralize any digression from goal adequacy by compensatory public action. This presupposes a public sector so organized that it can expand at short notice whenever the private sector fails to respond in accord with goal requirements. Over the long run, the transformation of economic incentives is a problem of 'education'. In this respect the anonymous pressures of the past—poverty and unbridled competition—were probably more effective than 'humanized' sanctions of public control will ever be. The former were truly inescapable, whereas the latter can, in principle, be resisted by countervailing political power.

However, we should not underestimate the potentialities of social learning, which have been so impressively demonstrated by the change in attitude toward fiscal controls on the part of the US business community, an educational advance achieved within one generation. The example highlights the significance of an enlightened public opinion that realizes the advantages which suitable micro-responses confer on the marketers themselves. A prime responsibility in this respect falls to economic science. If today we have some reason to anticipate a more co-operative reaction to public controls on the part of all economic strata, this is due not least to the more enlightened instruction that the present generation of economic leaders has received during its college days.

The Probabilistic Nature of Political Economics

Although they do not display the rigidity of engineering rules or the strict nexus that ties specific motivations to specific behaviour patterns, there are ascertainable links that relate particular action directives and expectations to particular environmental forces, especially to public control. These links are likely to grow stronger as public understanding of what is required for goal achievement widens and deepens. Predictions about the efficacy of public controls will then prove confirmable in proportion to the strength of those links. However, this does not alter the fact that as long as we deal with humans rather than with robots, 'social' causation will be weaker than 'natural' causation. Therefore, even if engineering rules and the behaviour–motivation nexus make the instrumental analysis of path, behaviour and motivations fully determinate, the last link in the regressive chain—suitable controls—can be established at best only with a high degree of probability.

This reservation hardly touches the instrumental part of political economics, whose earlier steps are unaffected by the uncertainties that surround the last step. But it has an important bearing on the deductive part, where the instrumental findings are applied as highest-level hypotheses. It is true that these hypotheses now have an empirical basis that the heuristic principles of traditional economics lack. Once the intermediate stage of the political–economic procedure—the activation of controls—has successfully been completed, a new reality confronts us which is 'ready made' for confirmable predictions. Still, the probability limitations that attach to the effect of controls on economic motivations are necessarily transferred to the highest-level hypotheses and thus to the predictive conclusions derived from them. Therefore, the explanations and predictions offered by political economics are essentially probabilistic.

From this one might draw the conclusion that political economics has little predictive superiority over traditional economics, since both are limited to stochastic propositions. Such a conclusion would miss the essential point made earlier, that it is precisely the *degree* of indeterminacy, as measured by the prediction interval, that matters for the practical utility of an economic theory. Under the conditions of mature capitalism, the odds are all in favour of the instrumental–deductive approach. By setting contrived limitations to the 'aberrations' of motivational and thus behavioural patterns, political economics approximates a state in which 'there is one and only one "mode" around which the observations . . . are grouped in such a way that the mean-square deviation is relatively small'.[27]

These considerations make us aware of the important auxiliary role which the probabilistic techniques of modern econometrics play in the context of political economics. As we now see, the doubts expressed earlier about the usefulness of these techniques in the framework of uncontrolled or haphazardly controlled market processes refer really to the *data* to which dynamic econometrics is currently applied rather than to the method itself.

Even a market in good working order is likely to exhibit a considerable range of tolerance for minor deviations from the rules which adequate patterning must obey. Determining the actual range of such deviations and predicting the most probable course of the macro-process within this tolerable range will then be a legitimate task of statistical techniques.[28]

What was said in a different context about mathematical programming can now be claimed for econometrics: far from running counter to the procedure of political economics, both approaches are indispensable in making the instrumental–deductive method an effective tool for economic practice.

At long last we are in a position to define precisely the logical relationship between political and traditional economics. Traditional economics is confined to the analysis of that special instance in which the automatic forces of the environment keep the 'aberrations' of the motivational and behavioural patterns within the 'tolerable' range—tolerable both for the system's steady provision and for the predictability of its movements. We saw, however, that the empirical validity of the ensuing theorems is at best limited to a passing phase in capitalist evolution. Contrariwise, political economics, by substituting contrived controls for automatic ones, establishes an analytical frame of reference which, *mutatis mutandis*, proves valid as an interpretation of all historical forms of economic organization. And thus one can assert that, logically, traditional economics is really contained in political economics as that marginal case in which the state of the environment makes it possible to keep controls near the zero level.

THE ECONOMIC POLICY OF POLITICAL ECONOMICS[29]

Conventional Economic Policy versus Instrumental Controls

[E]ven if most of the building blocks are available, the systematic construction of a Political Economics is a major task, and one that far transcends the scope of this study . . . Once more it must be emphasized that our purpose is didactic, and that no more is intended than a demonstration of some principles of economic reasoning within a highly simplified frame of reference.[30]

In a word, both my book and this paper move on a level of abstraction far removed from the field of economic–political action where the ideas discussed here are put to the real test.

It follows that important work remains to be done at the level of applied theory before political economics can serve as a reliable tool of policy framing. Among the major issues requiring intensive study I mention the proper balance between what in *OEK*[31] were labelled as 'manipulative' and 'command' controls, a distinction related to, though not identical with, that between indirect and direct controls; the differential measures suitable for eliciting adequate response from different socioeconomic strata; administrative techniques concerning the timing and sizing of intervention; and, last but not least, the political problems that public control of the economic process raises in democratic societies. Needless to add, the answers to these questions are bound to vary with the level of economic development and political maturity.

At this point I will confine myself to clarifying a distinction that was implied in my earlier comments on policy framing, the distinction between *instrumental controls* and measures of *conventional economic policy*. After all, in a general sense, economic controls have formed part of capitalist organization from its very beginning. Even if earlier measures of intervention were of a piecemeal and *ad hoc* nature, modern monetary and fiscal controls are certainly system oriented. What then is the peculiar characteristic of instrumental controls?

[Conventional controls] take the behavior of the micro-units for granted, confining themselves to modifying the natural and institutional framework within which micro-actions take their course. Making use of a physical analogy one can say that these controls operate like an outside force which compresses or releases a spring but leaves the elastic forces in the spring itself unchanged. In contrast, control as here understood includes a public policy that concerns itself with the shaping of the behavioral patterns themselves—by influencing the purposive and cognitive motivations of the actors immediately or, in a roundabout way, through reorganization of the system's structure.[32]

This is by no means to deny that measures of conventional policy—tariffs, taxation, or the monetary and fiscal controls of the new economics—are part, and an indispensable part, of the control system as applied by political economics. But though necessary, these measures are never sufficient for goal attainment. We can define them as *primary* controls, whose purpose is to modify the field of activity of the micro-units by opening or closing opportunities for transactions. But to be effective as means of goal attainment, they must be supplemented by *secondary* controls, whose purpose is to turn the responses of the micro-units in the right direction. In fulfilling this function, secondary controls cover a wider range than do primary controls, because they must govern the microeconomic response mechanism both when the stimulus consists of actions of other marketers and when it arises from measures of public policy.

After what was said above about the manner in which expectations as well as action directives can be brought under regulating influence, there is little need to detail the entire scope of secondary controls. They extend from information about the goal-adequate path to measures of persuasion and compensatory public action, not excluding in extreme cases even coercion. However, it may be helpful to illustrate their *modus operandi* through an example. Again the tax reduction under the Kennedy Administration can serve as a paradigm.

Though the tax measure was intended to stimulate the general activity of the system, no attempt was made to affect the behavioural responses and underlying expectations of investors and consumers. It was simply taken for granted that these responses would promote the policy goal, although, as was mentioned earlier, knowledgeable experts entertained grave doubts as to the repercussions of the tax cut on business psychology. In the face of such doubts, an instrumental strategy would have made marketers' responses its major target; for example, by supplementing the tax reduction with a well-advertised standby programme of public investment, which would go into effect if private spending did not rise promptly and to a sufficient degree. By thus reducing uncertainty about the trend of aggregate demand, the major obstacle to goal-adequate private behaviour would have been removed.

The literature on economic planning contains as yet little systematic exploration of the techniques of secondary control. But a cursory survey of the postwar economic policies of Scandinavia, Holland, or France gives the impression that practical experimentation is in full swing, and that the tenets of political economics, though largely unformulated, are in fact widely applied.

The Choice of Goals

I should like to conclude this essay with another word about the focal point of political economics: the choice of macro-goals. Earlier it was stressed that political economics *qua* economics must accept the stipulated goal or sets of compatible goals as data. This would be no different if, as economists, we were not wedded to 'scientific value relativism', but were prepared to commit ourselves to a definite hierarchy of goals with the apex of a *summum bonum*, as offered by rivalling theologies and philosophies. Even then our problem would be the suitability of the means rather than the validation of the ends.

So the problem presents itself as long as we are engaged in the preliminary work of instrumental analysis. But in order to advance to the level of predictive theory, we must, as we saw, pass through the practical stage in which the holders of political authority seek to modify the original institutional environment in accordance with their instrumental findings. This original environment, conceptualized as the structure of the initial state, reveals itself as a logical constraint in the analysis of the goal-adequate path. However, it is no less a practical constraint when the instrumental findings are to be applied. To give an example, it is in principle a feasible task for analysis to establish the path, the behavioural and motivational conditions, and even the controls suitable to transform a primitive subsistence economy into a mature industrial system. But when we ponder the practical application of the controls thus designed, we may come to the conclusion that the institutional transformation required would have to be purchased at the price of a social revolution which, rather than setting the primitive society on the road to development, might well throw it back to a still lower level.

What we encounter here is a conflict between a particular macro-goal and the socioeconomic environment from which the path toward the goal is to start. Stated in general terms, not all macro-goals are intrinsically compatible with any prevailing order of social relations. Whenever a conflict arises, we are compelled to choose between abandoning the goal or the existing order, the latter at the peril of applying means which may defeat the end.

Value absolutists may brush aside such pragmatic considerations, but

I must admit that they govern my own thinking as expressed in the concluding chapter of my book. Though I leave no doubt that the instrumental method is applicable to the elaboration of the means suitable to the attainment of *any* macro-goal, be it the size and composition of aggregate output, the level of resource utilization, the rate of growth, or the order of distribution,[33] I have confined the practical test cases selected for detailed investigation to two: full utilization of resources and balanced growth. Indeed, these particular goals pose problems of great analytical interest. But my choice was ultimately determined by political considerations. These are the only macro-goals which, I believe, are fully compatible with the institutional environment of mature capitalism.

The reasons for this belief are easy to state. Since decentralized decision making based on private ownership of the means of production is the core of capitalist organization, instrumental controls other than coercion will be effective within this framework only if the aim for which they are applied meets with the *consensus* of the large majority of micro-units. This consensus can indeed be anticipated for the two goals selected, since extending the opportunity for the utilization of present resources (stabilization) and assuring the absorption of newly accruing ones at a rising rate of productivity (balanced growth) seem to offer benefits to all.

I am aware that even in the pursuit of these goals, certain conflicts of interest may arise between particular sectors and social strata of the economy. But the ensuing resistance to public interference with the *functional* performance of the economy is certainly minor compared with the likely breakdown of consensus in the face of *structural* transformations such as the central planning of investment and output would require, not to speak of a fundamental redistribution of income and wealth. Fortunately, the politically feasible goals—stabilization and balanced growth—seem to satisfy the basic requirements for restoring to the market of mature capitalism that minimum of 'order' in the inclusive sense defined above on which the preservation of the fabric of Western society depends. Maintaining social consensus is a much more difficult and perhaps insoluble task in poor societies, which struggle not only for a more productive order but also for a more equitable one.

But it should be stressed once more that 'prudence' in the choice of macro-goals does not limit the universal validity of the scientific procedure of political economics, nor can such prudence itself be vindicated on scientific grounds. It expresses a value judgement emulating peaceful evolution even at the expense of uncompromising justice. If this reveals a conservative undercurrent in my thinking, as some critics have insinuated, I must bow to this, as to the opposite charge that my advocacy of political control of industrial capitalism 'gives aid and comfort to men who are neither wise nor gentle'. Since the political economist *contrives* his research object as much as he *observes* it, he too cannot escape the risks of decision making.

NOTES

1. Adolph Lowe, *On Economic Knowledge, Toward a Science of Political Economics*, Volume 35 of *World Perspectives*, planned and edited by Ruth Nanda Anshen (New York: Harper & Row, Publishers, 1965). Enlarged edition, with a Postscript, (New York: M. E. Sharpe Inc., 1977). For brevity I shall use the initials *OEK* when referring to the book in this text.
2. For an alternative presentation *see* Robert L. Heilbroner, 'Is economic theory possible?' *Social Research* (Fall, 1966), pp. 272–94.
3. *OEK*, Chapters 1–4.
4. Fritz Machlup, *Der Wettstreit zwischen Mikro- und Makro-Theorien in der Nationaloekonomie* (Tuebingen: J. B. Mohr [Paul Siebeck], 1960).
5. For an extensive treatment of this problem, *see* Alfred Schutz, 'Common sense and scientific interpretation of human action', in *Collected Papers*, Volume 1 (The Hague: Martinus Nijhoff, 1962), pp. 3–47.
6. *OEK*, pp. 52–6, 60–1.
7. For many more examples and for a discussion of the variety of predictive techniques employed, *see* Sidney Schoeffler, *The Failures of Economics* (Cambridge: Harvard University Press, 1955), Chapters 5 and 6.
8. *See Survey of Current Business*, US Department of Commerce, **46**, No. 5 (May 1966), pp. 13–29.
9. *See* Schoeffler *op. cit.* Chapters 4 and 8. *See also* Emile Grunberg, 'The meaning of scope and external boundaries of economics', in S. R. Krupp (ed.), *The Structure of Economic Science: Essays on Methodology* (Englewood Cliffs, NJ: Prentice-Hall, 1966), pp. 148–65.
10. Grunberg *op. cit*, p. 151.
11. *OEK*, p. 61.
12. Let me add a brief word of explanation for non-economists. What is meant by this state of expectations is that price changes are expected to be merely temporary, while quantities offered are expected to rise as prices rise and to fall as they fall.
13. For details *see OEK*, Chapter 2, Section 2.
14. *OEK*, pp. 46–9.
15. *OEK*, Chapters 5, 10, and 11.
16. *OEK*, p. 218.
17. I refrain from calling instrumental analysis a 'teleological' method of inquiry because this label is too often used to indicate that a given procedure is incompatible with causal analysis. That the instrumental approach is fully compatible with cause–effect relations follows from the subsequent application of its results to deductive inferences in which the originally unknown 'means' appear, after their instrumental determination, as known 'causes' of effects to be explained or predicted. At the same time it is true that the suitability of a 'cause' as a 'means' for bringing

about a stipulated goal cannot be judged without knowledge of the goal itself. In this sense a 'telos' enters the search procedure by which the suitable means–causes are to be discovered.

18. In order to establish full generality for this logic of goalseeking, we must speak of 'suitability', 'appropriateness', etc., rather than of 'requirements', because there are, as a rule, alternative paths, behaviour patterns, motivations and states of the environment which all can serve as means to the stipulated end. Thus we deal with sufficient rather than necessary conditions.

19. In this context I have sometimes been asked why I had to coin the term 'instrumental' analysis instead of simply speaking of 'normative' analysis in line with the recent practice of distinguishing between 'descriptive' or 'positive' and 'prescriptive' or 'normative' economics. In the latter dichotomy traditional theory is assigned to the first category, whereas welfare economics, for example, is placed in the second. My answer is that I have tried to avoid a confusion which seems to be inherent in the current terminology.

There is little danger of misunderstanding so far as the first category is concerned. But when we classify welfare economics as simply a normative procedure, we fail to take into account that it is concerned with two quite different problems whose solutions require quite different procedures. One refers to the choice of the most desirable objectives or, in another formulation, to the decision as to whether one collection of goods is greater in terms of welfare than some other collection. Such choices and decisions and the establishment of the guiding criteria indeed fall in the normative realm. But this is by no means so with the other problem of selecting the *means* for achieving these objectives or the *methods* of producing the chosen collection. These are issues that are open to discursive reasoning and are thus proper subjects of scientific analysis. This remains true even if the quest is for 'optimum' methods of goal attainment. In that case the discovery of the criteria for optimization is again a normative problem. But the subsequent application of such criteria to the selection of means is a purely analytical task.

What instrumental analysis tries to achieve parallels the analytical part of welfare economics—determining the means suitable for the attainment of given goals. And though drawing on the results of normative judgement for one of its *data*, it derives its own propositions by 'positive' reasoning.

20. *OEK*, p. 263.
21. *OEK*, pp. 141–3, 253, Chapter 11 *passim*.
22. This is not the place to reopen the dispute between the 'materialistic' and the 'praxiological' conceptions of economic theory. In *OEK*, Chapter 1, Section 2, and Chapter 8, Sections 3–5, I have restated the well-known reasons why the extension of economic theory into a 'generalized theory of choice' is bound to deprive it of any substantive content, reducing its propositions to mere tautologies. Professor Boulding's recent inclusion of painters among economic men because, just as the consumer may have to sacrifice 'a little ham for a little more eggs in a breakfast', the painter 'sacrifices . . . a little red for a little more green' (*Scientific American* (May 1965), p. 139), has only strengthened my conviction. Or are we to assume that 'optimum painting' amounts to maximization of colours by the square inch of canvas? Poor Rembrandt!
23. For details *see OEK*, Chapter 11, Sections 3–5. For a more extensive

treatment, including the quantitative determination of sector ratios and intersectoral equilibrium conditions, *see* my paper, 'Structural analysis of real capital formation', in M. Abramovitz (ed.), *Capital Formation and Economic Growth* (Princeton, NJ: Princeton University Press, 1955). [*See* Essay 2 above.

24. *OEK*, pp. 301–5.
25. *OEK*, pp. 67–8.
26. *OEK*, p. 155.
27. *See* Hans Neisser, *On the Sociology of Knowledge* (New York: James H. Heineman, Inc., 1965), p. 90.
28. *OEK*, p. 117.
29. *OEK*, Chapters 5 and 12.
30. *OEK*, pp. 250, 264–5.
31. *OEK*, pp. 148–50.
32. *OEK*, p. 131.
33. *OEK*, p. 255.

6 Economic Means and Social Ends: A Rejoinder*

The essays assembled in this volume [*EMASE* — ed.] raise a number of challenging questions. Limits of space make it impossible for me to discuss all of them in an adequate manner. Therefore, I will apply myself in the following observations to a few fundamental problems, on a satisfactory answer to which the theoretical soundness and practical relevance of a political economics as outlined in my introductory paper may well depend. [see Essay 5 above — ed.][1]

My ideas as originally formulated in the book *On Economic Knowledge* [see Essay 5 above, note 1 — ed.] have certainly not escaped the fate described by Professor Lerner—that of being rejected on the one hand as quite wrong, and, on the other hand, being played down as affirming only what is general knowledge and accepted practice. But whereas these critical responses usually follow each other as time passes, I have been exposed to them simultaneously. I shall try to defend myself to the best of my ability against the first charge. The second, however, about the absence from my 'message' of any revolutionary discoveries, I have myself stressed from the outset. Apparently the detailed description in my book of the gradual emergence of a political economics in the history of economic thought has not sufficiently clarified this point. So I should like to state once more and most emphatically that, notwithstanding certain reservations against conventional techniques of analysis and traditional economic policies, my entire undertaking aims at little more than a systematic formulation of the major trend in contemporary theory and practice. To make this implicit trend explicit, and to generalize and deepen the insights that we owe to the 'new economics' of Keynesian provenance, to the decision models of the Dutch school of econometrics, and to

---

* [In this rejoinder, Lowe reflects on the papers presented at the New School Symposium on his work cited in the opening editorial note to Essay 5 above. The proceedings were published in Robert L. Heilbroner (ed.), *Economic Means and Social Ends: Essays in Political Economics*, (Englewood Cliffs, NJ: Prentice-Hall, Inc., 1969). Below this work is referred to as *EMASE* — ed.]

other modern tool makers—these are the intentions that underlie my project.

As indicated earlier, even this modest endeavour is far from accomplished. It is the significance of these essays that they contribute notably to the furthering of this task, especially by scrutinizing closely my methodological approach, by pointing out the deeper implications, political and philosophical, of my position, and by the general fairness of their critical stance. As I did on the original occasion, I wish again to express my genuine gratitude for so productive a response to my ideas.

THE PROBLEMS UNDER DISPUTE

In order to locate the principal points at issue I will take my bearings from a comment with which Dr Machlup introduced the oral presentation of his paper. He found it characteristic of my approach that I am, at one and the same time, concerned with both the science of economics and the actual state of the Western economic systems. It is indeed true that I see the realms of economic theory and practice more closely interrelated than is customarily recognized. Of course no one denies that theoretical knowledge translated into rules for the framing of policy greatly affects economic reality. But there is a reverse and less obvious relationship, in which the actual states and processes of an economy influence our capacity for theorizing.

As I said above,[2] the link in this reverse relationship is the notion of *order* in the inclusive meanings of regularity of state and motion on the one hand, and of a satisfactory and stable level of provision on the other. The former trait defines a 'positive' concept of great generality, since it states a precondition for theoretical reasoning—that is, for generalizing explanations and predictions—in all sciences. The latter is a 'normative' concept and, as such, is limited to social research where human actions and their purposes are in the centre.

This difference in the logical status of the two constituents of economic order seems to suggest that they are also causally independent of each other. Certainly, as I pointed out earlier, one can conceive of regular and thus predictable economic movements which would result in what by modern standards would be regarded as unsatisfactory provision levels. However, the converse is by no means true, because, when judged by the same standards, satisfactory provision far from being independent of 'orderly' motions within the system, is conditional on a high degree of regularity and thus of the predictability of such motions.

This condition holds for all types of economic systems, centralized or decentralized, but it has a particular relevance for market systems. There predictability is a concern not only of the scientific observer but, before that, of the economic actors themselves who, in the absence of authoritative guidance, must be able on common-sense grounds to foresee the tendencies in their fields of action. Therefore, in an uncontrolled market, movements must be regular enough to enable the individual marketer to predict, at the least, all major changes in their *direction*. In the absence of such autonomous regularity, stable provision perforce depends on the contrived adjustment of these movements with the help of public control. But in order to choose, in a given instance, what measures of control are appropriate, we must be able to predict their effect—a task for the framer of economic policy and his scientific helpmate, the economist. Thus we arrive at the general conclusion that only economic systems whose movements are or can be made sufficiently regular to permit the prediction of major changes, will be efficient engines of provision.

On this basis we can now summarize the gist of political economics in the following propositions:

(1) The autonomous markets of industrial capitalism lack the required minimum of order. Their uncontrolled movements are too irregular for the individual marketer to predict major changes correctly and thus to achieve the interlocking patterns of behaviour which assure stability of aggregate provision.

(2) As a consequence, these markets have been progressively subjected to public control; however, without as yet displaying a satisfactory degree of stability.

(3) The main reason for this failure is the limited range of conventional market controls. These controls confine themselves to altering the micro-units' field of action by opening or closing marketing opportunities without, however, controlling their responses. I shall call such controls 'primary'.

(4) If orderly states and processes are to be brought about, to safeguard the viability of a system based on decentralized decision making, additional or secondary controls must be introduced. These must bring the response mechanisms of the marketers in accord with the behavioural requirements for stable aggregate provision.

(5) In order to discover what controls are likely to bestow order in any given instance, the first step is to specify the level and composition of aggregate provision to be obtained in a consistent set of macro-goals. From the knowledge of these macro-goals, of the initial state of the system, and of certain technological constraints, it is possible, with the help of a particular research technique called 'instrumental

analysis', to determine the goal-adequate movements of and within the system, as well as the goal-adequate motivational and behavioural patterns on the part of the micro-units, and the goal-adequate public controls that may be needed.

(6) The findings of instrumental analysis in terms of goal-adequate controls must then be applied as measures of economic policy, so that the actual motion of the system is transformed into goal-adequate motion.

(7) To the extent to which such transformation is successful, the practical demand for a satisfactory and stable level of provision will be met, as will the theoretical demand for such regularity of motion as permits generalizing explanations and predictions.

In the preceding essays, almost all of these propositions have, in one form or another, come under critical fire. They therefore offer a convenient framework for my defence. I will begin by restating the *facts* (propositions 1 and 2) that call for a transformation of traditional theory and practice in the direction of a political economics. Next comes a brief discussion of the nature of *macro-goals* and of the manner of their political stipulation, succeeded by an elaboration of the methodological principles underlying *instrumental analysis* (proposition 5). This will be followed by a review of the relationship between primary and secondary *controls* and their practical application (propositions 3, 4 and 6). Some reflections about the ultimate *criteria of goal setting*—a topic only lightly touched upon in Chapter 12 of *On Economic Knowledge* [hereafter referred to as *OEK* —ed.], but thoroughly explored in some of the foregoing writings—will bring my apology to a close.

THE FACTUAL BACKGROUND

My advocacy of a political economics and of instrumental analysis as its principal research technique derives from a particular evaluation of certain strategic facts. These facts concern the tendencies of the autonomous movements of modern industrial markets, which seem to me in conflict with the requirement of order in the sense defined above. In fact, in my book and in my position paper[3] I have gone farther by suggesting that, owing to the gradual relaxation of certain natural and social pressures and to the disappearance of some automatic escapements, and in the wake of the progressive immobilization of the industrial structure coupled with ever more rapid technological changes, these 'disorderly' tendencies are on the increase when compared with the competitive era of expanding capitalism.

It stands to reason that my diagnosis of the present state of affairs cannot be refuted by a different reading of the historical trend. Yet I readily admit that, as far as the latter is concerned, not only is the available factual material scanty but, as Dr Wallich rightly stresses, much that appears as 'new' may only reflect the growing sophistication of modern analysis. Perhaps my hypothesis will sound more plausible if one keeps in mind that it refers to the tendencies of *uncontrolled* industrial markets and should therefore not be judged by the manifestations of organized capitalism after the Second World War. Do we trust the 'self-equilibrating' market enough to acquiesce confidently in the abolition of all the micro- and macro-controls that have been installed since 1929?

But since historical evidence is inconclusive, let me concentrate on modern experience, especially since I include the recent past in my pessimistic diagnosis in spite of the widening range of public controls.

The case for a high degree of stability and predictability in modern business behaviour has been stated above by Dr Wallich,[4] and there is no better test for my own views that a confrontation with his. For this it is important that we seem to agree about the facts themselves, our disagreement beginning only when it comes to their interpretation.

A growing variety of action directives, among them the progressive substitution of 'satisficing' for 'maximizing' behaviour; uncertainty of expectations; prevalence of oligopolies and generally monopolistic manipulations and, as a consequence, a narrowing of price and wage fluctations; rapid technological progress—all these characteristics of the modern scene which Dr Wallich stresses also underlie my own argument. Dr Wallich concedes that some of them, in particular oligopolies and satisficing tendencies, reduce rather than enhance the predictability of business behaviour. But he sees compensating factors at work in the advance of professional management, interproduct competition and other antimonopolistic forces. And if administered prices and wages make the structure of the market more rigid, this should in his view only facilitate prediction.

If Dr Wallich and I draw such different conclusions from similar premises, the likelihood is that we focus on different aspects of the same phenomena. His is mainly a microeconomic discourse which studies the effect of the modern market organization on decision making in the individual firm. More precisely, his emphasis is on the professionally managed corporation, and he aptly describes the behaviour of what Professor Galbraith has labelled the 'technostructure'.[5]

There is no reason to impute to Dr Wallich the exaggerated notion Galbraith has of the significance of these oligopolistic corporations in the totality of modern business organization. If we give its due to the stratum of middle-sized enterprises, for whom the corporate form is little more than a legal convenience and whose transactions remain market bound, the range of managed predictability of costs, prices and sales shrinks considerably. More important—and this is my major objection to Dr Wallich's optimism—business planning, even at its most comprehensive, is still inadequate to establish *macroeconomic* order.

The decisive point has been well stated by Professor Meade in his review of Galbraith's book:[6]

Professor Galbraith asserts that each modern corporation plans ahead the quantities of the various products which it will produce and the prices at which it will sell them; he assumes . . . that as a general rule each corporation through its advertising and other sales activities can so mould consumers' demand that these planned quantities are actually sold at these planned prices. But he never explains why and *by what mechanism these individual plans can be expected to build up into a coherent whole* [my italics — A. L.] . . . In short, if all individual plans are to be simultaneously fulfilled they must in the first instance be consistent.[7]

In a competitive system it is, of course, the market mechanism, operating through price changes, which is supposed to bring about this consistency of business plans. Unfortunately this result can as a rule be achieved only *ex post*, and the respective adjustment processes are themselves a main cause of aggregate instability. Moreover, with the elimination of price flexibility and the weakening of competitive pressures, this adjustment mechanism is rendered inoperative, without there being any substitute as long as corporate behaviour is left to its own devices. And this is all the more so since, as even Professor Galbraith admits, 'there is no *a priori* reason why the policy pursued by any two mature corporations will be the same, for there is no reason to assume that the goals or intensity of commitment to goals will be the same in any two cases'.[8] Therefore, in contrast with a widely held opinion also voiced during our discussions, a privately planned capitalism is by no means superior to a competitive-market organization so far as predictability and macroeconomic stability are concerned.

The remedy is, of course, public control, to which Dr Wallich refers only in passing. This now leads to the cardinal question of whether existing controls, mainly derived from the 'new economics', have succeeded in overcoming the difficulties inherent in the modern industrial structure. With my critics I would agree that nowhere in the Western world has the economic process during the last generation exhibited the excessive fluctuations characteristic of the era preceding the Second World War. Moreover, a major share of fiscal and monetary controls in this achievement cannot be doubted, though rising military expenditures may have been the principal force of stabilization. For this reason neither national nor international experiences during the postwar era give any cause for complacency, not to mention the fact to which Dr Wallich and others have rightly pointed—namely, that as public insight into the manmade nature of most of our economic ills grows, we become much more politically sensitive to their social impact.

I have dealt with the relevant postwar events at length in my book,[9] and I want to refer here to only one further instance which may still be topical when this book appears. Earlier I discussed the serious gamble what was involved in the Kennedy tax reduction.[10] We are now engaged in the reverse experiment of the surtax of 1968. In rising protests over the tardiness of Congress in enacting the necessary legislation, it has been widely forgotten that, up to the end of 1967, economic experts were deeply divided as to the wisdom of a tax increase, because they could not agree on whether the likely consequences would be stabilizing or deflationary. And even now, in the summer of 1968, he would be a bold man indeed who dared to predict the ultimate effects of this surtax on the level of output and employment in 1969, leaving out of consideration any exogenous influences arising from military developments. But what I wish to stress is that this uncertainty on the part of scientific observers, as well as of investors, arises from the unpredictability of the responses of producers and consumers to this type of control. This uncertainty of response is the very basis of my argument.

As was shown earlier,[11] the same obstacle hampers experimentation with econometric prediction models. If it is true that the weak link in these models is their behaviour equations, no refinement in research techniques can yield a serious improvement in scientific macro-prediction. Only a modification of the research object itself—that is, the regularization of market behaviour—can achieve this professed aim of political economics.

THE NATURE OF MACRO-GOALS

Regularization of market behaviour is a function of public control. But one cannot exert control without being aware of the specific aims these controls are to attain. This introduces macro-goals as the fulcrum of the analysis, and leads to the 'inversion' of the conventional procedure in which terminal states are treated as unknowns to be derived from known patterns of behaviour. Now, however, order-bestowing behaviour patterns and the controls that are to establish them have become the major unknowns, which can be established only in relation to a stipulated terminal state or macro-goal.

I shall revert to the details of the 'regressive' method of analysis and its methodological justification in the following section. Here, in enlarging on my earlier remarks,[12] I should like to add some comments on the general nature of macro-goals, on the question of whether 'ends' can be stipulated independently of the 'means' with whose help they are to be realized, and on the different categories of possible 'goal choosers'. Discussion of the most fundamental problem—namely, the ultimate criteria that are to guide us in selecting the 'right' macro-goals—will be taken up later.

(1) My first concern is with dispelling a misunderstanding in Dr Machlup's rendering of my views. It relates to the question of whether pronouncements on macro-goals should be placed in the category of 'positive' or of 'normative' statements. Fortunately there seems to be agreement between us as to what the two critical terms are to mean in order to be useful in scientific discourse. To me the most plausible distinction between the two, which apparently Dr Machlup also accepts,[13] refers to statements about 'what is' as contrasted with statements about 'what ought to be', leaving alone for the moment the further questions of from whom the 'ought' is to issue, and of the criteria for his choice. In this interpretation we can also speak of the difference between factual statements and value judgements, one essential characteristic of the latter being that they 'cannot be tested by empirical procedures and cannot, therefore, be admitted into the body of positive science'.[14]

Now in the face of what I thought were unambiguous formulations to the contrary,[15] Dr Machlup takes me to task for overlooking the 'unquestionable plurality of macro-goals', choosing among which 'will always force us to engage in value judgments'. He also questions my treating these goals 'as legitimate data in positive analysis as long as they are clearly stated and are examined only in relation to the means suitable for their attainment'.[16]

The core of the misunderstanding is obviously the notion of 'data' and the precise sense in which value judgements and the macro-goals derived from them cannot be 'admitted' into the body of positive science. If Dr Machlup means to say that determination of the 'rightness' or 'wrongness' of a macro-goal is no task for positive science and that such rightness cannot be the subject of observations to be tested in accord with acknowledged scientific procedures, we are in full agreement. This does not, however, exclude any macro-goal, once it has been stipulated by some 'non-scientific' procedure, from serving as a 'premise' from which scientific reasoning can derive testable conclusions. Its logical status is then no different from that of any proposition serving as an axiom in a particular realm of knowledge. This, and this alone, is the use which instrumental analysis makes of the 'datum' macro-goal, a procedure that in Dr Machlup's own words 'does not involve the analyst's value judgement and is not normative in character'.[17]

This does not, of course, preclude further examination, logical or otherwise of such axioms, by submitting them to the critical principles of some different field of knowledge and, as I have made clear earlier,[18] I fully agree with the call for such a 'vindication of goals'. However, in line with a tradition which, I thought, had been abandoned as a result of the work of Kenneth Arrow and others, Dr Machlup assigns the function of a 'justification of values' and thus of the establishment of criteria for a choice among rivalling goals and means to a realm of knowledge called 'normative economics'. There indeed we disagree since, as I am going to explain in the last section of these comments, vindication of economic goals must be based on criteria which are relevant for every kind of social action and which therefore far transcend any field of inquiry that could legitimately be labelled 'normative *economics*'. Still, remembering Dr Machlup's sceptical verdict on welfare economics earlier in these pages, I wonder whether, notwithstanding our verbal contradictions, we are not in substantive agreement after all.

(2) In some remarks of Drs Edel, Nagel and Wallich, another doubt has been cast on my procedure of treating macro-goals as 'givens' in means analysis. Do we not, in our policies, as a rule, simultaneously pursue several macro-goals, whose feasibility and compatibility cannot be taken for granted? Do not such goals frequently change their role, so that what appears as an end in one context becomes a means in another? Moreover, do we not also apply value judgements to the selection of *means* irrespective of the instrumental test of their suitability? And more generally, does not the interdependence of all social phenomena nullify all specialist borders, thus on principle depriving the ends–means distinction of operational significance?

I have dealt with some of these questions before,[19] and will confine myself to indicating the direction in which the answers must be sought.

No doubt a set of macro-goals cannot be stipulated, as either a scientific premise or a political act, unless their feasibility and mutual consistency are assured. Mathematical programming was cited above as one of the techniques for investigating the feasibility of goals relative to the available resources, and thus as an auxiliary tool of instrumental analysis. The question of consistency raises subtler issues. To tackle them one must realize that, in the realm of economics, macro-goals are rarely incompatible in any absolute sense. What often makes them appear so is our reluctance to apply the specific means necessary for their joint realization. Take as an example the stipulation of full employment coupled with price stability, two goals which in our experience have so far proved irreconcilable. But were we willing to introduce severe wage and price controls accompanied by rationing or, in the extreme case, by the nationalization of key industries, the apparent contradiction might disappear. So it is ultimately our negative valuation of certain instrumentally adequate means that creates the semblance of incompatibility.

For this reason the real issue is how to relate the value judgements that we attach to certain means to the value judgements that underlie the selection of our goals. This is the *locus* of most practical conflicts, conflicts that can be resolved only by *another* value judgement—that is, which is of greater significance in a given instance: attaining the goal or preserving the integrity of our original evaluation of the means. Differently stated, the value criteria for means selection enter as criteria of optimization into the stipulation of the macro-goals themselves.[20]

Feasibility and compatibility studies are thus indispensable preliminaries of goal stipulation, and as such are a legitimate part of political economics. However, at the present stage in the development of social research, I expect little help in this or any other pursuit of political economics from what is widely advocated as 'interdisciplinary' work. In this respect I associate myself with a communication received from one of the participants in our discussions who himself is an advocate of a 'synthetic' approach. According to him, 'we do not appear to have a viable language or translation devices by which the different social sciences can be brought together into systematic cooperation'. This is not to deny that economic processes are embedded in a comprehensive social and cultural system and are interdependent with the latter's motion, nor that the eventual scientific conquest of this wider territory should enable us to extend and refine our specialist investigations. At the same time it should not be forgotten that all so-called metaeconomic influences can affect economic processes only through the channel of market behaviour. In other words, by ascertaining and controlling motivational and behavioural patterns as they operate *within* the economic sphere, we implicitly take care of the effects exerted by metaeconomic factors. Therefore, concentration on these intrasystemic phenomena is a legitimate shortcut.

(3) A shortcut of a different kind becomes necessary when we have to decide to whom we are to entrust the stipulation of the macro-goals. We are indebted to Dr Machlup for having shown once more in his lucid summary of the basic tenets of modern welfare economics that

any attempt at deriving such goals from the social preferences of the individual members of a larger community must fail. Even the 'heroic assumption' that we could determine the trade-off rates between all conceivable social goals acceptable to each member cannot bridge the gap between conflicting objectives. Therefore, a political decision must be 'imposed' in some sense—except in the case of a more or less perfect *consensus*, and even then the achievement of such a *consensus* is mainly a political task.

Dr Kaysen has presented us with a comprehensive survey of the political processes through which macro-goals are actually established in the framework of American institutions and, in particular, of the various roles which the 'economist as adviser' can play in this context. His paper fills a serious lacuna in my own work, and I gratefully accept it as an exemplary demonstration of the manner in which the level of abstraction of a theory can and must be lowered if it is to serve the framing and implementation of policy. But there are some issues in Dr Kaysen's paper on which I should like to offer a few supplementary rather than critical comments.

The first concerns the distinction between the stipulation of overall goals, such as full employment or a certain rate of growth for the system at large, and the specification of such goals, if possible, in terms of concrete, quantifiable targets. Dr Kaysen describes from experience the role, more often than not a clandestine one, which the professional economist plays in his capacity as adviser to promote overall goals. Frequently this task devolves upon him by default, when no other authoritative voice can make itself heard in the cross-currents of the democratic process. Still, as a matter of constitutional principle, one may doubt that this is a legitimate function of an expert who 'represents' only himself.

However, no one will deny the economist a major part in translating a politically accepted goal into concrete targets. To decide whether full employment should be spelled out as not exceeding a 4 per cent level of unemployment compatible with price stability, or as a maximum level of 3 per cent even if this has inflationary repercussions, requires an understanding of the remote consequences of both of the two states, as well as knowledge of the means required to achieve them—requirements which only professional competence can satisfy. At the same time we saw above that, in most of these decisions, more than detached analysis is involved—namely, a value judgement on the respective means to be applied. Therefore one must never forget that, even when he acts in what appears on the surface as a purely technical capacity, the economist is likely to step over—indeed, will have to step over—the boundaries of his 'positive' science.

All this fully agrees with Dr Kaysen's views. But the question remains as to what political criteria are to guide the value judgements of the advising economist or, for that matter, of anyone who stipulates macro-goals and specifies targets. Dr Kaysen himself recognizes a 'natural bias of economists . . . toward believing that consumers "ought" to get what they want, in some ethical sense of the word'.[21] A generation ago such may indeed have been the bias of the large majority in our profession, but I am not sure how true this is in an age so conscious of the frequent clashes between social and private benefits, and of the grave undersupply of public services. In any case, at this stage we are not looking for ultimate ethical criteria, but for a lodestar of political decision making.

The answer seems to lie in another distinction that Dr Kaysen introduces: the distinction between *settled issues* and *live issues*, with antitrust policy and international monetary policy as his paradigmatic examples. Issues are settled or live according to the degree of public *consensus* concerning the means by which we deal with them, and the economist looks like a merely technical adviser to the extent to which the value judgements underlying his decisions reflect the prevailing political aspirations. Take the example of fiscal and monetary controls. Since both are by now fully accepted by American public opinion, tax increases to fight inflation can be presented as merely technical advice derived from the new economics, whereas control of prices and wages—even if they were more effective as instruments of price stabilization—would still be treated as the offspring of a dubious ideology.

This leads us to the fundamental problem. The distinction between settled and live issues is equally applicable to the overall goals themselves from which all specific targets emanate. To clarify this point I must first introduce another distinction—that between *order-protecting* and *ameliorative* goals. The former express the minimum conditions for satisfactory provision as understood by majority opinion; the latter are propagated by reformers or revolutionaries as conditions for a provision optimum. Historically considered, the distinction is by no means rigid. What in one era is an ameliorative goal of a struggling minority, may well be regarded in the next generation as a minimum condition for social survival. Still, for any given period the distinction seems precise enough to serve as a point of orientation.

In my previous writings I have proclaimed stabilization and balanced growth—that is, the full utilization of available resources and the steady absorption of resource increments—as the major order-protecting goals of our age. No one familiar with the postwar history of the West will doubt that these goals are today settled issues that express the aspirations of the overwhelming majority. Their authoritative stipulation thus seems to be in full accord with our constitutional principles. Certainly this in itself does not confer upon them any 'absolute' dignity as expressions of a 'general will' based on some ultimate ethical standard. But when judged by the maxims of political practice, a macro-goal supported by public opinion at large can legitimately claim the place of an empirical 'datum'.

INSTRUMENTAL ANALYSIS ONCE MORE

Datum for what? With this question we re-enter scientific territory which, in submitting my position paper based on the methodological and substantive analyses in *OEK*, I thought I had exhaustively explored.[22] However, the challenging questions Dr Nagel has raised leave no doubt that neither my own statements nor Dr Gurwitsch's perspicacious exposition of my views, with which I fully concur, have succeeded in breaking down all barriers to a full understanding. Instrumental analysis being the core of political economics, I am most anxious to achieve a degree of clarification of its principles which will not only communicate its aims but also demonstrate its concordance with the accepted tenets of the philosophy of science.

Dr Nagel asks two questions that go the heart of the matter. Why should the conventional procedure of scientific inquiry, the hypothetico-deductive method, prove inapplicable in economics, considering its uncontested usefulness in the natural sciences? And secondly, once we probe the alleged 'regressive' procedure of instrumental analysis to the bottom, does it not reveal itself as another version of 'progressive'—that is, deductive—analysis.

In trying to give precise answers to these queries I shall also comment on the comparison between instrumental analysis and the technique recently used in constructing so-called 'decision models'. Furthermore, I want to enlarge on some earlier remarks concerning the 'knowledge–action' issue—namely, my contention that at the present stage of development the object of economic research can no longer be grasped by passive observation alone but must be 'created' by political intervention into the actual economic process.

(1) The reason that I find the hypothetico-deductive method inapplicable to the solution of the contemporary problems of economics is implied in my above diagnosis of the relevant 'facts'. It is that we do not possess any safe hypotheses or major premises from which we could deduce theorems capable of explaining and predicting the processes of industrial capitalism. This is only a formalistic restatement

of the substantive assertion that neither the macro-movements of modern markets nor the underlying micro-patterns of behaviour exhibit the degree of orderliness that is essential for scientific generalization.

What this amounts to in terms of scientific methodology can be illustrated by drawing some extreme conclusions from a comparison of economic motion with celestial motion. An analogue to the physical force of gravity has sometimes been seen in profit-maximizing behaviour. But whereas the strength and direction of the force of gravity are *uniquely* and *invariably* described in Newton's formula, no equivalent statement can be made about the actual forces ruling economic motion. Profit maximization is not the universal incentive in the era of organized capitalism, nor is its effect uniquely determined even where it operates as the dominating action directive. On the contrary, its effect on overt behaviour varies with the simultaneous state of expectations, so that the *identical* profit incentive will give rise to *different* responses—meeting a price rise at one time with an increase in supply, and at another time with a decrease. Nor can this uncertainty of prediction be overcome by inquiring into the determinants of the expectations themselves. For these in turn vary with the technical structure, the size, the financial commitments and other attributes of the firm. What makes the situation still worse is the fact that expectations cannot be simply correlated with objective states of the environment, but ultimately depend on the manner in which the potential economic actor *interprets* these states and their future changes—a contingency which the student of planets and cells is fortunately spared.

Now Dr Nagel is certainly right in insisting that in physics the relative strength of different forces also varies from field to field, and that, for example, gravitation is stronger in the solar system than in the atom. It is also true that, contrary to an oversimplified statement of mine, the interplay of several forces is not necessarily summative, but may result in very complex patterns. It is even quite possible that the content of the laws of nature themselves is subject to spatial and temporal variations. However, and this is the salient point, the structural order of these natural forces—though different in mechanics, electromagnetics, and genetics—is constant *within* any one of these fields, or, if it changes within them, does so at rates that are for all practical purposes negligible.

A logical parallelism would prevail—and from such an analogy Dr Nagel's queries seem to spring—if, say, nineteenth-century capitalism had displayed *one* ruling type of incentive coupled with *one* type of expectations, while twentieth-century capitalism showed a different but also stable pattern. Though then we might not be able to discover transhistorical laws of economic motion, some laws with a limited historical validity might well be established. But if my diagnosis of the contemporary scene is correct, not one but many patterns of interaction are at work within a wide spectrum of both incentives and expectations, and worse, this continuing situation is without any *ex ante* clue as to which of the possible combinations will emerge in a given situation.

To drive this point home, let me illustrate it by a fictitious example from astronomy. Suppose that on Mars gravitation were to operate inversely with the third power of the distance, whereas on Jupiter it was directly proportional with it. Though we could no longer have a universal mechanics, we could still have a special mechanics for each planet. But now assume that on this earth gravitation were sometimes to operate according to Newton's formula, sometimes inversely with the third power of the distance, and sometimes directly proportional with the distance, and that we could not know *ex ante* which of these alternatives would materialize at any given time. I wonder what sort of generalizations the hypothetico-deductive method could establish in the field of mechanics then. Under these assumed conditions, a 'theory' of mechanics would have to be replaced by taxonomic description. But this is not so in economics where, within limits, we can *create* order out of disorder, once we have made up our minds as to what our macro-goals are. For once we have stipulated them, they can serve as the major data from which we can derive whichever of the many possible forces—behavioural and motivational patterns, public controls—are 'orderly': namely, goal adequate.

(2) The technique for such derivation is instrumental analysis. In discussing its procedure, Dr Gurwitsch has drawn an interesting parallel with mathematical analysis. In both cases a certain state of affairs is posited—a macro-goal in economics, a geometrical figure with specified properties in mathematics—and the *quaesitum* is the set of conditions upon which the realization of the posited state depends. In both cases, in contrast to the 'progressive' technique of the hypothetico-deductive method, the analysis is 'regressive'—that is, proceeding from the knowledge of some terminal state back to its unknown determinants.

But is this true? In raising this question Dr Nagel advances two seemingly grave objections. The first concerns the construction problem in geometry. To solve it he rightly insists that we must know more than the posited state—namely, the specification by a set of axioms of the properties of the respective figures. Must there not also be, he asks, a corresponding set of 'axioms' for instrumental analysis? And if so, what else but some known laws of economic behaviour can fulfil this function? This leads to his second objection. For if there are such laws after all, why use regressive analysis? Why not proceed by progressive deduction from the knowledge of the initial conditions and those axiomatic laws to the terminal state?

The reply to the first question, which has also been raised with great emphasis by Dr Machlup, can only be an emphatic 'yes'. There is indeed in instrumental analysis an analogue to the axioms of mathematics: to wit, the engineering rules that tell us how, within the limits of our technical knowledge, the initial state of the system can be transformed into the goal-adequate state. But this set of technical operating rules is *all* that is necessary. *We have no need to know any laws of behaviour.* I have tried to demonstrate this above[23] through the fiction of a fully automated economy in which human action would be entirely confined to deciding the output menu, the technology to be applied, and the programming of the computers: that is, to goal setting. All production and distribution processes would 'move by themselves', so that to plan these motions *ex ante* and to understand them *ex post* would require no more than knowledge of the apposite engineering rules and the underlying laws of nature.

The insights imparted by this fiction are also fully valid for our present economic organization in which behaviour enters at strategic points. But the patterns of behaviour that may be suitable at these points cannot be known before we know the path the system is to follow. Therefore the suitable behaviour patterns are themselves among the unknowns of instrumental analysis that are to be derived from the technologically determined path.

To avoid any semantic misunderstanding I should like to clarify the distinction between an engineering rule and a law of behaviour by referring to an earlier proposition of mine where I stated that 'a rise of investment is a suitable means of promoting employment'. Dr Nagel interprets this statement as a law of behaviour. This would indeed be so if I were to assert that additional investment *will* raise employment. But all I claim there is that investment—that is, building more working places—will *create an opportunity* for more workers to be employed—a technical potentiality for, but no assurance of, subsequent economic action. In purely formal terms, an engineering rule says: If behaviour A—a rise in investment—occurs, a technical state B will follow—namely, more working places. On the other hand, a law of behaviour says: If behaviour A—a rise in investment—occurs, another behaviour C will follow—namely, more workers will be hired. Nothing about behavioural consequents following behavioural antecedents is pronounced in instrumental analysis, and therefore no laws or empirical generalizations of positive economics are implied.

This provides me with the occasion for a brief comment on the similarities and differences between instrumental analysis and the modern decision models, to which Dr Kaysen and Dr Wallich have alluded. There is indeed a formal similarity in so far as both approaches derive the 'means'—controls or 'instrument variables'—from knowledge of the initial and terminal states by applying certain 'structural relations' as constraints. The difference, and it is a fundamental one, concerns the nature of these structrual constraints. In the decision models they are, above all, behaviour equations, symbolizing the presumed or observed responses of the marketers to specific events. It should be clear by now that in instrumental analysis the structural relations are of a purely technological nature. True, the total set of all known engineering rules is also abstracted from observation, though obtained in the workshop rather than in the market place. But the criteria by which the *suitable* rules are selected in any given instance, from the total set cannot themselves be 'observed'.

(3) This now brings us to Dr Nagel's second question. If it is true that engineering rules are indispensable data for instrumental analysis, why bother with a regressive derivation of the suitable path instead of deducing it in the usual fashion from the knowledge of these rules and of the initial conditions? The answer is simple. Once we *know* which members of the total set of engineering rules are goal adequate, we can indeed deduce the path in the conventional manner. The first step of instrumental analysis is to provide us with precisely this knowledge.

Thus instrumental analysis reveals itself as a search procedure through which the suitable means to the stipulated end—or, if you will, the suitable causes of a desired effect—are to be discovered. It falls within the category of heuristics or of what Peirce called 'abduction', a mental technique of problem solving which is part and parcel of research in every field of science. Far.from being in methodological conflict with deductive reasoning, it is the technique by which the premises of any deductive syllogism are originally established.

Though they are really the source of all scientific knowledge and are unlikely to be displaced by even the most sophisticated computer, heuristic procedures do not at present constitute a major theme of methodological discussion.[24] Therefore it is difficult to deal with this aspect of instrumental analysis in abstract terms. This has been one of the reasons why I have supplemented my methodological exposition in *OEK* by a detailed description of some test cases in which the regressive technique is applied to substantive issues.[25]

Closer scrutiny of the manner in which, in these examples, the critical paths of the system are traced back to the pertinent technical rules of production, and these in turn to the macro-goal, should provide sufficient proof that heuristics has a logical and not merely a psychological status. It is quite true that there are no formal precepts whose observance would safely guide us to the solution. Ultimately we must 'hit' upon it through what Polanyi calls a logical 'leap'.[26] However, it is not a leap in the dark, but one directed by the nature of the problem, and by more or less rigid constraints which set narrow boundaries to the area within which a solution can be found.

We all have heard of Wolfgang Köhler's ape who longingly stares at a banana through the window of his cage, only to discover finally that if he wants to seize it he must move away from the window to the rear, which has an opening to the outside. In an analogous manner, an economic system in which the total capital stock is fully utilized can achieve growth (understood as an *increase* in the aggregate output of consumer goods) only if, to begin with, the current output of such goods is *reduced* so as to set free part of the available capital stock for expansion. There does not exist any technique of inference through which this conclusion could be reached. But the more precisely we circumscribe our problem—a purely logical task—the fewer the number of alternatives which include the solution for which we are searching.

We have now reached the point where my defence merges with Dr Nagel's charge. Once the heuristic task of instrumental analysis is successfully completed and the goal-adequate forces, private and public, discovered, the road is free for deductive generalizations of the conventional type. These generalizations extend the results obtained in the case analysed to all similar cases. For this reason I have labelled my procedure 'instrumental–deductive', in full awareness that the level of 'theory' is reached only when the instrumental findings can serve as highest-level hypotheses in the explanation and prediction of facts other than those which were the occasion for their discovery.

And yet an important reservation is in place. The apparent universality and constancy of forces in the world of nature permits, as a rule, a much wider range of theoretical generalization than is possible in the study of society. In the latter, the multitude of possible macro-goals makes it imperative to re-examine the conditions for suitability whenever a new terminal state is stipulated. It was with good reason that the question repeatedly came up in our discussions as to whether the instrumental–deductive procedure lends itself to the same inclusiveness of theorizing to which we are accustomed in the natural sciences, or whether it yields at best a number of unrelated sets of theorems, any one of which is applicable only to one class of cases.

(4) The answer to this question is bound up with what is perhaps the most startling feature of political economics—namely, its assertion that only 'prior ordering' of reality itself can provide us with a tractable object of theoretical investigation. As will be remembered, I have limited this thesis to the contemporary stage of organized capitalism, claiming that the environmental conditions of competitive capitalism

exerted a regularizing influence on the behavioural forces sufficiently strong to render conscious control of their interaction superfluous. But the impression has apparently been created that I regard the new constellation of forces as permanent from now on. Indeed, for purposes of policy framing, the present generation had better base its analyses on this assumption. But it would be rash to close one's mind to a possible future in which as yet unknown regularities might be discovered underlying the ostensible disorder of market movements, or in which even these surface movements themselves would again assume regular form.

The first alternative concerns an opening of scientific insight into new psychological laws that would permit us, after all, to predict which of the rivalling motivational and behavioural patterns will arise in each instance, and thus to construct an economic theory valid for all conceivable cases. Even such a scientific advance would not do away with the practical need for the discovery of the means suitable to establish order in the real world, and thus for instrumental analysis. But its findings would then acquire a generality comparable to natural-science hypotheses.

The second alternative is even more interesting. It amounts to speculating about a future state of society in which the anonymous forces making for socialization of behaviour become strong enough to bring about a spontaneous ordering of the behavioural field that assures the desired levels of provision. Under such conditions, observation of what actually occurs could, as in the natural sciences, lead to general hypotheses from which verifiable explanations and predictions might be deduced. A structure of this kind seems to prevail in traditionalist societies, though Dr Lerner has rightly stressed the extent of conscious experimentation with institutions and rules of conduct, which defies any romantic notions about a pre-established harmony of interaction in these societies. Even so, there the slow tempo of change allows both actors and observers to take the routinized patterns of stimulus and response for granted over long periods of time.

The image of such a stationary society has little in common with the political and technological dynamics of the modern world. But as victims of the disruptive tendencies of this dynamics, we are apt to underestimate the more temperate, but in the long run not necessarily weaker, forces of conciliation. The collectivist trend of the age may well bring about a new assimilation of incentives, while successive control of the environment may render expectations both more certain and mutually compatible. At the same time the cruder forms of command control seem everywhere on the wane. West and East show, as Dr Lerner has properly emphasized, a structural convergence toward a type of social organization in which considerable autonomy of the micro-units is combined with order-preserving manipulative controls,[27] made effective through the spontaneous affirmation of the controlled.

(5) These speculations about a possible future have a very practical bearing on the immediate present and, especially, on the usefulness of instrumental analysis as a tool for the framing of practical policy.

It will, I hope, be accepted by now that the suitability conditions for goal attainment can be determined without regard to the real social forces at work. But logically consistent as such a design is, it describes an imaginary world. To make the transition to reality—that is, to move toward goal *realization*—the real world must be approximated to the imaginary one through political action. But to do this is possible only if the last step of instrumental analysis has successfully been completed—namely, if a link has been forged between the motivations of the economic actors (incentives and expectations) and the forces of the environment, particularly public control.

As I pointed out before,[28] the forging of this link is obviously not a technological task. It is a problem of social psychology, of determining the social nexus through which specific environmental stimuli evoke *ex ante* determinable responses. So whenever instrumental findings— themselves discovered without reference to any *social* cause–effect relations—are to be applied, we enter a border region in which 'laws' or at least empirical regularities of a sociopsychological nature must rule. It is hardly necessary to emphasize once more that the *regularities in question are not the alleged laws of economic behaviour postulated by traditional economics*. The former are of much wider generality, referring to the effect of environmental stimuli on any type of social response, economic or otherwise. Indeed, one might say that to exist at all, specific laws of economic behaviour presuppose the logically prior existence of a lawful order of more comprehensive social relations.

The fact is (and there lies the connection with what was said above about anonymous forces making for socialization of behaviour) that the study of social causation has not as yet come up with safe generalizations.[29] Again I trace the reason for this failure to the state of the research object rather than to shortcomings of the research technique. At least in the so-called 'free societies' of the modern world, the responses of randomly chosen individuals to the same environmental stimulus vary widely, as do even those of the same individual at different times. And yet no social organization, large or small, can survive without a minimum of conformity and stability in the motivational and behavioural patterns of its members. Compared with most of the societies of the past and even with the contemporary societies outside of its boundaries, the 'free world' appears as an extreme case of 'non-conformity'. And yet its members, in their daily performances, continue to 'interact'. They succeed in doing so because the psychological heritage from more highly socialized stages of Western history and new agents of the 'public interest' sustain co-ordination.

In any event, it is this looseness of social structure that is mirrored in the vagueness of empirical generalizations, with whose help we try to anticipate the effect of social controls. If it is true that the trend is toward greater conformity, the chances for more accurate prediction of this effect will increase. To demonstrate that even under prevailing conditions these chances can be greatly improved will be the burden of the following remarks.

THE FUNCTION OF PUBLIC CONTROL

Public controls suitable to transform real economic states and processes into goal-adequate ones belong to two worlds. Their discovery is the final step of instrumental analysis and is thus part of the theory of political economics. Their application is a political act—the foremost practical task of political economics. But to make the theoretical findings amenable to practical application, the level of abstraction of the analysis must be lowered to the point where the general principles of controls can be specified in concrete measures of economic policy, taking into account the intangibles as well as the tangibles of the prevailing sociopolitical structure. This is an undertaking that calls for talents and experiences of which Dr Kaysen's paper presents a rare display, but which are not the ordinary equipment of the economic theorist. So it should not cause surprise that both my book and my Symposium position paper [Essay 5 above — ed.] show considerable gaps in this respect which I cannot even try to bridge in these summary remarks. Their purpose is rather to spell out in greater detail some of those general principles which underlie any specification of public controls.

(1) In my programmatic statement of the major propositions of political economics,[30] I have distinguished between primary and secondary controls. My first concern is to give this distinction precision beyond the cursory comments made earlier.[31] There I have subsumed all conventional measures of economic policy—taxation, tariffs and quotas, currency control and interest manipulation, social legislation, etc., as well as the techniques of monetary and fiscal controls as advocated by the new economics, under the concept of primary control. In stressing their inadequacy for goal attainment, I did not mean to imply that political economics could in any way dispense with such

controls. The contrary is true, and only in the context of these controls does the true problem emerge.

This problem was labelled above as the 'response mechanism' of the micro-units of the system—that is, their reaction either to actions of other micro-units or to primary controls imposed by public authorities. Because of the unrealistic assumptions concerning the motivational and behavioural patterns ruling in a modern industrial market, traditional theory and policy alike take the responses to such stimuli for granted. Concretely, the supposition is that tax reductions will *always* add to aggregate spending whereas tax increases *necessarily* reduce it, that public spending *always* raises aggregate employment, or that increasing labour supply *invariably* stimulates private investment, etc. It is against such a mechanical interpretation of the effects of primary or conventional controls that political economics argues. To put it in more practical terms, these controls are not to be replaced, but are to be supplemented by another type of control which assures that the intent which led to the introduction of the former controls is realized.

It is the function of *secondary* controls to bring this about by eliciting the goal-adequate behaviour of the controlled. In speaking of 'eliciting', I want to make it clear that we are dealing with a social and not a physical phenomenon, with a challenge that can be accepted or rejected. True, there are certain types of command control which, by threats to life and liberty, may perhaps evoke a pseudomechanical reaction. But, as a rule, responses to controls will be goal adequate only if the controlled *understand* and *affirm* both the macro-goals pursued and the policy instruments used in their service. This is even true in the case of 'restrictive' controls such as taxation or quotas on imports. These erect boundaries which the micro-units cannot overstep. But where actual behaviour will settle within these boundaries cannot be predicted *ex ante* unless the responses themselves are controlled. To promote such understanding and affirmation, and thus to give the impact of primary controls on micro-behaviour direction and strength, this defines the role of secondary controls.

What then are the concrete measures of public policy which promise to improve this causal nexus? It was admitted earlier that we have at this stage no sociopsychological laws to guide us in this inquiry, and that we must rely on certain empirical generalizations and rules of thumb. Generally speaking, techniques of secondary control lie between two extremes. At one extreme there is the ideal but exceptional case in which the stipulated macro-goals and the primary controls chosen for their realization coincide from the outset with the aspirations of the controlled. Spontaneous micro-behaviour is then intrinsically goal adequate, and no secondary controls are required. At the other extreme, we find the situation already alluded to in which, for lack of understanding of or radical disagreement with the macro-goals or the primary controls applied, the micro-units act obstructively. There secondary controls are indispensable, assuming the form of circumventing obstructive behaviour through compensatory public action, or coercion, or finally, by altogether supplanting private decision making in a collectivist regime.

The secondary controls appropriate to the mixed systems of the West, which are committed to maintaining a broad sector of private decision making, lie between these extremes. Their purpose is to 'convert' the micro-units to the realization that both macro-goals and controls coincide with their own long-term interests. In other words, they treat private decision making as open to a *learning process*.

I have shown earlier that, in particular, marketers' expectations are a highly promising object for goal-adequate restructuring through improved public information, in which the instrumental analysis of the given situation plays a major role.[32] Moreover, I could point to numerous instances in which education in the wider sense of the word, including the formation of a more enlightened public opinion, has profoundly affected the attitude of business and of the community at large toward policies that initially were hotly contested. Recent examples are the universal acceptance of collective bargaining, and of public spending as a means to counteract recessions. Since Dr Kaysen has placed such emphasis on the role of the economist as public adviser, I should like to stress his function as teacher and educator, a more subtle but over the long run even more effective instrument of secondary control.

How severe secondary controls should be in any given instance may be difficult to gauge from the outset. Incremental application of the respective primary controls can offer an important clue. If, for instance, in a state of depression, small doses of public spending lead to a rapid rise in private investment, the presumption is that the response mechanism in the private sector is goal-adequate. Conversely, as happened during the 1930s, a negative response of private investment demonstrates the need for supplementary secondary controls, a course of action which was not comprehended at the time.

(2) From improved information, the enlightening of public opinion, and effective teaching through the numerous techniques of 'persuasion' such as guideposts or indicative planning to compensatory public intervention and finally outright coercion—the arsenal of secondary controls is large indeed. Hence it is not surprising that again and again in our discussions an anxious question was raised asking to what extent these weapons are compatible with decentralized decision making.

More than one voice expressed the fear that once they have such means at their disposal the controlling authorities will be tempted into collectivist adventures.

It cannot be denied that there is always the danger that the insolence of office will grow with the strength of the powers that be. But the real problem, one that goes beyond bureaucratic ambition and misuse of political authority, has different roots. Whether controls, primary or secondary, will in fact be harsh or lenient is not determined first and foremost by the caprices of the controllers. It is, rather, a functional problem in which the nature of the macro-goal and of the initial state plays the dominant role. As far as the latter is concerned, the prevailing social and technical structure of a society is a rigid constraint for the adjustment processes that connect initial and terminal states.[33] From this it follows that certain goals are incompatible with the maintenance of the structure of the initial state, and can be attained only if this structure itself is altered. To give an example, an egalitarian distribution of income and wealth is not a feasible goal within a capitalist order of property relations. It can be accomplished only after these relations are abolished. This, however, would require the most extreme forms of command control.

Of greater practical importance at this historical juncture are goals, such as radical urban renewal, that in principle fit into the prevailing social structure, but run counter to the interests of powerful strata of society. These goals can be successfully pursued only if resistance can be circumvented, say, by attractive forms of compensation, or can be broken by more direct means. The primary controls required for this certainly lie outside the range of the manipulative controls of the new economics or of other conventional policies, and the secondary controls can hardly confine themselves to applying persuasion.

What we run up against here once more is the difference between 'settled' and 'live' issues. But now the context is much wider, including the popular attitude not only toward the goal itself, but also toward the means required for its attainment. In this wider context we can now define that difference more precisely. An issue is 'settled' when the goal in question and the primary controls associated with it are approved of by a politically relevant majority. It is obvious that in all such cases any secondary controls, if required at all, can be of the lenient kind. It is our good fortune that, as was mentioned earlier, the major order-preserving goals of the present age fall in this category; it can be shown that purely manipulative controls are very likely to assure their realization.[34]

This is by no means true of what I called 'ameliorative' goals, most of which are 'live' issues—that is, the fighting concern of pioneering minorities. So long as they have not conquered public opinion, such goals can be accomplished only if the sponsoring minority succeeds in imposing its will on an antagonistic majority. If it were only a question of 'extremist' groups pursuing sectional aims, the answer would not be too difficult, even in a democratic system. Alas, more often than not such dissent reveals a serious dilemma. It arises wherever an enlightened minority perceives as a long-term necessity what to a majority blinded by short-term concerns appears as a violation of its interests. In other words, the distinction between order-preserving and ameliorative goals is historically fluid, especially when we remember that our sensitivity to 'disorder' increases steadily. Under this aspect it is an open question whether stabilization and balanced growth still fulfil the minimum conditions of satisfactory provision, as I suggested earlier. Urban renewal, economic equality of opportunity among the races, pure air, clean water and, last but not least, greater distributional equity are today proclaimed as preconditions for social survival by vocal minorities supported by serious experts, in addition to such 'international' goals as population control and prevention of world-wide famine. If it is true that our very physical existence is threatened by short-sighted interference with ecological equilibria, can we wait with remedial action for a political consensus to be achieved through the democratic techniques of persuasion, or must such issues be 'settled' by other means?

In placing these alternatives before us I am raising grave questions of a constitutional nature. I have never cherished any illusions about the efficacy of lenient (manipulative) controls in underdeveloped societies that are striving for emancipation from the tyranny not only of nature but of oppressive rulers, domestic and foreign. But in writing my book I was perhaps too optimistic in relying on the social consensus prevailing in the mature societies of the West as a safe basis on which political economics can build. The symptoms multiply that the mere attempt at preserving our accomplishments for future generations will involve us in social conflicts for the resolution of which many of our present institutions may have to be restructured.

However, we should be aware that in attributing to certain ameliorative goals the function of 'preserving order', we have extended the notion of 'order' far beyond the original definition we gave it. It is now no longer a question of regularizing 'economic motion' and thereby assuring predictability of the system. Rather, the aspect of 'satisfactory provision', which was then stressed only as a complementary constituent of order, now takes over, and political economics reveals itself as the instrument for the discovery and application of means suitable to the attainment of whatever goal our welfare judgements regard as worthy of pursuit.

CRITERIA FOR GOAL SETTING

This wider scope of application is implied in the very concept of a political economics which tries to supplant what Dr Lerner calls the economic 'process of natural selection' by goal-oriented planning. But it brings to the fore an issue that we could evade as long as we assumed that the stipulated goals were accepted by a more or less unanimous public opinion. Stipulation was then little more than articulation of popular aspirations, and coincided with the legalization of these aspirations in the framework of prevailing political institutions. This is no longer so when popular consensus gives way to dissent over what the 'order-preserving' goals are in a given situation. The alternative to a struggle of brute force can then only be an appeal to criteria which, as the ultimate vindication of political action, are themselves above the power struggle.

There lies the crucial significance of Dr Jonas's radical assault on the agnostic position I have taken in all my writings as to whether there are any *scientific* criteria to guide our choice of goals.[35] This is the position conventionally labelled as 'scientific value relativism', of which the work of Max Weber contains the paradigmatic formulation. It is important to stress that the relativism proclaimed there confines itself to what scientific inquiry or discursive thinking generally can contribute to establishing 'intersubjective demonstrability' of norms. It remains open, and this is an important proviso, whether or not the choice among values and norms is yet amenable to a cognitive judgement, but in a realm in which we can communicate only by 'pointing to', as opposed to the realm of thought where propositions rule—a distinction which, in the words of Wittgenstein, is 'the cardinal problem of philosophy'.[36]

Now what Dr Jonas tries to do, and what to my knowledge has not been attempted in any other philosophical disquisition about economics, is to demonstrate that the essential criteria for goal selection can be explicated by rational analysis because they are intrinsic to the nature of economic organization as such. Of course, even if such a scientific explication of the 'true' goals proved possible, this by itself could not assure their acceptance as rules of political action. But it would certainly elevate political debate above the mere airing of 'opinions' and 'subjective judgements' and would provide us with a foundation for a self-contained science of political economics.

In my subsequent remarks, I shall have to raise a number of serious objections to Dr Jonas's demonstration. But I would like it to be understood that, even if he has not spoken the last word, he has addressed himself to the fundamental problem underlying all social research in an age which tries to transform the historical process from blind motion into responsible action.

(1) I will begin by briefly restating Dr Jonas's major propositions: (a) Rather than being stipulated from outside the economic field, a definite goal commitment is an indispensable condition for constituting this field. (b) This is so because economics deals with human institutions which cannot even be defined unless we include a 'causality of purpose'. (c) The intrinsic goals in which this basic commitment manifests itself are two, *provisioning* and *providence*—namely, providing the members of a group 'with the physical goods necessary to sustain their lives' and, in doing so, 'looking and planning ahead'. These basic economic goals are themselves ultimately grounded in two biological constituents: metabolism and reproduction; they express the 'basic self-affirmation of life', 'an *a priori* option'. (d) No extrinsic criteria are required to vindicate these basic goals. Rather they offer themselves as the criteria for the choice of more specific ones, at least by setting boundaries which separate legitimate goals from others. This yields us an 'unconditional economic imperative': 'Do not compromise the conditions for an indefinite continuation of some viable economy'.

In trying to comment on these propositions, I find myself in a strange quandary. I am in complete agreement with Dr Jonas's conclusion as stated in his economic imperative and, as a consequence, also with his counsel of caution when it comes to pursuing grandiose projects. But I cannot accept some of the premises from which this conclusion is derived, especially those which concern the intrinsic nature of provisioning and providence, as understood by Dr Jonas, and the treatment of the basic commitment as an '*a priori* option'. Moreover, even if the economic imperative is accepted unreservedly, in telling us only what *not* to do, it fails to offer guidance for our positive decisions within the permitted range.

(2) To vindicate my second and less fundamental objection, let us consider some of the topical choices among rivalling goals with which contemporary policy framers are confronted. Is it 'better' to reduce unemployment to the zero level even if this implies an actual price rise by x per cent to be borne by the recipients of fixed incomes—or to maintain price stability even if this will keep unemployment above the y per cent level? Or, as another example, 'should' a developing country keep consumption near the subsistence level to facilitate investment and a rapid rate of growth, or 'should' the present generation be favoured with a rising standard of living at the cost of reducing the gains of future generations?

Obviously, either of these decisions is covered by Dr Jonas's viability norm, some provision and some providence being assured in each case. But how are we to evaluate the relative advantages which alternatively accrue to different income groups and different generations? True, my examples do not refer to the category of global goals with which Dr Jonas is primarily concerned, but belong to what he calls 'measured alternatives of short-range planning'. But as a matter of fact, the overwhelming majority of goal choices that arise in political economics fall in the latter category, for which both the goals and the means can be spelled out with reasonable precision.

However, the same dilemma confronts our decisions on 'long-range, large-scale perspectives'. We agree that the new opportunities for communal choices and also the dangers implied in a wrong choice both derive from the same factor: rapid technological change. What then should our attitude be toward further technical progress? The general norm that states: 'Do not endanger economic viability', yields no guidance. Perhaps technical progress should be stopped altogether in the interest of safeguarding 'human wholeness'—a 'value' which, according to Dr Jonas, should form 'a legitimate part of hardheaded economic reasoning', making 'viability . . . rather a comprehensive concept in which the technical aspect . . . tends to merge with the humanistic aspect of man's well-being'.[37] But how can we decide on this unless we have an image of humankind in which we can read what human wholeness and the humanistic aspects of his well-being are?

(3) This question leads us to the fundamental issue of where to look for criteria—not only to help us choose among rivalling specific goals, but also to give precision to those basic goals: provisioning and providence. I agree with Dr Jonas that the overall purpose which constitutes economic activity can be formulated in these concepts. But I must disagree with his claim that these concepts provide us with any criteria other than the *successful functioning* of economic activity. And 'success' is measured here as the ability to make the 'best' of an altogether bad job, that of allocating scarce human and natural resources to our wants, where 'best' means 'most efficient', irrespective of any 'humanistic commitments'.

To see this clearly we must disabuse ourselves of the widely held notion that economic activity can be placed side by side with activities such as politics, science, or religion that pursue intrinsic *substantive* goals. When Dr Jonas speaks of provisioning as being concerned with supplying the physical goods necessary to sustain our lives, he comes dangerously near to the notion of there being a special type of wants called 'economic' or 'material' that concern *vital necessities*: food, clothing, housing, etc. In reality there are no particular wants that can justifiably be labelled 'economic'. There is only an *economic manner or technique* by which we provide for the satisfaction of *any* wants—vital, political, religious, etc.—a technique that comes into play whenever satisfaction is conditional on the application of scarce resources. Therefore, the construction of a church or—*sit venia verbo*—of the gas ovens of Auschwitz poses no less an economic problem than does the production of bread and shoes. Or even more pointedly: economic activity is not at all concerned with the actual satisfaction of any particular wants, but with overcoming the resistance a stingy Nature opposes to the satisfaction of all means-requiring wants. Thus economics deals exclusively with the realm of means, and is as such both narrower and wider than the other realms of human action: narrower because it is bare of any substantive goal, wider because it is subservient to all the other realms in so far as they require means.

Now what difference does it make whether we delineate the realm of economics as standing on a par with politics, science, or religion, or as a subsidiary and auxiliary realm of means disposal? The difference is far reaching indeed, because only in the latter conception does economic action reveal its historical relativity. All the realms pursuing substantive goals—vital, interpersonal, political, moral, etc.—are likely to remain fields of action as long as humans walk this earth. They sustain, to speak with a physical analogy, the 'voltage' of civilization—namely, the positive forces of human society. Not so economic relations. They are the 'ohms' of civilization, measuring the resistance of a stingy Nature to the fulfilment of our positive goals. They symbolize Adam's curse which, all through past history, has compelled men to sacrifice the potentialities of the 'good life' to the toil and trouble of procuring the means necessary for our most primitive—namely, vital—ends. But contrary to the Biblical prediction, technology is gradually emancipating us from this bondage, by progressively reducing the obstacles to means procurement. At least asymptotically we are moving toward a state in which the significance of economic activity dwindles relative to the opportunities for pursuing genuine goals.

But so long as it is with us, economic activity as such is *goal neutral*. The only imperative that can be derived from its intrinsic character commands us to apply the available resources as efficiently as possible to any extrinsically posited end. Even provision, in the sense of that which is to be provided, and providence, understood as the time span over which we are to provide, remain empty boxes unless they are related to a particular 'menu' stipulated from without. 'Indefinite continuation of a viable economy' may be an item in that menu, but need not be. If Hitler had decided in 1945 to bring about the final *Götterdämmerung*, the complete destruction of the German people and land, then the task of the economist *qua* economist, unmoved by extrinsic considerations, would have been to help in doing so most efficiently.

(4) Now in insisting that economics can provide us only with a functional criterion, I am far from proclaiming that in the economic realm 'everything is permitted'. But when I speak out against *autos-da-fé* and other destructive uses of 'means', calling them '*mala*' in accord with Dr Jonas, I transcend the intrinsic neutrality of economics by an appeal to extrinsic moral norms. As a matter of fact, such transcendence begins already when I try to define what 'legitimate' wants are. True, on the primitive subsistence level, 'choices' and thus normative decisions are in practice almost excluded, because vital needs claim all the available resources. I say 'almost', because even there, 'affirmation of life' and 'interest in being' remain a genuine 'option' and, contrary to Dr Jonas, are no *a priori* of economic action. But certainly above that level, the opportunities for choices steadily expand, and with them the need for criteria beyond the functional command of efficiency.

As a matter of historical fact, these criteria are rooted in the dominant system of cultural values, which determines the legitimate range not only of wants but also of means: to a pious Jew pork is no food. Thus only by surrendering its autonomy in favour of the rule of such extrinsic moral, aesthetic, and other values in which 'human wholeness' comes to fruition, will economic activity remain within the boundaries of what is 'constructive', and will economics be able to fuse its criterion of technical efficiency with the 'humanistic aspect of man's well-being'.

At the same time it cannot be the business of economics and its adepts to pronounce on these values. In spite of Dr Jonas's modest disclaimer, this is a philosophical task, more precisely one of philosophical anthropology. Practically, if not in principle, its services might be dispensed with if our age were dominated by one and only one cultural value system. Here our present discussion merges with our prior reflections on the conflict of rivalling macro-goals in Western public opinion, not to speak of the ideological conflict between East and West or between traditional and modern societies generally. Seen in this light even terms such as 'humanistic aspect of man's well-being' lose precision because they point to a very singular image of human kind, as it has been formed through the blending of the classical heritage with the Judaeo-Christian tradition. I sympathize with Dr Jonas's fear and trembling when confronted with such a Promethean task—but to whom else if not to the philosopher can we appeal in our search for a 'just' solution of these conflicts?

(5) In conclusion, a word must be said about another objection

which Dr. Jonas has raised. It concerns the feasibility of instrumental analysis, an objection which, if sustainable, would be truly crushing. Optimistic as he is when the establishment of ultimate criteria for goal setting is at stake, he turns into a radical sceptic when these criteria are to be applied to spell out the concrete features of the terminal state in which the stipulated goal is to materialize, and also of the intermediate stages which represent the suitable path. This scepticism arises from our inability to foresee the long-term effects of any action, because any terminus projected today is 'spotlighted . . . out of a darkness of collateral unknowns with which it is inextricably inter-twined'. Therefore, 'in the last resort, the directed and "controlled" alternative is cognitively little better off than the "automatically" self-realizing one'.[38]

It may be useful to emphasize that Dr Jonas's reservations to instrumental analysis are different from and more radical than Dr Machlup's stress of our 'ignorance of what bridges may be crossed' in the course of carrying out our instrumentally established policies. What bothers Dr Machlup is not our inability to foresee the long-term effects of our present actions, but the multitude of alternative paths and behavioural patterns through which a stipulated goal can be reached, and between which the choice can only be made on the basis of a value judgement. In other words, Dr Machlup's problem is the abundance rather than the dearth of our cognitive findings, to be solved by stepping over the boundaries of positive economics into the realm of what he calls 'normative economics'. Though, as should be clear by now, I regard a normative economics in which values can be 'justified' as a scientific mirage, I fully agree with Dr Machlup that we must transcend the realms of positive economics or of instrumental analysis if we are to find criteria for such choices.

Dr Jonas, on the other hand, stops short from the very outset, because he denies the feasibility of any cognitive propositions on means. Fortunately, he confines his sceptical reasoning to 'long-range, large-scale perspectives', and thus opens the way for political economics after all. This is so because the collateral unknowns of a distant future play a minor role in the short-range projects with which political economics is mainly concerned. Certainly stabilization and balanced growth, our paradigms of order-preserving goals, do not refer to a Utopian future, but point to an ongoing struggle against ongoing threats of economic dislocation. And the darkness in which even the proximate future may be shrouded can be lightened by the trial-and-error technique of incremental control. All this has been stated very clearly and convincingly in Dr. Edel's comments, with which I fully associate myself.

I should even go farther and assert that the typical goals that political economics stipulates and the typical measures it advocates are in strict comformity with Dr Jonas's cautionary warning, because they are all in the service of viability, which is only another term for what was defined above as 'order' in the comprehensive sense. On this level it would be a gross misreading of the facts were we to place the 'automatically self-realizing alternatives' on the same footing with the planned ones. As the experience of the Great Depression has demonstrated only too forcefully, the former alternative threatens us with the very destruction of economic viability. Even if political control is, and to some degree will always remain, an imperfect tool, it would be a surrender to a negative eschatology were we to prefer the risks of 'natural selection', a view which again seems to accord with Dr Edel's position.

But I must not end in this critical vein. I said at the outset, Dr Jonas's paper has opened a debate which is bound to challenge both economists and philosophers for some time to come. I admit that, with all his concern about the intrinsicalities of economics, I still see him wearing the philosopher's crown rather than the bowler hat of the economist. But when he tells us that economics is 'interdisciplinary by its nature'[39] dealing with an indivisibly 'compound situation' in which the physicist, the biologist, the anthropologist, the psychologist, etc., are also involved, I begin to wonder whether for him that crown and that hat are not really the same. I wrote some time ago that for the solution of its basic problems, economics is in dire need of another Aristotle,[40] meaning a philosopher sufficiently at home with the economic issues of his time to be able to provide it with its ultimate norms. Though for the time being Jonas's answer is not Aristotle's, he has retrieved Aristotle's quest.

NOTES

1. In doing this I will not confine myself to commenting on the symposium papers but also, at least implicitly, I will refer to the discussion that followed their delivery at the two Symposia. It is only natural that my rejoinder should deal mainly with my critics, referring to affirmative voices only occasionally when they improve on my own argument. The text itself follows the line of several statements I submitted during the proceedings. But it tries to present the issues in a more systematic fashion independent of the chronology in which they arose at the time and also of the order in which they are taken up in this volume. [*EMASE* — ed.]
2. *See* Essay 5 above.
3. *See OEK*, Chapter 3, and Essay 5 above.
4. *See EMASE*, pp. 156–8.

5. *See* J. K. Galbraith, *The New Industrial State* (Boston: Houghton Mifflin, 1967).
6. J. E. Meade, 'Is "The New Industrial State" inevitable?', *Economic Journal*, **LXXVIII**, No. 310 (June 1968), pp. 372–92.
7. *ibid*, pp. 377–8.
8. *See* Galbraith *op. cit*, p. 159.
9. *OEK* Chapters 2 and 3.
10. *See* Essay 5 above.
11. *ibid*.
12. *ibid*.
13. *See EMASE*, p. 103.
14. *See EMASE*, p. 111.
15. *See* Essay 5 above, and *OEK*, Chapter 12.
16. *See EMASE*, p. 128.
17. *See EMASE*, p. 116.
18. *OEK*, Chapter 12.
19. *See OEK*, Chapter 12, especially for the reversibility of ends–means relations.
20. *OEK*, pp. 260–1.
21. *See EMASE*, p. 149.
22. *See* Essay 5 above and *OEK*, Chapters 5, 10, 11.
23. *See* Essay 5 above.
24. *See*, however, the enlightening comments in N. R. Hanson, *Patterns of Discovery* (London: Cambridge University Press, 1958), especially Chapter IV; and the writings of G. Polya.
25. *See OEK*, Chapter 11, especially the re-enactment of the 'discovery' of the circular nature of an industrial structure of production, on pp. 266–71.
26. Michael Polanyi, *Personal Knowledge* (Chicago: University of Chicago Press, 1958), p. 123.
27. For the distinction between manipulative and command controls, *see OEK*, Chapters 5, and 12.
28. *See* Essay 5 above.
29. *ibid*.
30. *See* above pp. 194–6.
31. *See* Essay 5 above.
32. *ibid*.
33. *OEK*, Chapter 10.
34. *OEK*, Chapter 11.
35. *See OEK*, Chapter 12, and pp. 18, 34.
36. In a letter to Bertrand Russell. *See Autobiography of Bertrand Russell*, Volume II (London: George Allen & Unwin, 1968), p. 172.
37. *See EMASE*, p. 82.
38. *See EMASE*, p. 70.
39. *See EMASE*, p. 83.
40. 'The normative roots of economic value', *Human Values and Economic Policy*, ed. Sidney Hook (New York: New York University Press, 1967), pp. 170–80.

7   What Is Evolutionary Economics?: Remarks Upon Receipt of the Veblen–Commons Award*

It was in Paris in 1863 that a small group of artists dared to exhibit their paintings in what was called the *Salon des Refusés*. This group, among them Cézanne, Manet and Whistler, had been refused display space in the official halls of the Academie Royale. Although neither the critics nor the wider public took much note of it, one can well say that this event marked the beginning of modern art as a collective enterprise.

Almost exactly a century later, the Association for Evolutionary Economics was established. It was not a *salon des refusés*, but a *salon des refusants*, a band of refusers—refusing to be tied down by the ruling dogma of neoclassical economics. Since then, other rebellious groups have organized themselves—social economists, radical economists, post-Keynesian economists and more. But it was your Association that pioneered in offering a platform for views that had long been banished, in J. M. Keynes's word, to the underworld of economics.

Speaking of myself, I am pleased to admit that I have dwelled in that underworld for more than fifty years. Having been brought up by my teacher, Franz Oppenheimer, on Ricardo and Marx, I found it easy to look through the formal brilliance of the Walrasian system or even the persuasive common sense of Marshall, to the barrenness of neoclassical economics when judged by its applicability to problems of the real world. Thus, in this critical sense, I have been your ally from the very outset. And my convictions were fortified when, later on, I studied your original masters—Thorstein Veblen and John R. Commons. For these reasons I am deeply grateful for and really proud of the honour you have bestowed on me. Even if truth does not depend

---

* [Adolph Lowe received the 1979 Veblen–Commons Award from the Association for Evolutionary Economics. The present essay records the text of Lowe's remarks on the occasion of the receipt of the award and was first published in the *Journal of Economic Issues*, **14**, (1980).

The publication details of Lowe's books cited in this essay are given in the Bibliography at the end of this volume. — ed.]

on public acclaim, your recognition strengthens and encourages the struggler in his will to persevere.

I thought hard how best I could express my appreciation through the statement that it is both my duty and my pleasure to submit to you. I have concluded that I could do no better than to relate what I regard as the essence of my own work to the aims and aspirations of evolutionary economics as I understand the term. This is not quite easy because, as some of you may remember, I have in the past expressed some reservations to certain tenets that 'institutionalists' seem to propogate. I realize that evolutionary economics, as your Association represents it, is a wider concept than what traditionally goes by the name of institutionalism, and different even from what Veblen meant by evolutionary economics. But I also recall the self-searching debate you conducted a few years ago, aiming at a clarification of the true distinction between orthodox and evolutionary economics. I take it that this debate is not closed, so that a comment on this problem, brief as it must be, may not be untimely.

THE ORIGIN OF EVOLUTIONARY ECONOMICS

The crucial issue is *theory*. What is the function, if any, of theory in evolutionary economics? Even more basic, what do evolutionary economists mean when they speak of theory?

I confess that my reading in the literature has not provided me with a clear answer to either of these questions. I find a wide spectrum of opinion. At one extreme, the hypothetico-deductive method is emphasized in much evolutionary economics as strongly as it is in traditional economics. At the other, this procedure is rejected as totally unrealistic and is replaced by the Baconian methods of observation, description and classification of economic institutions.

My perplexity increased when I recently went back to the writings of your founding father, Veblen himself. He denounced the traditional method, as classical and neoclassical economists practiced it, as non-causal and normative. At the same time, he accused the German historical school, on the surface a congenial undertaking, as being content with 'emuneration of data and a mere narrative account', without offering 'a theory of anything'. (All quotations are taken from Veblen's essay, 'Why is economics not an evolutionary science?' in *The Place of Science in Modern Civilization*, 1898.) In contrast, he insisted that 'any evolutionary science . . . is a close-knit body of theory . . . a theory of a process', and even more precisely of 'a cumulative process of adaptation of means to ends'. Now, we shall presently see that emphasis on the relationship between means and ends, as opposed to the traditional concern with causes and effects, indeed points to a new departure for theorizing. But to my knowledge, nowhere did Veblen follow up this idea in specific terms. Rather, he concluded with the call—more befitting a Spengler or a Toynbee—that 'evolutionary economics must be a theory of cultural growth as determined by the economic interest'.

Exposed to such conflicting views, you will, I hope, not find it pretentious if I now try to indicate what, in my opinion, evolutionary economics *should* be, and especially what role is to fall to theory in that context. Let me present my position as an answer to the following three questions: (1) Why, at the present stage of economic development, is a purely taxonomic approach unable to provide us with the insights necessary for a practically relevant economics? Why, in other words, must an up-to-date economics rest on theory, that is, on a body of propositions logically derived as consequents from stated antecedents? (2) Is the conventional hypothetico-deductive method the only technique of constructing such a theory, or is there an alternative method better suited for the purpose? (3) If so, on what grounds can such an alternative claim to represent the core of an evolutionary economics?

THE ROLE OF THEORY

Why do I put such emphasis on the fact that, under the present conditions of organized capitalism, theory has gained immense *practical* importance? Was this not always so? What about the practical function of that large body of theory developed since the days of Hume and Cantillon? My answer, to put it bluntly, is that once liberal capitalism had been established—not least under the impact of classical analysis—theory became more or less an intellectual luxury. In that vanished world of *laissez-faire*, the role of the economist differed little from that of the astronomer. He was a passive observer, and his predictions, correct or incorrect, did not affect the course of events any more than did the incantations of a shaman.

All this has drastically changed during the present century. Even if the specter of *laissez-faire* still haunts some lecture halls, we live in an era in which the many ill-fated effects of the free play of economic forces are no longer accepted as acts of God, and in which the processes of the market are progressively subjected to public control. With this shift in public attitude, the role of economics has undergone an equally drastic change. From a medium of passive contemplation, it is being converted into a tool of active interference. Increasingly, the economist is called upon to advise the public planners in the framing of their policies. But to do so, he must be able to foresee the effects of the measures he advocates. Thus, prediction—and a theory from which the consequences of antecedent actions can be derived—is no longer an intellectual pastime, but the very precondition for the fulfilment of a practically indispensable task.

THE CONVENTIONAL 'AXIOMS' OF THEORIZING

I expect that, up to this point, the guardians of convention, and certainly their Keynesian wing, agree with my proposition. However, the roads part when we ask how to construct a practically relevant economic theory.

Let me start with a more general question. Are there any universally valid principles—let us call them 'axioms'—that, according to the ruling methodology of science, are implied in *any* act of theorizing? In fact, there are two such axioms.

To clarify this proposition, I turn for a moment to the natural sciences. There, all scientific thinking—as opposed to magic—takes for granted the existence of *an outside world, moving independently of man's volition.* Whether natural processes are seen as activiated by inherent tendencies of goal seeking (the Aristotelian view) or whether, in the modern vein, they are regarded as subject to efficient causality, science treats them as 'autonomous', that is, as unaffected by what the scientist does. Where, as in the subatomic realm, we cannot prevent the act of observation from impinging on the phenomena observed, such intrusion actually diminishes our knowledge by shrouding it in 'uncertainty'.

Autonomy of the research object is one axiom, *inherent orderliness* of the research object is the other. The scientist aims at more than a mere registering of episodical events. His tool chest—observation, experiment and ratiocination—is expected to reveal regularities of state and motion: 'laws' or at least probabilistic generalizations.

It is noteworthy that those axioms of autonomy and orderliness have been at the root of the science of nature from its beginnings in Greek natural philosophy to our own day. But it is no less noteworthy that those axioms were introduced into social and especially economic thought only during the modern era. Previously, it was a predominantly *normative outlook*, issuing in moral postulates, that directed the inquiries of ancient and mediaeval thinkers. Even during the mercantilist period, when this moral concern was replaced by the political interest in national expansion, the social cosmos was by no means regarded as autonomous, but as in need of and open to human intervention.

Only with the classical and neoclassical notion of a competitive equilibrium did economics adopt the natural science axioms. In analogy with the movement of the planets, the spontaneous actions of the autonomous bargaining partners in the market were supposed to create a macro-order, an order that any attempt at planned interference could only distort.

What is essential for a full understanding of the orthodox methodology is to lay bare the ultimate postulate on which this faith in a prestabilized order rests. It rests on the postulate of a *universal and uniform behavioural vector*, originally personified in a receipt-maximizing and expenditure-minimizing economic man, but nowadays formalized as a colourless maximum or minimax principle. In analogy with gravitation, this behavioural principle issues in an *immutable law of economic motion*. With the help of this law, traditional economic theory derives from any given state of the system the future state induced by a change in the initial conditions—the hypothetico-deductive method.

No one besides Marx has denounced the harmonistic pretense of this construction more bitterly than Veblen. In fact, he may have gone too far. During the liberal era of capitalism, a unique *combination of external pressures*—mass poverty, unbridled competition and Puritan work ethic—did enforce a high degree of maximizing behaviour, as the very condition of economic survival. Therefore, Ricardian economics, when qualified by certain Marxian insights, did not do so badly as a theory of nineteenth-century capitalism.

I need not bore you with a lengthy exposition as to why this is no longer the world in which we live. Growing affluence of all strata, monopolistic organizations on both sides of the social fence, and a boundless desire for instant gratification has loosened those order-bestowing pressures. As a result, *market behaviour is today the great unknown*. In many a large corporation, profit maximization has been diluted by homeostatic tendencies. But quite generally, considering the ever-expanding time horizon of decision making, *any* action—increasing or decreasing output, raising or lowering prices—may in different circumstances serve the aim of receipt maximization. Thus, actual behaviour no longer can be predicted. Moreover, technological change, the major vehicle of this transformation, adds to destabilization. Its disturbing effect was mitigated so long as vast opportunities for economic expansion prevailed. Now the self-assertion of the Third World and our growing awareness of the ecological dangers are rapidly closing this safety valve, and the result has been instability, the progress of which has become our daily experience.

ECONOMIC THEORY AND PLANNING— INSTRUMENTAL ANALYSIS

Speaking to this group, I need not waste time in demonstrating that, in the absence of the earlier behavioural constraints, a return to anything resembling *laissez-faire* must bring about the total breakdown of the system. To advocate such a return makes good sense as a subversive plot of revolutionary Marxists, but not as a panacea in the mouth of old-style liberals and neoconservatives. The only feasible alternative is a public plan for restabilization. This now brings us back to the role which falls to economic theory in devising such a plan. I said early that no public controls can be formulated unless they can base themselves on a reliable anticipation of the consequence of any act of policy. To provide this information has become the prime task of the economist today. But how is he to go about it *in the absence of a law of motion?*

There is only one conclusion: To cope with an altered reality, *we need an altered method of inquiry.* Now it is interesting that without methodological fanfare, precisely such a change in theoretical procedure has come about in recent years. Under various labels—programming, operations research, decision theory—a new orientation has emerged. Common to all these attempts is that, in contrast with the traditional procedure which derives future effects from present causes, *they try to discover the means suitable to attain previously stipulated ends.*

All I have done in my own work is to draw the systematic conclusions from this approach. Obviously, this is not the place to go into details. Those interested in my present thinking about what I have called 'instrumental analysis' are referred to the second edition of my book *On Economic Knowledge* and to the application of instrumental analysis in *The Path of Economic Growth*. I should also mention a very lucid exposition of my main ideas by Robert Heilbroner in an article published in the *Journal of Economic Issues*.[1] Here I shall give only a very brief account of the essentials.

Since it is no longer possible to deduce an unknown future state, and thus the consequences of any measure of public policy, from the initial conditions and a law of motion, I have inverted the problem. I no longer treat the future state of the system as unknown; I treat it as a *known goal*, established by political decision; therefore, I speak of political economics. Examples for such goals are full employment with a rate of inflation not exceeding 4 per cent, or a 5 per cent growth rate, of which the rise in productivity is no less than 3 per cent, or any other politically desirable goal. The first task of analysis then is the derivation of one or more *paths* over which the initial state can be transformed into the terminal state. By a *path* I mean a sequence of positions the system must assume on its way to the stipulated terminal state. Such positions can be described in terms of physical and price relations between the major variables, such as inputs and outputs, employment and income, consumption and investment, and so forth. Once we know that path, we can establish the *behavioural patterns* that will act as forces to set the system on the goal-adequate trajectory. Thus, behaviour, although initially an unknown, can be determined from the knowledge of the goal-adequate path and certain technological rules.

In this manner we obtain knowledge of the structural and behavioural conditions suitable for the attainment of the goal. But we cannot assume that these *suitable* conditions coincide with *actual* conditions. This now leads us to the final step in instrumental analysis—establishing *measures of public control* suitable to transform actual into required behaviour. The potential arsenal of such controls is quite large. It includes mild measures, such as guideposts and other techniques of persuasion; compensatory public investment; but also wage, price, profit and investment control; and, in extreme cases of resistance, outright coercion.

This is quite a superficial description of the instrumental procedure, which leaves more than one question unanswered. Again I must refer you to my writings, especially to the postscript I have added to the second edition of *On Economic Knowledge*. However, one question comes up again and again that I must not dodge. Will not such behavioural controls do away with the freedom of individual decision making? The answer depends on what we mean by such freedom. Was economic behaviour 'free' while it was shaped by the impersonal but relentless pressures of the *laissez-faire* era? Obviously, no market system can function unless the behaviour of its participants is somehow constrained. What a political economics proposes is to substitute for the irrational constraints of an anonymous environment the rational constraints of an effective welfare state—constraints that are themselves subject to the checks and balances of the democratic process.

EVOLUTIONARY ECONOMICS TODAY

I must leave it at that. But I have still to answer my third question: What right do I have to claim that such a revised idea of theory has an affinity with evolutionary economics?

It is now almost fifty years since I tried to show in my *Economics and Sociology* that the notion of a 'pure economics', namely one whose generalizations are valid for any conceivable social order, is an illusion. Such a pure economics, as is still found sometimes in textbooks, either proclaims banalities—such as that humans have wants of different urgency, that they use scarce means for the satisfaction of those wants, and so on—or it points to so-called laws of physical returns which, to the extent to which they are true, are actually technological statements. But when it comes to universal *behavioural* 'laws', *exempli gratia*, that humans in any social order try to maximize their utility, be they Trobriand Islanders, American consumers, or Soviet *apparatchiks*, we are confronted with a tautology consistent with any behaviour, while refutable by none. Only within a well-defined institutional and sociopsychological framework in which maximization of utility refers to testable alternatives, for instance, preference for more goods over less in contrast with homeostatic tendencies, does such a proposition make sense.

But I have gone further. In my view, institutional and sociopsychological factors separate not only traditional orders from market economies or market economies from command systems. Even *within* the capitalist order itself, I emphasize the effect, especially on behaviour, of any large changes in the conditioning framework, such as growing affluence, monopolization, rise of consumerism and so on.

Even this is not all. I finally extend the evolutionary way of thinking from the research *object* to the *method* of its treatment. There I digress even from some early champions of institutionalism such as Raymond Bye and Frank Knight. They insisted that when it comes to method there is no such thing as evolution. In contrast with this view, which is of course also the orthodox dogma, I stress the limits of the hypothetico-deductive method by pointing to the need for instrumental analysis if we want to handle the problems of the postliberal present.

I need hardly assure you that I am most eager to learn, when an occasion arises, your response to these suggestions. They come from a former outsider whom you have so graciously turned into an insider.

NOTES

1. R. L. Heilbroner, 'On the possibility of a political economics', *Journal of Economic Issues*, **4**, December 1970.

8   Is the Glass Half Full or Half Empty? A Self-Critique*

Criticism of other people's work is a legitimate part of scientific activity. After all, science is a co-operative enterprise, and though we might sometimes help one another more by publicly stressing points of agreement, raising questions and finding fault, when properly done, can act as a spur.

Publicly to criticize one's *own* work is a less frequent preoccupation. It is implicitly done when we issue a 'revised' edition of a book, and in rare cases an author even admits that 'I myself held with conviction for many years the theories which I now attack' (preface to Keynes's *General Theory*).

I say that these occasions are rare. And yet we are often less assured about the rightness of our position than might be suspected. This comes to the surface in an experience which, I am confident, many of my fellow workers share with me. It concerns the reaction to a censorious review of one of our writings, namely, the ironical feeling: how much more effectively could I have done this myself! The reason is obvious. As a rule we know better than our readers the weak spots, the strands in the argument which we left dangling, the points where the evidence is shaky.

But there is another kind of self-examination which digs more deeply. It is not concerned with mistakes, oversights and other imperfections which a better mind would have avoided. It understands the term 'critical' in the philosophical sense in which Kant or Marx used it—as a clarification of the presuppositions of our work. It is critique in this sense that I shall attempt here to apply to some of my thinking in economic theory.

The problem intrigues me because of its closeness to a mystery story, for those presuppositions—sometimes in the form of auxiliary

* I wish gratefully to acknowledge the comments of my friends and colleagues Ron Blackwell, Robert L. Heilbroner, and, especially, Hans Jonas on the first draft of this paper.

[This essay was first published in *Social Research*, **49** (1982). — ed.]

hypotheses—do not lie on the surface but must be ferreted out. Moreover, and this anticipates a major point I am going to make, some of these presuppositions fall outside the range of issues that are amenable to what we call 'scientific procedure'. How then can they be vindicated?

I would still hesitate to risk my old bones on such slippery ground were it not that concern about the validity of such presuppositions has recently acquired some respectability. Norwood Hanson's *Patterns of Discovery*, Gerald Holton's 'thematic hypotheses', Thomas Kuhn's 'paradigms', Michael Polanyi's *Personal Knowledge* are expressions of the same interest.[1] And they all claim that the conflict, say, between Ptolemaic and Copernican astronomy, between Aristotelian and Galilean or Newtonian and Einsteinian physics, cannot be fully resolved on the planes of either observation or ratiocination. Rather, these scientific 'beliefs'—note the term which recurs in all these writings—are said to contain ingredients which are refractory to both experimental and analytical procedures.

I shall presently elaborate one of these problematic ingredients through a concrete example. But let me first note that most of the work done in this field until now has confined itself to the natural sciences. Kuhn even doubts that the social sciences have progressed to the point where its 'beliefs' can be formulated as 'paradigms'. And though Holton regards the 'soft' sciences as particularly 'themata-prone', his examples too are all taken from physics. So it may not be redundant to illustrate the nature and significance of these problematic elements on work done in the social sciences. Since economics is by common consent—which does not mean common approval—the most 'scientific' of the social sciences, it can serve as a good test case. And as one is best qualified to discuss what one is familiar with, it is only fair that I offer myself as guinea pig.

ORDER OR DISORDER?

Now let me be specific. Some years ago the New School organized, under the aegis of President Everett, two symposia devoted to a review by social scientists and philosophers of my work in *Political Economics*. In his introduction to the published version of the papers delivered on that occasion, Professor Heilbroner expressed the challenge I had thrown out to conventional economics in two propositions.[2] First, 'contemporary economic theory is not—and, worse, cannot be—an adequate tool for the control of our social destiny because the very premises on which that theory is based are no longer relevant to social reality'. Secondly, 'a restructured economic theory might become such a tool if economists understood the *changed relationship of theory and reality* in the milieu of industrial capitalism, and altered the nature of their procedure accordingly' (my italics — A. L.).

Indeed, this formulation reveals the salient points of my position. It emphasizes the fact that the premises of economic theory, if they are to lead to operational conclusions, must reflect social reality and must therefore change with changes in that reality. This, I assert, prevailing theory has not done and cannot do within its traditional framework of detached observation. Why? The answer is the cornerstone on which both my critique and my attempt at reconstruction rest. It asserts that the *autonomous markets of industrial capitalism lack the required minimum of order*. This absence of 'order' shows in the recurrence of wide discrepancies between quantities supplied and demanded in the markets for commodities and productive factors, with the result of large and long-lasting underutilization of available resources, alternating with periods of overutilization accompanied by inflation, not to speak of the most recent paradox of 'stagflation', when mass unemployment and high inflation combine.

Now I was certainly not the first to make this observation. But I went on to point to a secondary aspect of this imbalance that had to my knowledge not been stressed before. This aspect concerns not the 'facts' but the ability of the economic theorist to *analyse* those facts. His efforts are bound to end in frustration because, however refined his techniques of observation and analysis, with the absence of stability his *Erkenntnisobjekt* lacks the precondition for any scientific generalization, not to say prediction—that is, *regularity of state and motion*.

Faced with this dilemma, I drew the radical conclusion that, in the interest of human welfare as well as of successful theorizing, *economic reality itself must be changed by public controls*—directed toward the restructuring of certain institutions, but above all toward streamlining economic behaviour. I should add that, in my evaluation of the historical trend, this need for a prior reconstruction of the *Erkenntnisobjekt* is of relatively recent date. In agreement with prevailing theory I recognize that the economic processes of nineteenth-century capitalism displayed a self-correcting mechanism which kept instability within definite limits—too wide for a *laissez-faire* regime always to achieve satisfactory provision and employment levels, but narrow enough to permit theoretical generalizations with a high level of probability.

These are the propositions which I want to subject to a fundamental critique. I shall be greatly helped in this by the response which my challenge found in the papers and discussions at the two conferences—all the more so since on that occasion the defenders of the orthodox belief in the inherent stability of the industrial market and its scientific tractability were a clear majority.

To start with, let us look a little more closely at my basic premise that the prevailing degree of instability or disorder defies scientific generalizations. In this respect the New School symposia were especially illuminating because we participants all appealed to 'facts' and even to the same facts, namely, a growing variety of business incentives, rapid technological change, and a largely monopolistic environment. But we drew radically opposite inferences from these facts. In the view of my opponents, the very rigidity of market structures not only produces stability but, linked with the advance of professional management, facilitates prediction. I retorted that this might be valid for the process of decision making *within individual firms*, though even then only within a minority of big corporations. But there was no assurance whatever that these individual business plans, however rational in a *micro*economic context, would automatically integrate themselves into a coherent *macro*economic order—the true locus of instability, as far as both provision and prediction were concerned. Whereupon a question was raised that laid the analytical ambiguity of our discussion bare: Considering the spotty record of the past, I was asked, how can I be sure that capitalism today is less stable than it was 100 years ago—an era for which I grant retrospectively the possibility of prediction? Perhaps what has changed is not *reality* but the *standards* by which we judge it?

This comment reminds us that, in speaking of stability or instability, we use terms which are not strictly defined. Or, to put it more precisely, we are discussing 'threshold' problems, which can be solved only after first determining what is the critical threshold. Obviously, no one asserts that market processes, now or at any time in the past, have been perfectly regular, that is, invariable in structure and motion. Nor can we reasonably impute to them perfect instability or randomness— after all, we still survive. The relevant range lies between these extremes, a range that might be called with equal right 'semiorganized' or 'semidisorganized'. We may give them the former label when we focus on the fact of our survival. If we recall the waste of effort and resources and the potential wealth we have forgone, we may be inclined to use the latter label. But which is the viewpoint that we 'should' adopt, that we could impose by logical argument on our opponent?

ARE THERE REMEDIAL CONTROLS?

Let me now turn to my second proposition—that economic reality can be made amenable to theory only if public controls establish a necessary degree of stability. There we shall meet with a different but no lesser dilemma. To point it out I must first state specifically where I see the sore spot in the modern body economic.

I admitted already that my general diagnosis of instability of modern capitalism is far from novel. It has been the constant theme of critics of the system from Marx to Keynes. Now what unites these and other critics, and even allies them with the champions of capitalist stability, is their *belief in an inexorable mechanism* which is supposed to direct all market motions. The critics differ from theoretical orthodoxy only in the manner in which they see this mechanism operate. It is the conviction of classical and neoclassical orthodoxy that market processes bear all the characteristics of a *negative-feedback mechanism*, which automatically corrects any deviation from stability. The critics, on the other hand, point to certain institutional factors, such as property relations, income distribution, absence of investment opportunities, which are alleged to produce *positive feedbacks*, amplifying partial distortions into general disequilibrium.

I do not deny that such institutional factors and even some others actually designed to strengthen the compensatory mechanism—for example, certain policies of the 'welfare state'—are contributory sources of destabilization. But I see the principal cause in a weakening of the *behavioural forces*—those forces which, in the early stages of capitalism, sustained the operation of negative feedbacks. Of course, everyone agrees that economic behaviour is the strategic agent of market movements. But it is a dogma of all previous theory, upheld by Marx no less than by Adam Smith and Paul Samuelson,[3] that market behaviour can be treated as invariant, dominated by the universal incentive of receipt maximization and expenditure minimization. In fact, this incentive is far from universal. It neither 'comes with us from the womb', as Smith thought, nor is it a generally applicable 'heuristic principle', as Milton Friedman has put it. It did indeed rule in the early stages of capitalism for very special reasons related to the then-prevailing socioeconomic environment: mass poverty, unbridled competition and an untamed spirit of accumulation—circumstances which made maximization a condition for economic survival. That is the reason why, in adopting the maximization principle as basic behavioural premise, the classical economists were indeed able to reproduce a fairly realistic image of the economic processes of their own age.

But is it proper to cling to a premise when neither the premise itself nor the conclusions drawn from it can be verified any longer? At that point analytical and descriptive economics diverge sharply. The former, including its econometric offspring, faithfully adhere to the classical creed. The latter readily admits a wide spectrum of economic behaviour patterns and of the underlying action directives. Professors Boulding, Galbraith and Simon have presented us with an impressive catalogue of both business and household incentives—ranging from maximization of the growth rate rather than of profits to 'satisficing' and the homeostatic principle of maintaining the value of assets, from preference for routine purchases irrespective of price differentials to conspicious consumption.

As I see it, this growing freedom and thus unpredictability of action is the direct result of rising affluence, especially during the postwar period, of the lessening of competition in an ever more highly organized market structure, and of a new style of life in which pecuniary considerations play the role of means rather than of ends. In other words, the classical pressures have been yielding under the impact of the strongest dynamic force of industrialism: technical progress with its consequence of rising productivity on the one hand and of growing immobility strengthened by a new sense of security on the other. But it is these very consequences that paralyse the negative-feedback mechanism which, in the past, assured to some extent automatic correction of destabilizing tendencies.

If this diagnosis is correct, the remedial controls must be quite specific. They must try to co-ordinate the spontaneous behaviour of producers and consumers, savers and investors. To put it differently, contrived pressures of public policy must take the place of the former impersonal pressures emanating from the environment. However, this poses a grave dilemma. Let us admit that the new variety of economic decision making reflects our gradual emancipation from the fetters of poverty and primitive social organization—a development which, under the aspect of human progress, can only be applauded. But this same emancipation reveals itself as a grave threat because it undermines the stability of the market—itself not only the most efficient technique of allocation but also a bulwark against totalitarian dominion.

We can pinpoint the dilemma by asking: How much control and what kind of control? To preserve as much as possible of our newly gained freedom, we are inclined to favour the minimum of controls compatible with stable provision, and to prefer 'indicative' controls to 'command' controls, that is, to *induce* appropriate behaviour rather than to *enforce* it. This view lies at the root of the fiscal and monetary controls of the no-longer-so-new 'new economics' of Keynesian provenance. But recent world-wide experience with stagflation has radically polarized the opinions of experts and the general public, with far-reaching consequences for governmental policies as demonstrated in the United States and Britain on the one hand and in France on the other. Whereas the socialist regime in France has assumed a more radical position, supplementing indirect controls by direct interference with the free market, the conservative governments of the two former countries make pre-existing controls themselves responsible for the growing instability and seek salvation in a return to the *laissez-faire* practices of the last century.

CAN THE 'HARD' SCIENCES HELP?

On the surface we witness an analytical contest in which the entire arsenal of theoretical concepts is being mobilized and even new ones—for example, supply-side economics—are being invented. But if this is really an issue that can be settled by observation and logical inference, one wonders why so far no *rapprochement* is in sight. Judging by the tone of the debate, in which emotion plays more than its customary role, one begins to suspect that *conflicting values* are at stake. But before accepting this conclusion we propose a detour. Perhaps our big brothers, the hard sciences, in particular astronomy and physics, may point a way toward an objective standard for the basic propositions also in the social sciences. It is in this context that the writings of Hanson, Holton, Kuhn and Polanyi referred to above become significant for our undertaking.

Let me illustrate what is at stake through an example which looms large in some of the writings quoted. It concerns Copernicus's heliocentric model of the universe as opposed to the geocentric model of his Ptolemaic predecessors. On what grounds did Copernicus claim superiority?[4]

Reading the introduction 'To the reader of this work' with which *De Revolutionibus* begins, we find an answer to this question which might have been written by Ernst Mach. The palm belongs to Copernicus, it is stated there, because of the greater simplicity of his assumptions and the greater accuracy of his predictions. And the positivistic interpretation goes even further. Copernicus is said to present not physical truth but only mathematical devices suitable to determine precisely the positions and changes in position of the heavenly bodies. The 'phenomena are to be saved' rather than the underlying reality revealed.

As a matter of fact, this introduction was not written by Copernicus himelf but by his friend Osiander, a Lutheran divine who hoped to protect the author in this manner from the wrath of the theologians.

But, however useful as a political ruse, his positivistic claims can by no means be confirmed. As far as the assumptions are concerned, Ptolemy had postulated forty-two circles. Copernicus reduced them to thirty-four—perhaps a quantitative but hardly a qualitative gain in simplicity. And by common accord his calculations of observable phenomena are today regarded as no more in accordance with the facts than those of the Ptolemaists.

Now it is very interesting that Copernicus himself offers quite a different, and by no means positivistic, justification for what amounted to the overthrow of a world view held for more than a millennium. He claims to have rehabilitated the true nature of the universe, namely, the uniformity of circular motion which the Ptolemaists, by combining circles with epicycles and eccentrics, had given up. This re-affirmation of circular motion was certainly not derived from the 'facts', as Kepler was to demonstrate two generations later. It was a relic of Aristotelian metaphysics, according to which circular movement is the most 'natural' as well as the most 'perfect' motion. This motion is in Copernicus's opinion 'naturally' engendered by the spherical shape of the celestial bodies, in both of which—spherical shape and circular motion—the Earth participates. From this certainly 'meta'-physical starting point all his revolutionary physical propositions follow: the Sun as the centre of the universe, the common motion of all planets including the Earth about the Sun, the unmasking of our naive illusion that we stand still while the universe moves around us.

We must, of course, distinguish between the content of a theory, as it was shaped in the mind of its originator, and its subsequent elaboration in which it found general acceptance. Kepler's, Galileo's and Newton's modifications of the heliocentric hypothesis finally produced an astronomical theory the explanatory and predictive power of which vastly exceeded the range of any earlier construction. But are all the propositions used to 'close' the system demonstrable? What about 'action at a distance' or later on an all-pervasive 'ether', auxiliary hypotheses that one after the other were introduced in order to bestow a physical meaning on the mathematical formulation of the operation of gravity? Were they more clearly demonstrable than the Aristotelian propositions?

It is true, all this is by now old hat, since General Relativity theory presents us with a finite, curved universe, a conception which permitted Einstein to eliminate those mechanistic hypotheses, and to relate the physical laws of the universe to a set of geometric theorems. But again we must ask: How safe is the empirical ground on which this new world view rests?

The likely answer can only confirm the hunch that all the known models of the universe rest on propositions *which are not open to direct verification*. And what is true of the physics of stellar phenomena is equally true of physics generally, best illustrated by quantum theory. In other words, the physical sciences are compelled to substitute a methodology of indirect testing for direct testing, that is, to seek vindication of undemonstrable hypotheses through the verification of conclusions drawn from them.

But now we are back on familiar ground. As in our economic deliberations, we may now ask: How closely must a conclusion agree with the facts—or rather, over how large a range of independent observations must such agreement extend—in order to vindicate the assumption? As we realized then, there are no objective criteria, but the subjective factor of judgement plays a decisive role. In referring again to General Relativity, although it solved some problems which had baffled the Newtonians, there are rival hypotheses for the explanation of those particular Newtonian 'anomalies'. Thus the question arises whether the indirect evidence so far accumulated in favour of the Einsteinian construct of the universe is strong enough to justify the transition from a mechanical to a geometrical explanation.

No. If Newton's system reigned supreme for more than two centuries, or if D. C. Miller's demonstration of yet a noticeable 'ether drift' could not shake the scientific community's trust in Relativity Theory, the reason must lie in a dimension other than the realm of experimental findings. In this respect it is highly enlightening to listen to Norwood Hanson's[5] pronouncements: 'If you accept the law of gravitation, the laws of Galileo and Kepler, the lunar motions and the tides will, as a matter of course, be *systematically explained* [my italics — A. L.] and cast into a universal mechanics . . . what could be a better reason [to accept these laws]?' Even more revealing are his comments on the neutrino, which was postulated by Wolfgang Pauli twenty-five years before its actual discovery, for no other reason than to be able to retain the principle of conservation of energy. Mind you, it was not the discovery of that particle which was used as a confirmation of the conservation principle. Rather, in order to keep this principle intact in the face of serious empirical counterindications, an energy-balancing factor was conjectured. Again Hanson asks: 'What could be a better reason?' and we may perhaps conclude that for him the reason would not have been any worse if the actual neutrino had never been detected. In the same vein speaks Poincaré: 'Whatever fresh notions of the world may be given to us by future experiments, *we are certain beforehand* [my italics — A. L.] that there is something which remains constant and which may be called energy'.[6]

PRINCIPLES, THEMATIC HYPOTHESES AND PARADIGMS

What is it that physicists are 'certain about', irrespective of the facts which future experiments may disclose? Thematic hypotheses, tacit coefficients of knowledge, patterns of discovery, shared paradigms— these are some of the answers which the new methodology offers. Alas, none of these terms has so far been clearly defined in the writings referred to. Professors Kuhn and the late Polanyi may insist that conceptual vagueness is in the nature of the problem: *wenn Ihr's nicht fuehlt, Ihr werdet's nicht erjagen*. In spite of this warning, I will now try to introduce some taxonomic distinction between these related but—as I see it—by no means identical notions.

(1) There are, first of all, what Professor Margenau calls 'metaphysical requirements' or 'ideal principles'.[7] They represent the highest level of generalization by pointing to certain ideas which regulate our constructs, without themselves being conveyed to us by sensory data. Among them we find, for example, causality and, in a different dimension, the postulate of 'simplicity'. For us the most important metaphysical requirements are 'permanence' and 'stability' of constructs as a reflection of the permanence and stability of nature itself. Note well, both are postulated as an indispensable guide to experience rather than inferred from observation and experiment.

We are not interested here in the epistemological status of these principles. But it should be stated that those mentioned above are all implied, and carry an identical meaning, in the physics of Aristotle, Newton and Einstein.

(2) This is not true of a second level of generality. If the metaphysical requirements are *formal* conditions for the very act of theorizing, here we deal with *substantive* propositions, such as force, conservation, atom, evolution, to mention only a few. They serve as axiomatic premises, though they are, in Bertrand Russell's words, 'neither empirical nor logically necessary' and have even been labelled as 'prejudices' (Karl Popper).[8] It is these notions for which the term 'thematic hypothesis' seems best suited. They present the basic themes, as it were, for the more elaborate structures ('paradigms') of specific systems. But as is the case with musical themes, they are open to many variations. Thus Aristotle's 'energeia' and Newton's concept of 'force' (as embodied in his second law) are different conclusions drawn from the common thematic hypothesis of a basic 'active principle'. On the other hand, Holton points to a striking analogy between the ancient Milesian cosmology with its three-step scheme of evolution and the dominant hypothesis of

modern cosmology—neatly balanced by the 'steady state' hypothesis as a revival of Parmenidian ideas. Though sometimes ruling over long stretches of scientific history, specific interpretations of these thematic hypotheses may undergo radical changes, and some of them may altogether disappear in certain epochs, like evolution during the Middle Ages.

(3) We now move to a third level, defined by Kuhn's notion of 'paradigm'. There we find different overall views of the physical world, views in which metaphysical requirements combine with certain thematic hypotheses in a specific 'matrix' (Kuhn's term). These matrices determine and limit the direction of both fact gathering and theorizing in a given field during major scientific epochs. They crystallize in particular 'models', the concept understood as including also non-intuitive constructs (quantum theory!). In this sense we have then different Aristotelian, Newtonian, Einsteinian and Planckian physical paradigms.

Toward the end of his book Kuhn raises a problem that no one can evade once he realizes the historical sequence of radically divergent paradigms referring to the same subject matter. Are the 'revolutions' which bring about these changes stages in an unbroken chain of scientific progress? Is the later paradigm necessarily the 'better'?

In contrast with the practitioners in, say, art or philosophy, the majority of scientists will answer this question in the affirmative.[9] Kuhn, on the other hand, offers two answers. Considered as a technique of 'problem solving', Newtonian physics must indeed be regarded as superior to Aristotelian physics as Einstein's is superior to Newton's. But if scientific 'truth' is understood in the ontological sense of a 'representation of what nature is really like', Kuhn cannot discover in the succession of paradigms 'a coherent direction of ontological development'.[10] And indeed for this position he can quote the most recent revolution in which 300 years of celestial mechanics—once a triumph over the Aristotelian tradition—have been superseded by a return to Aristotle's finite universe, and to the Pythagorean view according to which mathematics is more than a tool for computation, namely, the revelation of the true meaning of the laws of nature.

PARADIGMS IN ECONOMICS

Where does this leave us? It is not difficult to discover specimens of metaphysical requirements, of thematic hypotheses and even of paradigms in the history of economic analysis. As far as the first is concerned, the supreme importance of the 'orderliness' of economic

processes and their 'permanence and stability' for theoretical generalizations were stressed here from the outset. The maximization postulate,
on the other hand, is a characteristic thematic hypothesis in both
classical and neoclassical economics. Finally, the application of this
postulate as *the* motor force bestowing permanence and stability gives
us the paradigm of a self-correcting feedback mechanism.

As is well known, this economic paradigm is of relatively recent
origin. It was preceded in ancient and mediaeval economics by a
'normative' model, which distinguished between the 'natural' forms of
household management and the 'unnatural' art of trade devoted to
unlimited acquisition of money. On the other hand, as has often been
pointed out, the classical model of a self-sustaining market shows an
affinity to the Newtonian theory of mechanics, with the maximization
principle being next of kin to the physical principle of least action. If
one likes such speculations, one can even see in the *ad hoc* propositions
with which neoclassical theory tries 'to save the phenomena' (e.g. with
the help of special business-cycle theories) an analogue to the epicycles
of the later Ptolemaists. Finally, the normative underpinning of the
paradigm of political economics and other goal-oriented modern
approaches (welfare economics, operations research) may be interpreted
as a return to the Aristotelian paradigm.

But when all is said, such analogies do not take us very far toward
the understanding of the roots of thematic hypotheses or paradigms in
economics, nor of the causes of their historical change. As far as
changes in physical paradigms are concerned, we must acknowledge
the trivial fact that, within the limits of historical time, physical processes
must be regarded as *invariant*—a fact which is difficult to reconcile
with contradictory paradigms of equal validity. Fortunately, by acknowledging the *historical nature* of all social phenomena, we easily evade
this dilemma in economics. In other words, a sequence of antithetic
economic paradigms, each one of which can be validated by the special
conditions of a particular epoch, appears as the natural consequence
of the variability of the *Erkenntnisobjekt* itself. This is even true of the
Marxian 'vision' of economic evolution. Though subject to a 'general
law of accumulation', the capitalist process is supposed to move through
several stages—competitive, monopolistic—each one of which displays
a particular structure.

ACTION OR INACTION

However, such an appeal to the historical character of economic
paradigms cannot account for the presuppositions that underlie conflict-

ing paradigms constructed *for one and the same period*. So we are back at the beginning and must ask once more: On what ultimate grounds can I reject the prevailing construct of a self-steering market mechanism in favour of that of a political economics?

Perhaps an experience that preceded the present doctrinal split can point the way after all. Direct interference with the mechanism of the free market was not always the panacea of only the political left. In the summer of 1971 a Republican government introduced wage and price controls in the United States, and this at levels of inflation and unemployment far below the present ones. This unorthodox step was taken because, though the momentary situation was hardly intolerable, the likely trend of events was feared to turn catastrophic if uncontrolled. In other words, what was and is at present at stake is an evaluation of the *long-term tendencies of the present state*. Using the terms introduced earlier, the question was and is: Are the feedbacks at work negative, that is, self-balancing, or are they positive, tending to progressive disintegration?

Obviously, it was the identical issue that set my own views against those of my opponents when we argued about the stability or instability of modern capitalism generally. We all looked at the same glass of water and even agreed on the level up to which it was filled. But my opponents saw it *half filled*, trusting that the automatic mechanism of the market forces would gradually fill it to the brim. I, on the contrary, saw and still see it as *half empty*, anticipating a growing danger of runaway leaks. Where then can we turn to find a criterion that will enable us to 'predict the trend'?

The answer to this question goes to the root of economics as a practical science. To discover it, I take my bearings from an analogous problem in biochemistry, to which Ernest Nagel has drawn attention:[11]

Suppose that, before a fresh batch of medicine is put on sale, tests are performed on experimental animals for its possible toxic affects because of impurities that have not been eliminated in its manufacture, for example, by introducing small quantities of the drug into the diet of one hundred guinea pigs. If no more than a few of the animals show serious after-effects, the medicine is to be regarded as safe, and will be marketed; but if a contrary result is obtained the drug will be destroyed. Suppose now that three of the animals do in fact become gravely ill. Is this outcome significant (i.e. does it indicate that the drug has toxic effects), or is it perhaps an 'accident' that happened because of some peculiarity in the affected animals? To answer the question, the experimenter must *decide* on the basis of the evidence between the hypothesis H_1: the drug is toxic, and the hypothesis H_2: the drug is not toxic. But how is he to decide, if he aims to be 'reasonable' rather than arbitrary? Current statistical theory offers him a rule for making a reasonable decision, and bases the rule on the following analysis.

Whatever decision the experimenter may make, he runs the risk of committing either one of two types of errors: he may reject a hypothesis though in fact it is true (i.e. despite the fact that H_1 is actually true, he mistakenly decides against it in the light of the evidence available to him); or he may accept a hypothesis though in fact it is false . . . In consequence, before a reasonable rule can be proposed, the experimenter must compare the relative importance to himself of the two types of error, and state what risk he is willing to take of committing the type of error he judges to be the more important one. Thus, were he to reject H_1 though it is true (i.e. were he to commit an error of the first type), all the medicine under consideration would be put on sale, and the lives of those using it would be endangered; on the other hand, were he to commit an error of the second type with respect to H_1, the entire batch of medicine would be scrapped, and the manufacturer would incur a financial loss.[12] However, the preservation of human life may be of greater moment to the experimenter than financial gain; and he may *perhaps stipulate that he is unwilling to base his decision on a rule for which the risk of committing an error of the first type is greater than one such error in a hundred decisions* [what statisticians call a 'K-rule of rejection' — A. L.]. If this is assumed, statistical theory can specify a rule satisfying the experimenter's requirement, though how this is done, and how the risk of committing an error of the second type is calculated, are technical questions of no concern to us. The main point to be noted in this analysis is that *the rule presupposes certain appraising judgements of value*. In short, if this result is generalized, statistical theory appears to support the thesis that value commitments enter decisively into the rules for assessing evidence for statistical hypotheses.

Now Nagel adds an important qualification which pinpoints the significance of the example for our purpose. He emphasizes that such prior commitment to a value judgement comes into play only if 'alternative decisions . . . lead to *alternative actions having immediate practical consequences* upon which different special values are placed'.[13] This is by no means the general case in scientific research. In his quest for laws of nature a physical scientist is, in principle, indifferent to the character of his results, even if they present themselves as rival hypotheses, as in the apparent antinomy between particle and wave. In the same manner, the study of social processes yields the researcher often conflicting propositions—Nagel cites as an example the relative frequency of childless marriages under certain arrangements—without his associating any values with either one.

Now as far as our immediate problem is concerned—the prediction of economic trends—we must remember that we are emerging from a tradition that conceived the 'laws' of economics as depicting an inexorable mechanism upheld but never for long deflected by human action. On the basis of that axiom, both Adam Smith and Karl Marx offered unconditional (even if contradictory) predictions about the future of capitalism. In a formal sense their predictions resembled the rival speculations according to which our distant descendants either must perish from 'heat death' or will happily live ever after because the second law of thermodynamics is only a probability statement that anyhow applies only to closed systems. Either way those concerned will not be able to do anything about it.

This now points to the crux of the matter. In contrast with our classical forebears and many of our neoclassical contemporaries, there is a growing number of those who think that *something can be done about preventing large-scale economic disorder*. In the present context I am not interested in any specific policies that might achieve at least the necessary minimum of stability. What matters here is that we are confronted today with the *open alternatives of action or inaction*, forcing upon us willy-nilly a deliberate choice. Thus we find ourselves in the same predicament that troubles Nagel's biological experimenter. We, that is, those responsible for our economic welfare, must weigh the risks of erroneous expectations that may be implied in either decision—either to introduce what we regard as stabilizing measures or to let matters take their course.

However, in trying to do so, we are in a much worse position than Nagel's experimenter because it is in the nature of our *Erkenntnisobjekt* that no 'K-rule of rejection' can be established, such as how many errors may occur in a hundred decisions. Economics is no experimental science that could base its findings on any number of laboratory tests. What observations are available stem from the experiments that history performs. And those are not only much too few to permit probability statements in terms of frequency. The very historical nature of economic processes makes it highly unlikely that either the 'mode' around which the available observations group themselves or the 'residuals' will remain what they are when observed in the present. Thus all the conclusions we can draw from the most thorough analysis of the present are mere hunches, and the assessment of the respective risks remains highly speculative.

Even so, in order to come to a decision we must spell out to ourselves these hunches. On the one hand, if nothing is done though destabilization progresses, we may be faced with runaway inflation and/or a level of unemployment surpassing even the dimension of the Great Depression, ending in what might be not only an economic but a political catastrophe. If, on the other hand, stringent controls are introduced though the automatic forces of the market would have been capable of re-asserting themselves, a large measure of decentralized decision making would have been sacrificed needlessly in favour of an expanding bureaucracy that may not only be incompetent or even worse but would restore a fusion of economic with political power from which the liberal era had largely freed the Western world.

This is not to imply that the option must be an all-or-nothing affair, excluding a feasible compromise. But even the terms of such a compromise can be established only after the guardians of the general will—a parliamentary majority or an enlightened autocrat and his advisers—have made up their minds about the relative value of what is to be gained and what is to be sacrificed in any option.

Crucial as such decisions are for the survival of a viable economy, they are by no means an isolated case. It is a distinctive characteristic of our era that, in contrast with a fatalistic past, more and more of the macro-processes of society are conceived by more and more observers as objects suitable to, and even in need of, planned intervention. The consequences of this transformation are far reaching not only in practice. They are also at variance with the so-called 'objectivity' of social research.

The salient point is this. Assume that a new phenomenon is drawn into the circle of objects amenable to 'social engineering', but our investigation confines itself to a diagnosis of 'what is'. By not acting upon our findings, though we could do so, we pass an implicit judgement upon 'what will be', expressing our trust in the salutary operation of impersonal mechanisms. Such trust in turn implies that we evaluate even an eventual failure of those mechanisms as less 'damaging' to the social process than would be the consequences of any kind of intervention.

But the 'subjectivity' of such trust and the implied value judgement is of course fully matched by my own distrust, from which all the postulates of a political economics emerge. In a word, once alternatives of behaviour with different practical consequences are present, we cannot any longer escape—in R. B. Braithwaite's words—'judgements as to the future we want'.[14]

An inquisitive mind might go further, probing the deeper sources from which such value judgements spring. I prefer to leave this exploration to the students of Erik Erikson and Karl Mannheim. More to the point is a final observation. What started out as a critique of apparent shortcomings of my own work has turned into a critique of the foundations of economic theorizing generally under the conditions of the modern world. But at least this proposition—that analysis in a world of alternatives of action contains a 'subjective' element—is itself value free.

NOTES

1. *See* Norwood R. Hanson, *Patterns of Discovery* (Cambridge: Cambridge University Press, 1958); Gerald Holton, 'Presuppositions in the construction of theories', in Harry Woolf (ed.), *Science as a Cultural Force* (Baltimore: Johns Hopkins University Press, 1964); and Thomas S. Kuhn, *The Structure of Scientific Revolutions*, 2nd edn. (Chicago: University of Chicago Press, 1970). Also, with reservations, *see* Michael Polanyi, *Personal Knowledge* (Chicago: University of Chicago Press, 1958).
2. *See* Robert L. Heilbroner (ed.), *Economic Means and Social Ends: Essays in Political Economics* (Englewood Cliffs, NJ: Prentice-Hall, 1969), p. viii.
3. *See* Samuelson's Nobel Memorial Address, reprinted as 'Maximum principles in analytical economics', *American Economic Review*, **62** (1972), pp. 249–62.
4. In what follows I have leaned heavily on Alexandre Koyré's paper 'Copernicus', published in the *Quarterly Bulletin* of the Polish Institute of Arts and Sciences in America (July 1943), pp. 1–26. *See also* Thomas S. Kuhn, *The Copernican Revolution* (Cambridge: Harvard University Press, 1957).
5. Hanson, *Patterns of Discovery*, pp. 108, 125.
6. *See* Henri Poincaré, *Science and Hypothesis* (New York: Dover, 1952), p. 166; also Holton, 'Presuppositions in the construction of theories', pp. 96–7.
7. *See* Henry Margenau, *The Nature of Physical Reality* (New York: McGraw–Hill, 1950), Chapter 5.
8. Quoted in Holton, 'Presuppositions in the construction of theories', pp. 93–4.
9. This seems implicitly true also of Hanson's evaluation of successive 'patterns'. Holton's appraisal of the sequence of thematic hypotheses is not clear.
10. Kuhn, *The Structure of Scientific Revolutions*, p. 206.
11. *See* Ernest Nagel, *The Structure of Science* (New York: Harcourt, Brace & World, 1961), Chapter 14, especially pp. 496–8.
12. To point up the dilemma, I should prefer as alternative risk 'depriving people suffering from a serious illness of an effective cure'. — A. L.
13. Nagel, *The Structure of Science*, p. 497; my italics — A. L.
14. *See* R. B. Braithwaite, *Scientific Explanation* (Cambridge: Cambridge University Press, 1955), p. 174.

Bibliography of the Works of Adolph Lowe*

BOOKS

Arbeitslosigkeit und Kriminalität. Eine kriminologische Untersuchung, (Berlin, 1914).
Wirtschaftliche Demobilisierung, (Berlin, 1916).
Die rechtliche Entwicklung und Ausgestaltung des Kriegsernährungsamtes. Eine Studie zur Entwicklung der verfassungsrechtlichen Ideen im gegenwärtigen Krieg, unpublished dissertation, (Tübingen, 1918).
Economics and Sociology: A Plea for Co-operation in the Social Sciences, (London: Allen & Unwin, 1935).
—Japanese edition, (Tokyo, 1953).
—Portugese edition under the title *Economia e Sociologia*, (Rio de Janeiro, 1956).
The Price of Liberty. A German on Contemporary Britain, (London: Hogarth Press, 1937).
The Universities in Transformation, (New York: Macmillan, 1940).
On Economic Knowledge: Toward a Science of Political Economics, (New York: Harper & Row, 1965).
—second, enlarged edition, (White Plains, New York: M. E. Sharpe, 1977).
—German edition under the title *Politische Ökonomik*, (Frankfurt am Main, 1968).
—second, enlarged German edition, (Königstein im Taunus, 1984).
—Portugese edition under the title *A Ciencia da Economia Politica*, (Rio de Janeiro, 1969).
—Japanese edition, (Tokyo, 1973).
The Path of Economic Growth, (Cambridge: Cambridge University Press, 1976).

* [This bibliography was prepared by Harald Hagemann with the assistance of Claus-Dieter Krohn. It was originally published in Hagemann, Harold und Kurz, Heinz D. (Hrsg.), *Beschäftigung, Verteilung und Konjunktur: Zur Politischen Ökonomik der modernen Gesellschaft: Festschrift für Adolph Lowe*, (Universität Bremen, 1984), S. 262–8.
Minor amendments have been made in order to cater for English-speaking readers. — ed.]

The Prospect for Freedom, (provisional title—in preparation).
Has Freedom a Future? (to be published in 1988).

PUBLICATIONS IN JOURNALS

'Zur Methode der Kriegswirtschaftsgesetzgebung', *Die Hilfe*, **21** (1915), S. 333–5.
'Die freie Konkurrenz', *Die Hilfe*, **21** (1915), S. 385–7.
'Rücksiedlung aufs Land', *Heer und Heimat*, **2** (1917).
'Mitteleuropäische Demobilisierung', *Wirtshaftszeitung der Zentralmächte*, **2** (1917), S. 563–5.
'Die ausführende Gewalt in der Ernährungspolitik', *Europäische Staats-und Wirtschaftszeitung*, **2** (1917), S. 542–6.
'Die Massenspeisung im System der Volksernährung', *Europäische Staats-und Wirtschaftszeitung*, **2** (1917), S. 657–61.
'Die Fragen der Übergangswirtschaft', *Die Woche*, **20** (1918), S. 612–3, S. 637–8.
'Die Arbeiter- und Soldatenräte in der Demobilmachung', *Europaische Staats-und Wirtschaftszeitung*, **4** (1919), S. 89–94.
'Die neue Demokratie', *Der Spiegel*, **1** (1919), S. 8–14.
'Zur Soziologie des modernen Judentums', *Der Spiegel*, **2** (1920), S. 8–12.
'Chronik der Weltwirtschaft', *Weltwirtschaftliches Archiv*, **22** (1925), S. 1*–32*.
'Wie ist Konjunkturtheorie überhaupt möglich?' *Weltwirtschaftliches Archiv*, **24** (1926), S. 165–97.
'Weitere Bemerkungen zur Konjunkturforschung', *Wirtschaftsdienst*, **11** (1926), S. 1271–6 und 1516–17.
'Zur Möglichkeit der Konjunkturtheorie, Antwort auf Franx Oppenheimer', *Weltwirtschaftliches Archiv*, **25** (1927), S. 380–4.
'Reparationspolitik', *Neue Blätter für den Sozialismus*, **1** (1930), S. 37–41.
'Lohnabbau als Mittel der Krisenbekämpfung?' *Neue Blätter für den Sozialismus*, **1** (1930), S. 289–95.
'Lohn, Zins – Arbeitslosigkeit', *Die Arbeit*, **7** (1930), S. 425–30.
'Der Sinn der Weltwirtschaftskrise', *Neue Blätter für den Sozialismus*, **2** (1931), S. 49–59.
'Das gegenwärtige Bildungsproblem der deutschen Universität', *Die Erziehung*, **7** (1931/2), S. 1–19.
'Über den Sinn und die Grenzen verstehender Nationalökonomie', *Weltwirtschaftliches Archiv*, **36** (1932), S. 149*–62*.
'Some theoretical considerations of the meaning of trend', *Proceedings of the Manchester Statistical Society*, (1935), pp. 40–5.
'Economic analysis and social structure', *The Manchester School*, **7** (1936), pp. 18–37.
'The social productivity of technical improvements', *The Manchester School*, **8** (1937), pp. 109–24.
'The task of democratic education: pre-Hitler Germany and England', *Social Research*, **4** (1937), pp. 381–98.
'The turn of the boom', *Manchester Statistical Society Transactions*, (1938), pp. 10–15.
'Social transformation and the war', *The Christian-News-Letter*, No. 29 (1940).
'A reconsideration of the law of supply and demand', *Social Research*, **9** (1942), pp. 431–57.

'The trend in world economics', *The American Journal of Economics and Sociology*, **3** (1944), pp. 419–33.

'Freiheit ist nicht umsonst zu haben'. Aus der Broschüre 'The Price of Liberty' (1936), *Neue Auslese*, **2** (1947), S. 1–9.

'On the mechanistic approach in economics', *Social Research*, **18** (1951), pp. 403–34.

'A structural model of production', *Social Research*, **19** (1952), pp. 135–76.

'Lowe's "mechanistic approach". Rejoinder to James Parsons', *Social Research*, **19** (1952), pp. 497–500.

'Lowe's "structural model". Rejoinder to Gerhard Colm', *Social Research*, **19** (1952), pp. 503–7.

'The classical theory of economic growth', *Social Research*, **21** (1954), pp. 127–58.

'The practical uses of theory'. Comment, *Social Research*, **26** (1959), pp. 161–6.

'Wirtschaftstheorie—der nächste Schritt', in: Zur Ordnung von Wirtschaft und Gesellschaft. Festausgabe für Eduard Heimann zum 70. Geburtstage, *Hamburger Jahrbuch für Wirtschafts– und Gesellschaftspolitik*, **4** (1959), S. 174–81.

'In Memoriam Franz Oppenheimer', *Year Book of the Leo Baeck Institute*, **10** (1965), pp. 137–49.

'Is present-day higher learning "relevant?"' *Social Research*, **38** (1971), pp. 563–80.

'What is evolutionary economics? Remarks upon receipt of the Veblen–Commons Award', *Journal of Economic Issues*, **14** (1980), pp. 247–54.

'Is economic value still a problem?' *Social Research*, **48** (1981), pp. 786–815.

'Is the glass half full or half empty?' *Social Research*, **49** (1982), pp. 927–49.

CONTRIBUTIONS TO COLLECTED WORKS

'Die Reichseinkommensteuer im künftigen Steuersystem', in: *Parlament und Wissenschaft zu den Kriegssteuern*, (Berlin, 1916), S. 10–21.

'Der Entlassungsplan', in: *Der Tag der Heimkehr, Soziale Fragen der Übergangswirtschaft, Schriften der Gesellschaft für soziale Reform*, Heft 59 (Jena, 1918), S. 57–62.

'Zur ökonomischen Theorie des Imperialismus', in: *Wirtschaft und Gesellschaft. Beiträge zur Oekonomik und Soziologie der Gegenwart. Festschrift für Franz Oppenheimer zu seinem 60. Geburtstag*, (Frankfurt a.M., 1924), S. 189–228.

'Der gegenwärtige Stand der Konjunkturforschung in Deutschland', in: Bonn, M. J. und Palyi, M. (Hrsg.), *Die Wirtschaftswissenschaft nach dem Kriege. Festgabe für Lujo Brentano zum 80. Geburtstag*, (München und Leipzig, 1925), Bd. 2, S. 329–77.

'Uber den Einfluß monetärer Faktoren auf den Konjunkturzyklus', in: Diehl, K. (Hrsg.), *Beiträge zur Wirtschaftstheorie*, 2.Teil, Konjunkturforschung und Konjunkturtheorie, *Schriften des Vereins für Socialpolitik*, Bd. 173/II (München und Leipzig, 1928), S. 355–70.

'Kredit und Konjunktur', in: Boese, F. (Hrsg.), *Wandlungen des Kapitalismus. Auslandsanleihen. Kredit und Konjunktur. Schriften des Vereins für Socialpolitik*, Bd. 175 (München und Leipzig, 1929), S. 335–47.

'Diskussion über "Die Konkurrenz"', *Verhandlungen des Sechsten Deutschen*

Soziologentages, (Tübingen, 1929), S. 107–8.

Diskussion über '"Die Wanderung"', ebenda, S. 203–7.

'Sozialismus aus dem Glauben'. Verhandlungen der sozialistischen Tagung in Heppenheim, Pfingstwoche 1928, (Zürich and Leipzig, 1929), S. 117–21 and 219–22.

'Das Reparationsproblem', 2 Teile, *Veröffentlichungen der Friedrich-List-Gessellschaft*, Bde. 1 u. 2, (Berlin, 1929), Teil 1, S. 89–91, Teil 2, S. 155–6 und 299–303.

'Fragen der Kartellpolitik', *Veröffentlichungen des Enquete-Ausschusses über Kartellpolitik*, (Berlin, 1930), S. 323–34.

'Kapitalbildung und Steuersystem, Verhandlungen und Gutachten der Konferenz von Eilsen', 2 Teile. *Veröffentlichungen der Friedrich List-Gesellschaft*, Bde. 3 u. 4, (Berlin, 1930), Teil 1, S. 76–82 und 428–31, Teil 2, S. 143–4.

'Der Stand und die nächste Zukunft der Konjunkturforschung', in: Clausing, G. (Hrsg.), *Der Stand und die nächste Zukunft der Konjunkturforschung. Festschrift für Arthur Spiethoff*, (München, 1933), S. 154–60.

'Nationalism and the economic order', in: *Nationalism. Report of the Royal Institute of International Affairs*, (London, 1939), pp. 217–48.

'The study of world affairs', in: *The Study of World Affairs. The Aims and Organization of the Institute of World Affairs*. Two Addresses delivered at the Inaugural Meeting on 17 November 1943, (New York, 1944), pp. 9–24.

'Cyclical experience in the interwar period: the investment boom of the twenties and business cycles in a planned economy', in: National Bureau of Economic Research (ed.). *Conference on Business Cycles*, (New York, 1951), pp. 222–3 and 390–6.

'National economic planning', in: Haley, B. F. (ed.), *A Survey of Contemporary Economics*, Volume II, (Homewood, Ill.: R. D. Irwin, 1952), pp. 405–7.

'Structural analysis of real capital formation', in: Abramovitz, M. (ed.), *Capital Formation and Economic Growth*, (Princeton: Princeton University Press, 1955, pp. 581–634.

'Technological unemployment reexamined', in Eisermann, G. (Hrsg.), *Wirtschaft und Kultursystem. Festschrift für Alexander Rüstow*, (Stuttgart und Zürich: Eugen Reutsch Verlag, 1955), S. 229–54.

'Über eine dritte Kraft. Uber das Verhältnis von theologischer und politischer Wissenschaft', in: Hennig, K. (Hrsg.), *Der Spannungsbogen. Festgabe für Paul Tillich zum 75. Geburtstag*, (Stuttgart, 1961), S. 109–27.

'S ist noch nicht P', in: Unseld, S. (Hrsg.), *Ernst Bloch zu Ehren*, (Frankfurt a.M., 1965), S. 135–43.

'The normative roots of economic value', in: Hook, S. (ed.), *Human Values and Economic Policy*, (New York: New York University Press, 1967), pp. 167–80 (dt: 'Die normative Wurzel des wirtschaftlichen Wertes', in: *Interdependenzen von Politik und Wirtschaft. Beiträge zur Politischen Wirtschaftslehre. Festgabe für Gert von Eynern*, (Berlin, 1967), S. 135–43.

'Toward a science of political economics', in: Heilbroner, R. L. (ed.), *Economic Means and Social Ends. Essays in Political Economics*, (Englewood Cliffs, NJ, Prentice-Hall, 1969), pp. 1–36.

'Economic means and social ends. A rejoinder', in: *ibid*, pp. 167–99.

'Toward a science of political economics', in: *Phenomenology and Social Reality. Essays in Memory of Alfred Schutz*, (The Hague, 1970), pp. 140–73.

'Adam Smith's system of equilibrium growth', in: Skinner, A. S. and Wilson T. (eds.), *Essays on Adam Smith*, (Oxford, 1975), pp. 415–25.

'Über das Dunkel des gelebten Augenblicks', in: Bloch, K. und Reif, A. (Hrsg.), *'Denken heißt Überschreiten'. In Memoriam Ernst Bloch 1885–1977*, (Köln und Frankfurt a.M., 1978), S. 207–13.
'Prometheus unbound. A new world in the making', in: Spicker, S. F. (ed.), *Organism, Medicine and Metaphysics*, (Dordrecht, 1978), pp. 1–10.
'Die Hoffnung auf kleine Katastrophen', in: Greffrath, M., *Die Zerstörung einer Zukunft. Gespräche mit emigrierten Sozialwissenschaftlern*, (Reinbek, 1979), S. 145–94.
'Briefwechsel Adolf Lowe—Ernest Bloch 1943–75', in: *Ernst Bloch Briefe*, (Frankfurt a.M. 1985), pp. 728–823.

OBITUARY NOTICES

'F. A. Burchardt, Part I: Recollections of his work in Germany', *Bulletin of the Institute of Statistics*, Oxford, **21** (1959), pp. 59–65.
'In memoriam: Eduard Heimann 1889–1967', *Social Research*, **34** (1967), pp. 609–12 (dt. 'Übersetzung: Nachruf für Eduard Heimann', *Zeitschrift für die gesamte Staatswissenschaft*, **124** (1968), S. 209–11.
'Hans Philipp Neisser 1895–1975', *Social Research*, **42** (1975), pp. 187–9.
'Hans Staudinger', *Social Research*, **47** (1980), pp. 201–3.

EDITED WORKS

Soziale Forderungen für die Übergangswirtschaft, (Leipzig und Berlin, 1918).
Wirtschaft und Gesellschaft. Beiträge zur Oekonomik und Soziologie der Gegenwart. Festschrift für Franz Oppenheimer zu seinem 60. Geburtstag, (Frankfurt A.M., 1924)—zs. mit R. Wilbrandt und G. Salomon.
Ausschuß zur Untersuchung der Erzeugungs-und Absatzbedingungen der deutschen Wirtschaft (Enquete-Ausschuß). *Verhandlungen und Berichte*, I. Unterausschuß (Allgemeine Wirtschaftsstruktur), 5. Arbeitsgruppe (Der deutsche Außenhandel), Bde. I–XX, (Berlin, 1930/1)—zs. mit J. Marschak.
Studies of the Institute of World Affairs, (New York, 1943–51).
Four posthumous volumes of the writings of Karl Mannheim, (Oxford, 1951–6).

OFFICIAL GOVERNMENT PUBLICATIONS (to which Adolph Lowe made a major contribution)

Verordnung, betreffend Maßnahmen gegenüber Betriebsabbrüchen und- stillegungen vom 8. 11. 1920, *RGBl.* (1920), S. 1901–4.
'Wirtschafts- und Handelsfragen Deutschlands im Rahmen der Weltwirtschaft', in: *Sammlung von Material für die Konferenz in Genua*, (Als Manuscript gedruckt, Berlin, 1922).
'Deutschlands Wirtschaft', in: *Material für ein Studium von Deutschlands Wirtschaft, Währung und Finanzen*, (Als Manuscript gedruckt, Berlin, 1924). Nach Überarbeitung von der Deutschen Kriegslastenkommission und der Reichsbank veröffentlicht unter dem Titel: *Deutschlands Wirtschaft, Währung und Finanzen*. Im Auftrage der Reichsregierung den von der Reparationskommission eingesetzten Sachverständigenausschüssen über-

geben, (Berlin, 1924), Abschnitt A, S. 35–49.

Die weltwirtschaftliche Lage Ende 1925. Hrsg. vom Statistischen Reichsamt und vom Institut für Konjunkturforschung, (Als Manuscript gedruckt, Berlin, 1925)—Denkschrift zur Gründung des Deutschen Instituts für Konjunkturforschung.

Acknowledgements

All of the papers included in this volume have been published previously. Permission from the following copyright holders to republish here is gratefully acknowledged:

— *Social Research* and the Graduate Faculty of The New School for Social Research, New York, for Essays 1, 3, 4 and 8.

— The National Bureau of Economic Research, Cambridge, Massachusetts, for Essay 2, 'Structural Analysis of Real Capital Formation'; originally published in M. Abramovitz (ed.), *Capital Formation and Economic Growth*, (Princeton: Princeton University Press, 1955), pp. 581–634.

— Robert L. Heilbroner, Norman Thomas Professor of Economics, The New School for Social Research, New York, for Essays 5 and 6.

—Essay 7 is reprinted from the *Journal of Economic Issues* by special permission of the copyright holder, the Association for Evolutionary Economics.

—The Bibliography of the works of Adolph Lowe is reprinted with the kind permission of Harald Hagemann and Klaus-Dieter Krohn.